Language Issues

Ireland, France, Spain

P.I.E. Peter Lang

Bruxelles · Bern · Berlin · Frankfurt am Main · New York · Oxford · Wien

Wesley HUTCHINSON
& Clíona NÍ RÍORDÁIN (eds.)

Language Issues

Ireland, France, Spain

We gratefully acknowledge the financial support of Prismes
(EA 4398) in the publication of this volume

The cover image is a print from a collectors' box set by Richard Gorman
entitled 'Sept' (2006). Commissioned by the Beckett Project Paris to
mark the centenary of Samuel Beckett's birth, the box set was made at
the Atelier Michael Woolworth in Paris, with support from Culture
Ireland, the Centre Culturel Irlandais in Paris, and the Ireland Fund of
France.

© P.I.E. PETER LANG S.A.

Éditions scientifiques internationales

Brussels, 2010

1 avenue Maurice, B-1050 Brussels, Belgium

info@peterlang.com;   www.peterlang.com

Printed in Germany

ISBN 978-90-5201-649-8
D/2010/5678/63

Library of Congress Cataloging-in-Publication Data
Language issues : Ireland, France, Spain / Wesley Hutchinson & Clíona Ní
Ríordáin, (eds.).   p. cm. Text in Engish and French.
This book emerged out of contributions to a bilingual conference that was
organised at the Institut du Monde Anglophone and the Bibliothque Sainte-
Barbe in Paris on December 5 and 6, 2008. The conference was entitled
«Indigenous Minority Languages in Ireland: A Comparative Perspective,»
translated into French as: «Les langues regionales et minoritaires en Irlande:
Perspectives croisies.»   ISBN 978-90-5201-649-8 1.   Irish language—Political
aspects—Northern Ireland—Congresses. 2.   Irish language—Social aspects—
Northern Ireland—Congresses. 3.   Language policy—Ireland—Congresses. 4.
Sociolinguistics—Northern Ireland—Congresses. 5.   Language minorities—
Congresses. I. Hutchinson, Wesley. II. Ríordáin, Clíona Ní.
PB1298.N67L36 2010   306.44'9416—dc22   2010032612

CIP also available from the British Library, GB

Bibliographic information published by "Die Deutsche Nationalbibliothek"

"Die Deutsche Nationalbibliothek" lists this publication in the "Deutsche National-
bibliografie"; detailed bibliographic data is available on the Internet at <http://dnb.ddb.de>.

Contents

Acknowledgements

We would like to thank the following people and institutions for allowing us to reproduce material for this book:

Éditions Apogée, Rennes, for permission to reproduce a section of a map which originally appearedin Alain Croix & Jean-Yves Veillard (2001), *Dictionnaire du patrimoine breton*, Rennes, Apogée;

The Inspection académique des Pyrénées-Atlantiques and the CRDP Aquitaine for permission to reproduce a map featured on the following site: http://crdp.ac-bordeaux.fr/langues/basque/cartbasq4.htm;

Marc Moreau, copy editor, *Réforme*, for his help in locating an article by René Fréchet.

Introduction

This book grew out of interest in the issue of language in Northern Ireland, an area that has been at the centre of much heated debate since at least the early 1980s. Initially, much of the debate centred exclusively on the Irish language which, having long been excluded from the public space in the North, was undergoing a strong revival, actively and very vocally supported by elements within the republican movement. Since the end of that decade, and – arguably – under the influence of the two traditions policy put in place under the auspices of the Anglo-Irish Agreement (1985), the "language question" subsequently widened to take in Ulster-Scots. Although much energy has been spent trying – in vain – to convince opposing parties that Ulster-Scots should be seen alternatively as a fully-fledged "language" or merely as a dialect of English, an essential subtext to the often acrimonious discussion has been the apparently inextricable links between Ulster-Scots and unionist politics. The result is that, independently of one's political position, many in the North believe that language issues have been hi-jacked by the (radical) politicians...

Indeed, such is the ongoing intensity of this debate that it would have been quite conceivable to envisage yet another book, focusing solely on the situation of language in Northern Ireland or alternatively, in a more comparative logic, in examining the radically different situations and representations of the two languages North and South of the border. However, it was felt that more might perhaps be gained by comparing and situating the language movements in Ireland in relation to developments elsewhere within the European Union. Given that the research group is based in Paris, the obvious choice was of course to look at the situation in France. Indeed, France presents quite a different picture to that prevailing in Ireland or in Great Britain, not only in terms of the number of languages identified as being present on the territory of the French Republic (a total of 75, if the 1999 Cerquiglini report is to believed!), but also in terms of the attitude of the French state which appears to be more concerned with protecting the French language as it fights its losing battle with English on the world stage than with the status of the lesser-used languages which fall within its jurisdiction. Indeed, despite the fact that the Constitution was amended in 2008 to give (half-hearted) recognition to "regional" languages, the French authorities have repeatedly refused to ratify the European Charter for Regional or Minority Languages. The fact that, as with Irish and Ulster-

Scots, several of these languages are present in two jurisdictions, led us to push the comparative logic one step further and look at policy on the other side of the Pyrenees where the various *autonomias* have put in place strategies which contrast sharply with the centripetal tendencies that dominate thinking in the French "hexagon."

The result is a book that looks at the situation of a number of lesser-used western European languages within three broad frames: cultural politics, the education system and relations with the state (or states) in which they are spoken. While Irish runs off with the lion's share of the attention, the reader will find work on Ulster-Scots, Welsh, Breton, Basque and Catalan.

The book also reflects broader choices made by Irish studies in France which are structured within a strongly transdisciplinary frame. Concretely, this involves students and researchers operating increasingly on the interfaces between literature, "civilisation" and language. Such a transdisciplinary strategy presided over the selection of the texts that feature in the present volume and which operate in various, sometimes interconnecting fields: literature, history, geopolitics, linguistics and cultural studies.

In conclusion, we would like to express our thanks to the Groupe de Recherche en Études Irlandaises at the Université Sorbonne Nouvelle-Paris 3 (EA 1775) which financed this publication. The group has been renamed "Pôle Irlande" and is part of a new Équipe d'Accueil called Prismes (EA 4398), created in 2009.

Wesley Hutchinson & Clíona Ní Ríordáin

PART I

IRISH AND ULSTER SCOTS: CULTURAL POLITICS

"Something of a Cultural War"

Linguistic Politics in Northern Ireland

Aodán MAC PÓILIN

ULTACH Trust

The title of this paper comes from a statement made in June 2008 by Peter Robinson, leader of the Democratic Unionist Party and First Minister of the Northern Ireland Assembly. According to the *News Letter*, a local unionist newspaper:

> The DUP is launching a fightback against republican attempts to erode the British identity in Ulster.
>
> Party leader Peter Robinson yesterday revealed plans for:
>
> ▪ a Unionist Academy, which will promote the unionist culture and the advantages of the union […]
>
> ▪ a British Cultural and Equality Unit to provide legal advice to the public on fighting the removal of British emblems from Northern Ireland society.
>
> The twin-pronged initiative […] comes amid unionist anger at an unrelenting Sinn Féin campaign to promote the Irish culture and target British structures and symbols throughout the country.
>
> The DUP leader told a briefing for journalists at Stormont: "There has been something of a cultural war in Northern Ireland. We intend to fight back."
>
> "Our unionist way of life will not be put in some drawer in the back of an office.
>
> We are British and intend to stay that way" […].
>
> He insisted the fightback would not destabilise government.[1]

No-one expects politically motivated pronouncements on culture to be subtle, nuanced or complex. But when a politician who had never before shown much interest in culture begins to pronounce on cultural issues, it is not unreasonable to wonder at his motivation. The proposed Unionist Academy juxtaposes 'the promotion of the advantages of the union and the promotion of the unionist culture' as if the two issues are

---

[1] "DUP fights back against 'erosion of Britishness'," *News Letter*, Belfast, 25/6/2008.

coterminous. This is worth unpicking. The 'advantages of the union' involves a reasonably clear agenda, the defence of a constitutional status quo, which is essentially a political question, although it might have economic or possibly social aspects. The term 'the unionist culture' is much more problematic. Why the definite article: is there only one unionist culture? If unionism is essentially a political or constitutional ideology, does it have a cultural correlative? How can unionist culture be defined? How do the responses to any of these questions relate to the wide diversity of cultures in Britain and Ireland? And what exactly is meant by the term 'cultural war'?

"War," said Carl von Clausewitz, "is not a mere act of policy but a true political instrument, a continuation of political activity by other means."[2] It may not be unfair to interpret Peter Robinson's cultural war as the continuation of political activity by other means; his version of 'unionist culture' will certainly be seen by many in Northern Ireland as being driven less by an interest in culture than by a political imperative.

What is not in doubt is the fact that culture is now a political issue of some importance for Northern Ireland's political class, important enough for the First Minister to declare a cultural war against his Deputy First Minister and nearly half of his Cabinet. The *News Letter* article is interesting in that it appears to conflate 'the unionist culture' 'the unionist way of life', and 'the British identity' as if the terms were interchangeable, and closely related to 'British emblems' and 'British structures and symbols'. This paper will look at the background to the cultural war, with particular emphasis on the place of language in it.

The most cynical interpretation is that when our politicians engage in cultural and linguistic head-butting and coat-trailing, they are in fact providing a diversion, a distraction, a game of smoke and mirrors designed to maintain the comforting illusion that the dreary integrity of our historic quarrel is intact, while behind the scenes they are busy with their daily round of compromise and pragmatic accommodation. According to this theory, the politicians are fighting a phoney war around a number of highly symbolic and emblematic issues about which few of them really care. That Robinson was confident that his cultural war would not destabilise the government is significant.

I would argue that there is an element of truth in this analysis. Certainly the public pronouncements of our politicians do not reveal any great depth of engagement with or understanding of cultural issues. However, I would also argue that, on one level, our politicians do take culture – or cultural identity – very seriously. In fact, I would argue that

---

2   Michael Howard and Peter Paret (ed. & trans.) (1976), Carl von Clausewitz, *On War*, [*Vom Kriege*, 1832] Princeton, Princeton University Press, p. 87.

many of them see cultural identity as central to the long term political future of Northern Ireland.

The cultural war can only be understood as a response to the particular constitutional situation of Northern Ireland, and I will try to summarise this with a broad brush. Politics in Northern Ireland are dominated by two main political blocks, nationalism and unionism. Unionism involves a desire to maintain the current constitutional union – the United Kingdom of Great Britain and Northern Ireland. Nationalism involves a wish to break up that particular union and to form an alternative union with the Republic of Ireland. Until recently, there has been a high correlation between political and religious affiliation, and this perception is still alive and well – one of the few points of cross-community agreement in Northern Ireland is the widely accepted proposition that Protestants are overwhelmingly unionist and that Catholics are overwhelmingly nationalist.[3]

To get the full picture, it is also important to know that Northern Ireland was formerly a disputed territory, held within the United Kingdom but claimed by the Republic of Ireland. This situation has changed in recent years. It is clear that Britain no longer particularly wants to keep Northern Ireland within the United Kingdom. The Republic of Ireland formerly had a constitutional imperative to re-unite the country; this was changed by referendum in May 1998 to a constitutional aspiration involving re-unification by consent.[4] In reality, however, its political class and a large element of its population do not want a united Ireland. Nobody really wants us, but, in their different ways, both Britain and the Republic are stuck with us.

For both governments, Northern Ireland has presented an intractable conundrum, in that the principles and aspirations of the two main political blocks in Northern Ireland are utterly irreconcilable. The two states have responded to this by imposing a political settlement which forces

---

[3] In the 2007 *Life and Times Survey*, 76% of respondents (74% Catholics and 79% Protestants) agreed with the statement "Britishness and Protestantism are strongly intertwined." 80% of respondents (77% Catholics and 84% Protestants) agreed with the statement "Irishness and Catholicism are strongly intertwined." 'Britishness' is generally equated with unionism, and 'Irishness' with nationalism. Available at: www.ark.acc.uk/nilt/2007/Identity/BRITPROT, www.ark.acc.uk/nilt/2007/Identity/IRISHCAT (accessed 18/06/2009).

[4] The relevant text, in the *Nineteenth Amendment of the Constitution Act, 1998*, reads: "It is the firm will of the Irish nation, in harmony and friendship, to unite all the people who share the territory of the island of Ireland, in all the diversity of their identities and traditions, recognising that a united Ireland shall be brought about only by peaceful means with the consent of a majority of the people, democratically expressed, in both jurisdictions in the island." 94.39% of voters in the Republic voted in favour of the Amendment.

unionists and nationalists to share power. The Northern Ireland Assembly is a devolved jurisdiction within the United Kingdom, but involves certain agreed powers of interference from the Government of the Republic. The Assembly is the political equivalent of a shotgun marriage – it is certainly not a love-match. It is about as harmonious as you would expect a shotgun marriage to be – politics in Northern Ireland lurch between a state of venomous stasis and one of theatrical inertia.

This settlement also has an inbuilt instability, as, in theory, Northern Ireland can transfer to the Republic of Ireland if a majority of its citizens wish it to do so. In that context, it is important to note that the Catholic/ Protestant balance of the population is shifting. The 1991 Census provided a dramatic indication of the growth in the Catholic proportion of the population over the previous decades: 34.9% (1961), 36.8% (1971), 38.4% (1981), 42.1% (1991).[5] In 1991 the Catholic community also had a much lower age profile than the Protestant community: 51% of children under ten were Catholics, but only 30% of those over 75 years of age.[6]

The 2001 Census showed a further growth of Catholics to 43.8%, against 53.1% Protestants,[7] while under tens were 49.3% Catholic and 44% Protestant.[8] The Irish edition of the *Mirror* greeted these last figures with an extravagant if somewhat innumerate headline: "Catholic Boom: Census shows Protestants will be minority in 10 years."[9] One nationalist party, Sinn Féin, took the additional step of assuming that the seemingly inevitable development of a Catholic majority would translate into a nationalist majority:

> Mitchel McLaughlin, Sinn Féin chairman, said yesterday it was a question of "when, not if, a majority in the north favours Irish unity." Another Sinn Féin source said that some analysts were even predicting a united Ireland by

---

[5] Edgar F. Jardine (1993/1994), "Demographic Structure in Northern Ireland and its Implications for Constitutional Preference," *Journal of the Statistical and Social Inquiry Society of Ireland*, Vol. XXVII, Part 1, p. 197.

[6] Edgar F. Jardine, *ibid.*, pp. 199, 201.

[7] Table KSO7b "Community Background: Religion or Religion Brought Up In," *Northern Ireland Census 2001: Key Statistical Tables*: (2002) p. 22. Figures have been rounded out to one decimal place.

[8] Table S306 "Age by Community Background: Religion or Religion Brought Up In," *Northern Ireland Census 2001: Demography: People, Families and Households*: (2002) p. 30. Percentages have been extrapolated from statistics.

[9] *Mirror*, 14/01/2002. Quoted in James Anderson, Owen McEldowney, Ian Shuttleworth, "Discourses of Ethno-National Demography: Northern Ireland from the 1991 Census to the Census of 2001," International Population Geography Conference, University of St Andrews, 11-14/08/2004.

2016, the centenary of the Easter Rising. "The momentum is gathering fast," he said.[10]

Alex Maskey, former Sinn Féin Lord Mayor of Belfast, was even more unequivocal in linking religious and political allegiance:

> The publication of the new census figures has shown that the Catholic population has increased significantly and, indeed, is set to grow further in the next few years.
>
> This increase has long been expected and predicted by observers and academics alike, with the nationalist population in the Six Counties now at its highest point ever since the partition of Ireland and the pro-unionist population shrinking to the extent that for the first time it will represent just over 50% of the population.[11]

The assumption that a potential Catholic majority is likely to emerge at some time in the future is widely, if not universally, accepted. Besides the issue of when that might come about, the really important issue, the constitutional issue, is whether or not that potential religious majority will also turn out to be a political majority. The chief source of scientific attitudinal studies is the longitudinal *Northern Ireland Life and Times Survey*, and some use will be made of its evidence in the following pages, with the caution that, as well as the inherent weaknesses of attitudinal surveys everywhere in identifying long-term political outcomes, the NILT sometimes throws up wildly contradictory evidence. NILT does, however, identify some interesting patterns. In 2001, for example, it was widely assumed that a united Ireland was imminent. Responding to the question "At any time in the next 20 years, do you think it is likely that there will be a united Ireland." 44% Catholic and 43% of Protestants thought this outcome to be either very or quite likely (as opposed to 37% and 39% respectively who thought it would be very or quite unlikely).[12]

There are two possible developments which will influence the political outcome of the religious demographic shift. On the one hand, if and when Catholics become a voting majority, some unknown proportion of them is likely to be unionist – there is already a small number of Catholic unionists.[13] It is also likely that there will be a significant number of

---

[10] Dan Buckley, "North moving closer to Catholic majority," *Irish Examiner*, 19/12/2002.

[11] Alex Maskey, Irelandclick.com (accessed 3/01/2002).

[12] *Northern Ireland Life and Times Survey*, (2001). www.ark.ac.uk/nilt/2001/Political _Attitudes/UTDIRE (accessed 18/06/2009).

[13] *Northern Ireland Life and Times Survey*. In NILT, Catholics rarely identify themselves as unionists (the 2008 survey identified 1% of Catholics as unionists), but other indicators in the same survey contradict this. In a question of whether the ma-

what could be described as functional unionists, Catholics who no longer care whether or not Ireland is re-united. This is already a large category – between 1989 and 2008, an average of 41% of Catholics in the NILT survey defined themselves as neither nationalist nor unionist.[14] Some unionist strategists have argued that the union will be safeguarded into the foreseeable future by these groups of Catholic voters.

On the other hand, there is also a small proportion of Protestants who are political nationalists.[15] It is possible that, within a generation or two, a larger number of Protestants may be nationalists; others may be indifferent to whether they live in a British or in an Irish state. It is almost certain that, as the Republic of Ireland becomes more secularised, Protestants will be less and less worried at the prospect of being sucked into a confessional state in which the Catholic Church wields enormous direct power. Nationalist strategists believe that, in these circumstances, they can persuade a reasonably large proportion of the Protestant population to either embrace or tolerate the idea of a united Ireland.

Even using a broad brush, it has taken me some time to get here, but we are now at a critical point in my argument. If our society begins to emerge from the sectarianism that has plagued the region for hundreds of years, the strong correlation between religious allegiance and political allegiance that has characterised it may begin to fade. It is possible that at some time in the future, the vote which will decide Northern Ireland's constitutional position will no longer be decided by religious allegiance, but by cultural identity. This is certainly the perspective of a significant number of our politicians, and is one explanation of why cultural identity is now such a live issue in our politics.

Most of the debate revolves around a single word, and how that word is interpreted. The word is 'Irish' I would argue that, in the context of the Northern Ireland constitutional debate, the other terms in use in the identity debate, Ulster, British, Ulster-Scot, tend to be promoted as

---

jority of people in Northern Ireland ever voted to become part of a united Ireland, 2% of Catholics would find this almost impossible to accept. Significantly, 21% of Catholics would not like it but would accept the wishes of the majority. www.ark.ac.uk/nilt/2008/Political_Attitudes/FUTURE1.html (accessed 18/06/2009).

[14] Responses to this question fluctuate widely, between 27% and 59%. www.ark.ac.uk/sol/surveys/community_relations/time_series/encycidentity.htm (accessed 18/06/2009); www.ark.ac.uk/nilt/2001/Political_Attitudes/UNINATID.html (accessed 18/06/2009).

[15] Protestants identifying themselves as nationalists are statistically insignificant, rarely meeting the 1% threshold. However, responses to the survey between 1989 and 2007 show between 3% and 8% (average: 4.74%) of Protestants agreeing that the long-term policy for Northern Ireland should be for it to reunify with the rest of Ireland. www.ark.ac.uk/sol/surveys/community_relations/time_series/crcconstit.htm (accessed 18/06/2009).

alternatives to the word 'Irish'. The key to the importance of this word is that both nationalist and unionist politicians assume that people who identify themselves as 'Irish' will either give their primary political allegiance to a united Ireland or be relatively content with an all-Ireland polity.

Peter Robinson's cultural war is based primarily on this assumption. I should add that Robinson is by no means the first unionist politician to engage in the cultural war. David Trimble, Nobel Peace Prize winner, and the first ever First Minister in the Northern Ireland Assembly, was himself something of a cultural warrior. His response to being labelled 'Irish' is always intense. Once, when "[...] described in the press as a 'Northern Irish politician', he became quite upset, declaring that, while he didn't mind being described as a 'Northern Ireland politician', he was in no way, shape or form to be categorised as 'Irish'."[16]

Before becoming leader of the Ulster Unionist Party, he was cultural spokesman for the party. As early as 1985, not long after Sinn Féin's own cultural campaign began to gather steam,[17] he identified Irish culture as a threat to unionism and founded the Ulster Society for the Promotion of Ulster-British Heritage and Culture, usually referred to as the Ulster Society. In 1989, speaking as chairman of the Ulster Society during a speech to a community relations conference, he took exception to both the Irish traditional music played during the social events and the title of the conference ('Varieties of Irishness'). He defined his own cultural allegiance as follows: "The term I use to describe the culture I grew up in is 'Ulster-British'. I do not like using the term 'Protestant' because of the sectarianism encouraged by the use of religious labels."[18] He was rather less careful in avoiding the sectarianism encouraged by the use of religious labels when defining what he called the 'competing' culture:

> [...] what for want of a better word one will call the Irish Gaelic/Catholic culture. The latter has, in the course of the last century or so, tried to de-velop, or redevelop, its own self-contained culture. It was clearly bound up with the development of political separatism. It was to be 'ourselves alone' politically, culturally and, or, especially, linguistically.[19]

---

16 Arthur Valentine, letters to the Editor, *Independent* [London], 19/06/ 2000.

17 Sinn Féin's Cultural Department was set up in 1982, see: Feargal Eamonn Mac Ionnrachtaigh (2008), "'An Ghaeilge faoi Ghlas': Republican Prisoners and the Irish language in the North of Ireland – Power, Resistance and Revival," PhD Thesis, Queens University Belfast, pp. 200-201.

18 Maurna Crozier (ed.) (1989), *Cultural Traditions in Northern Ireland: Varieties of Irishness and Proceedings of the Cultural Traditions Group Conference*, Belfast, Institute of Irish Studies, QUB, p. 47.

19 *Ibid.* 'ourselves alone' is a slightly inaccurate translation of "Sinn Féin".

The Society's journal says that the Ulster Society was founded: '[...] with the aim of promoting and preserving the distinctive culture and heritage of the Ulster-British people, embracing: language, drama, poetry, music, folk customs, symbolism, and history'.[20] One edition of the journal attacked the Irish language movement for attempting '[...] to dye Ulster's cultural tartan a solid emerald green'[21] (in Northern Ireland's iconography, green is the colour of Irish nationalism). Trimble's Ulster-British culture is defined less by what it is than by what it is not: it is definitely not Irish, definitely not Gaelic, and, if we can infer the sectarianism encouraged by religious labels, not Catholic.

While Trimble placed the Irish language somewhere in a matrix that involved cultural, religious and political elements, some unionist politicians have concentrated almost exclusively on the language issue. Shortly after Peter Robinson's launch of the cultural war, David McNarry, a UUP Member of the Legislative Assembly and Assistant Grand Master of the Grand Lodge of Ireland, took up the issue during a Twelfth of July Orange demonstration in Broughshane. For McNarry: "The most dangerous threat to Britishness in Northern Ireland is the creeping 'application of cultural apartheid,' in the form of the Irish language agenda."[22] He went on to argue that:

> [...] the number 1 threat was now Sinn Fein's use of Irish language and cultural (*sic*) to attack the unionist way of life. He said Gerry Adams was using "the intensity of an Irish language onslaught to strangle our sense of Britishness."

> Mr McNarry offered a dire warning that Sinn Fein wanted an Irish Language Act "to run rampant throughout our country" – and would have got it under Direct Rule.

> "The plan was that in all schools, public places, especially where republicans are in control, British cultural symbols will be thrown out to be replaced with romantic Provo symbols.

> In courts, in street names, road signage, emergency warning signs, the list is endless, republicans will push to have dual English and Irish language displayed, to make unionists uncomfortable and erode the British identity. [...]

---

[20] Back cover blurb, *New Ulster, the Journal of the Ulster Society*, No. 2, Lurgan, 1994.

[21] Quoted in Gordon McCoy (1997), "Rhetoric and Realpolitik: the Irish language movement and the British Government," in H. Donnan, and G McFarlane (eds.), *Culture and Policy in Northern Ireland: Anthropology in the Public Arena*, Belfast, Belfast Institute of Irish Studies, p. 128.

[22] *News Letter*, 14/07/2008, p. 46. I would like to thank my colleague Gordon McCoy for drawing my attention to this article.

> If left uncountered the Irish language issue will plague Northern Ireland in the same way the reckless chase for Irish unity by the Provos has resulted in sectarianism, bitter division.[23]

McNarry's somewhat apocalyptic comments are focused primarily on the legal status of Irish, on its public profile, and on the emblematic significance of that profile. At one level, Irish is depicted as the linguistic equivalent of painting the kerbstones green, white and orange, a territorial marker that indicates that nationalists control the area. There is the added threat that an Irish Language Act could also have brought bilingual signage into "all schools, public spaces," in other words, into spaces not controlled by nationalists. The main threat is that bilingual signs will "erode the British identity." However, in the context of this intemperate speech, and the occasion of its delivery, McNarry takes a more nuanced approach than David Trimble to the issue of culture, making an explicit distinction between culture and its symbolic and political use: "Orangemen and unionist (*sic*) were not and should not be against Irish culture or freedom of expression. But a grave situation has developed in which the culture is being used by republicans in the new-look war in [*recte* on] Britishness."[24] This distinction may be entirely sincere; however, it is reasonably common for unionist politicians to claim that they are not against Irish language and Irish culture, but against their misappropriation for political ends. It must be added that, in practice, opposition to the political use of the language is generally indistinguishable from opposition to the language itself.

The definition of Britishness to which unionist ideologues like David Trimble subscribe is in sharp contrast to that of the rest of the United Kingdom, which prides itself – not always unjustifiably – as a polity in which a wide variety of cultural identities can co-exist, and in which a variety of national identities can be maintained and nurtured within a multi-national state. Until very recently, it has been quite easy for the Welsh and the Scots to identify themselves as Welsh or Scottish in cultural terms, and as British in political terms, and this position is still possible in the post-devolution era. The state itself, well before devolution, has been highly supportive of the Welsh language and, to a lesser extent, of Scottish Gaelic. From an historic perspective, unionists in Ireland happily described themselves as both Irish and British throughout the 19th century, and in some cases into the 20th, but from a very early stage in the 20th century Ulster unionism has tended to reject all forms of an Irish identity, certainly in public discourse.

---

[23] *Ibid.*

[24] *News Letter*, 04/07/2008, p. 46.

The definition of Ulster British culture subscribed to by politicians like Robinson and Trimble appears to me to be based, essentially, on an acceptance by unionists of the nationalist definition of Irishness that was developed in the late 19th and early 20th centuries; it also appears to have been constructed in contrast to and in reaction to that definition. In this context, the term 'British' is not without its difficulties. Northern Ireland is not in Britain, it is in the United Kingdom of Great Britain and Northern Ireland. Politically, Northern Ireland is the only part of the United Kingdom that the British government is happy to give up without a fight. In terms of cultural identity, 'Britishness' on the larger island is widely varied in its cultural expression. British cultural identity in Northern Ireland is rather less straightforward. A Britishness that rejects an Irish identity in a place called Northern Ireland can seem rather anomalous. It also excludes from Britishness those who might want to identify themselves as culturally Irish, while accepting, or even embracing, membership of the British state.

One way of understanding unionist hostility to an Irish identity is to look at the nationalist version of the concept. All nationalists and most Catholics in Northern Ireland identify themselves as Irish. The word Irish, however, spans a range of meanings. You can be Irish because you are a citizen of the Republic of Ireland. You can be Irish because you were born on the island of Ireland. As we have seen, this is disputed, and not only by David Trimble; the Duke of Wellington, when accused of being an Irishman, is said to have responded that "being born in a stable does not make a man a horse." Critically, you can call yourself Irish to describe your political identity – used in this sense it means you are a nationalist. You can also have an Irish cultural identity – a complicated state of mind that we do not have time to explore. For a nationalist, these various meanings of the word 'Irish' can blend seamlessly into each other, and, for a nationalist, the geographical, cultural and political meanings tend be used interchangeably.

To make it even more complicated, the noun 'Irish' is also the term usually used for the ancient language of Ireland, sometimes called 'Gaelic', that manages to be both the first official language of the Republic of Ireland and a fragile and threatened minority language. The Irish language can present a rather more difficult problem for nationalists, only a minority of whom speak it. While many find themselves in the same position as WB Yeats: "Gaelic is my national language, but it is not my mother tongue,"[25] it is not uncommon for nationalists, including those who are monoglot speakers of English, to speak of Irish as

---

[25]   W. B. Yeats (1937), "General Introduction For My Work," in Edward Larrissy (ed.) (2001), *The Major Works*, Oxford University Press, p. 385.

'our language', or 'my native language'. Not surprisingly, support for the language revival in Northern Ireland is mainly to be found among nationalists. For some nationalist strategists, particularly among republicans, the language holds a central place in their political ideology. These people may indeed see the language in terms of cultural enrichment, linguistic ecology or cultural repossession, but the dominant ideological thread in their thinking sees the language as the ultimate act of psychic decolonisation, or as another weapon in their political armoury.

In 1982, Sinn Féin set up a Cultural Department, whose work involved high-profile promotion of the Irish language. Indeed, it involved little else, as can be seen from the following quotation from the party's cultural spokesperson:

> Sinn Fein is committed to the cultural revival because we believe the cultural oppression of our people by Britain, combined with the political, social and economic oppression, prevents us from obtaining national sovereignty.

> The Irish language is a great sign of our nationality, and by learning and speaking it we are not only resisting cultural domination but also strengthening our national identity, and asserting our determination to exist as a free and distinctive nation.[26]

The Cultural Department was extremely active, particularly in Belfast, but had a tendency to regard the language movement with a somewhat proprietorial eye; in 1990 one former Cultural Officer claimed that republican activists were the leaders of the Irish language revival.[27] The Department published a pamphlet in 1984 which gives some flavour of its priorities. The seminar on which the pamphlet was based was organised for students at Irish classes in Belfast: "[…] to introduce learners to the revolutionary ideology of their teachers in relation, first and foremost, to cultural oppression."[28]

> I don't think that we can exist as a separate people without our language. Now every phrase [of Irish] you learn is a bullet in the freedom struggle. Every phrase you use is a brick in a great building, a re-building of the Irish nation.[29]

---

[26] Diarmuid Ó Tuama, "Cultural Revival," *Sinn Féin, West Belfast Bulletin*, Issue 1, No. 1, March 1983.

[27] Máirtín Ó Muilleoir, "Cothódh lucht na Gaeilge a n-acmhainn ghrinn in aghaidh ionsaí na nGall" (Irish-speakers should keep their sense of humour against the attacks of the foreigner), *LÁ*, Belfast, 29/08/1990.

[28] Máirtín Ó Muilleoir (ed.) (1984), Foreword, *Learning Irish/Ag Foghlaim na Gaeilge*, Sinn Féin, Belfast, p. 1.

[29] Pádraig Ó Maolchraoibhe, Sinn Féin Councillor, in Máirtín Ó Muilleoir (ed.) (1984) *ibid.*, p. 4.

Sinn Féin is pledged to resisting not only the economical and political oppression but also the cultural and social controls imposed by the British and
their allies on the Irish people. [...] it is our contention that each individual
who masters the learning of the Irish language has made an important personal contribution towards the reconquest of Ireland.[30]

Gerry Adams, the Sinn Féin President, also sees politics and culture
as a seamless garment: "My own conviction is that the restoration of our
culture must be a crucial part of our political struggle and that the
restoration of Irish must be a central part of the cultural struggle."[31]
Adams specifically identifies the Irish language as a tool for persuading
Protestants to adopt a nationalist identity: "[...] for the Protestant people
to embrace the Irish language today would be for them to reject loyal-
ism."[32]

This seems to me to be a profound misreading of the complex relationship between cultural identity and political allegiance. It is also a
statement that will do little to ameliorate unionist prejudice against the
language. Indeed, it is likely have the opposite effect – in the political
culture of Northern Ireland, opposing sides tend to believe each other's
propaganda.

While unionists born on the island of Ireland may not be able to es-
cape their geographical fate, they neither have nor want any variety of
the political identity that defines itself as 'Irish'. Publicly, as we have
seen, particularly among the political class, it tends to involve a total
rejection of Irishness – public discourse in Northern Ireland is dominated by a reductive, ideology-driven, hard-line polarization, an almost
theological rejection of the weaknesses inherent in ambiguity, paradox,
complexity, honourable confusion or the drunkenness of things being
various.

On an individual level, the relationship of many unionists with Irish
culture is more nuanced, more problematic, and far more interesting.
This is not always easy to identify; social discourse in Northern Ireland
involves a complex interplay of defence mechanisms and avoidance
strategies. In social situations, controversial issues are either avoided, or
escalate to the point where people, reacting to their assessment of their

---

[30] Máirtín Ó Muilleoir (ed.) (1984) *ibid.*, p. 2.

[31] Quoted by Mairéad Nic Craith, "Language and the Creation of Boundaries: The Irish
Case," in Malcolm Anderson and Eberhard Bort (eds.) (1999), *The Irish Border:
History, Politics, Culture*, Liverpool, Liverpool University Press, p. 191.

[32] Gerry Adams (1995), *Free Ireland: Towards a Lasting Peace*, Dingle, Brandon
Press, p. 139. Quoted in Gordon McCoy (2006), "Protestants and the Irish language
in Belfast," in Fionntán de Brún (ed.), *The Irish Language in Belfast*, Dublin, Four
Courts Press, p. 167.

interlocutor's ideological position, tend to take a more extreme position than they actually hold.

It is easy to see why unionists, almost invariably in public and often in private, tend to be hostile to the ideological bundle the word 'Irish' carries with it – indeed, the number of Protestants who identify themselves as Irish in the NILT surveys rarely rises above 3%.[33] If nationalists tell unionists that they are Irish – as nationalists often do – unionists will react to the hidden implication – which is often present – that they should therefore be Irish nationalists. Because nationalists often promote Irish culture to unionists in the hope of persuading them to adopt, or accept, an Irish identity, unionists will react against the implication – which is often present – that an Irish cultural identity is synonymous with an Irish political identity. They will react accordingly, even if the person they are talking to has no intention of converting them to nationalism. If someone is promoting the Irish language to unionists, it will be assumed that decolonising and proselytising political agendas outlined above lurk somewhere in the background. The unionist tendency to associate the Irish language movement with republicanism is partly grounded in a highly effective PR campaign intended to have that very effect.

Unionist politicians face another problem. Anyone who has engaged with Anglo-Irish literature will be aware of just how complex, multilayered and paradoxical an Irish identity can be, but it is a model of clarity and coherence compared to the Ulster British identity peddled by unionist politicians. Irish culture can also present a very attractive package, particularly to an outsider. I believe that unionist ideologues are deeply worried about this very attractiveness. They are worried that nationalists may be correct in their belief that unionists who engage with Irish culture, and adopt an Irish cultural identity, will finish up either as nationalists or as unionists who will accept a united Ireland with relative ease. They believe that any weakening of unionist hostility to Irishness, any large-scale engagement with Irish culture, could ultimately undermine the union. Trimble's fear of the threat to unionism of Irish culture was made explicit in his 1989 speech: "One of the enduring folk memories of the Ulster-British people is the fear of massacre – the fear that the people may cease to be, at least culturally."[34]

---

[33] See for example: *Northern Ireland Life and Times Survey.* www.ark.ac.uk/sol/sur veys/community_relations/time_series/CRencycidentity.htm (accessed 18/06/2009). This represents an averaging out of the responses, which ranged from 1% to 7% between 1989 and 2007.

[34] Maurna Crozier, *op. cit.*, p. 50.

Neither the nationalist nor the unionist analysis of the political importance of cultural identity is necessarily true. Terence Brown has argued that: "It seems that Ulster unionists, Ulster Protestants, whatever one wishes to call them, have felt no need of the concept of national identity,"[35] and suggests a number of theories why this may be so. He concludes his analysis with a warning against nationalist assumptions on this issue:

> It has always been the pious aspiration of the nationalist and the cultural nationalist, that if only the Ulster Protestants could see the error of their ways, once they fall upon the riches of Irish literature, the richness of Irish political culture, they will see that their error is massive, and become converted to Irish separatism, or some kind of Irish independence. That seems to me an improbability in the current circumstances and, if we are to make progress, we have to understand, even if we find the task difficult, why the Ulster Protestant, at this stage, sees no need of that concept of identity. 'I have no need of that hypothesis,' said La Place to Napoleon, when discussing the existence of an explanatory deity. In Ulster Protestant culture, there is a strong sense that they have no need of the hypothesis of national identity, and to discover why it is not needed, and what kind of inter-relationship there can be between them and nationalists, is a major project for social and intellectual historians and for the politically-engaged in Ireland.[36]

If Brown is correct in his analysis, not only are nationalists wrong in their belief that they can use culture to convert unionists to nationalism, but unionists are equally mistaken in seeing Irish culture as a threat.

It can also be argued that both nationalist and unionist ideologues are misled in their assessment of future constitutional options. Northern Ireland is no longer in a zero-sum game, where the only two perceived options are to become exclusively bound either to a British state or to an Irish state. In thirty or forty years this society may have internalised the fact that, through the EU, national sovereignty is not what it was, and could well come to the conclusion that the blurring of national boundaries is a better option than a zero sum game. Indeed, it is arguable that this process is already under way. The NILT surveys have shown a consistent pattern, the emergence of a new, regional identity, under which an average of 41% Catholics and 27% Protestants identify their primary political allegiance as "neither unionist nor nationalist."[37] If this

---

[35]   Terence Brown (1992), "Identities in Ireland: the historical perspective," in Jean Lundy and Aodán Mac Póilin (eds.), *Styles of Belonging: the Cultural Identities of Ulster*, Belfast, Lagan Press, p. 42.

[36]   *Ibid.*, p. 45.

[37]   *Northern Ireland Life and Times Survey.*www.ark.ac.uk/sol/surveys/community_ relations/time_series/CRencycidentity.htm (accessed 18/06/2009). These figures represent an average of the responses between 1989 and 2008.

trend continues, it is possible that both nationalism and unionism will become much less intense, much less rigid, much less exclusive, and much less sectarian. The evidence appears to indicate that the formal union is not under threat, but it is likely that the Republic will have a greater formal say in the internal affairs of Northern Ireland. I believe that in thirty or forty years we – or those of us who are still alive – will be relaxed about living in a society in which people adhere to different national identities and a wide range of cultural identities. It is likely that, in the long term, there will not be enough people who will be passionate enough about a united Ireland to bring it about. Some unionists are already saying this. It is unfortunate that few of the unionists who make this case act as if they believe it themselves.

Both the Irish language and Ulster Scots have been caught up in the politics of the constitutional issue. Both have benefited from this politicisation, in that both have gained recognition and accessed government funding that would not otherwise have been available to them. Both, I think, have suffered and will suffer from having been drawn into a cultural war that is, essentially, the continuation of political activity by other means, and has little or nothing to do with cultural values.

Culture and politics are inextricably bound one to the other, in a constant state of complex interaction, and it is neither possible nor desirable that they be entirely divorced. However, when people interested in culture find that culture being appropriated as an appendage of some short-sighted political agenda, when they see it being reduced to the brutal simplicities of our politicians' thought processes, they have no choice but to fight for cultural autonomy. A language that is of interest to politicians mainly as an emblem to mark out territory may not suffer more than a temporary setback if it is vibrant and secure, but a fragile linguistic tradition that finds itself in this position and depends on these politicians for its very survival is in a very dangerous situation.

Political agendas at their best tend to cramp cultural debate; at their worst they become nothing more than a battle-ground for ideological tub-thumping. Jim Shannon, a member of the Democratic Unionist Party, indicated in 1996 that his commitment to Ulster Scots culture was primarily driven by a unionist political agenda: "We are Ulster-Scots descended from a proud and fiercely independent people with a longer tradition than that promoted by nationalists. Their language is a dead language for a dead people."[38] This was no more than a mirror-image of statements made by spokespersons for Sinn Féin's Cultural Department. In 1984, Máirtín Ó Muilleoir indicated that his party's cultural struggle

---

[38] Jim Shannon, Democratic Unionist Party Councillor, quoted in *Irish News*, 25/09/1996.

mirrored, and indeed was subservient to its broader political and military aims:

> We see the armed struggle as the highest point of the cultural revival. We see no contradiction. [...] I see no difference between fighting imperialist political control with guns on the street, and fighting imperialist cultural control through this department! [...] All [genuine liberation] movements have acknowledged a need for a cultural attack on oppression to partner a military one.[39]

Ó Muilleoir's approach was echoed in 1990 by Gearóid Ó hEara, then head of Sinn Féin's Cultural Department: "It is impossible to de-politicise the cultural struggle or to separate it from the struggle for self-determination,"[40] and: "[...] there is now a greater awareness of the importance of culture as part of our revolutionary struggle than ever before."[41]

The common element between all these statements is that each of these cultural warriors promotes his chosen cultural movement as the exclusive property of one section of the population. It does not seem possible for their proponents to imagine that society in Northern Ireland could learn to embrace linguistic diversity without reductive political baggage. Ulster Scots is a valuable cultural resource. The dialect of English that I was brought up in Catholic west Belfast had some Irish words in it (gub, slug, clabber), but many more Scots. We hirpled and hirstled and sprachled and cowped into seughs with the best of them. We redd up the house and hepped up against the cold. People you didn't like were grulshy, gaukey or gormless, or were geeks, gaums, gaunches, gits, glumphs, glipes, gorbs, gomerils, glunters, skittery goats, gabs and gabshites, and that's only the words beginning with 'g'. Ulster Scots as spoken in its heartlands is infinitely richer and infinitely more expressive.

Ulster Scots and Irish are both under threat. Ulster Scots is being eroded towards an English norm. One generation of neglect could see the death of Irish. Both linguistic traditions are fragile, something they share with most of the world's languages. Both of them are worth maintaining. Jim McCluskey has made this point better than I can:

> Every language that succumbs to the economic, political and cultural pressures being applied all over the globe today, takes to the grave with it an en-

---

[39] Interview with Máirtín Ó Muilleoir, Damien Gorman (1984) "With a bodhrán in one hand [...]" *Belfast Review*, Issue 7, Summer 2007, p. 2. I am grateful to Gordon McCoy for drawing my attention to this article.

[40] Interview with Gearóid Ó hEara, "Advancing the cultural struggle," *An Phoblacht*, 25/01/1990, p. 10. I am grateful to Gordon McCoy for drawing my attention to this article.

[41] *Ibid.*

cyclopaedia of histories, mythologies, jokes, songs, philosophies, riddles, superstitions, games, sciences, hagiographies – the whole cumulative effort of a people over centuries to understand the circumstances of its own existence. It is an enormously frightening thought that nine tenths of that accumulation of wisdom, speculation and observation is to be lost within the next century or so.[42]

And again, speaking specifically of Irish:

In a broader, global perspective, there are excellent reasons for trying to maintain Irish, but those reasons have nothing to do with nationalist sentiment, nor with any search for an authentic, distinctive, or exclusive *Irish-ness* (whatever that might mean). Far from being driven by an insular or inward-turning impulse, the effort is worth making because it is our contribution to a much larger effort, a global struggle to preserve a kind of diversity which human society has enjoyed for millennia, but which is being lost in our time. Like the Maori and the Inuit, we have the good or the bad fortune to be sole custodians of one threatened strand of that diversity.[43]

In conclusion, it is more than probable that the cultural war in Northern Ireland is indeed a phoney war. However, it may not be a phoney war in the sense of being a cynical manipulation of public opinion. Much of the evidence points to the conclusion that our politicians have misread the situation and are engaged in an elaborate and sincerely felt struggle over an issue that is ultimately meaningless. As Flaithrí Ó Maoil Chonaire put it in his acid comment on the 16th century *Contention of the Bards*, in which, while the Gaelic world fell apart around them, the leading Gaelic poets of Ireland argued over whether the north half of Ireland or the south had primacy:

Lughaidh, Tadhg agus Torna
ollaimh oirrdheirce ar dtalaimh,
coin iad go n-iomad feasa
ag troid fa an easair fhalaimh![44]

Lughaidh, Tadhg and Torna
Famed poets of our land,
Hounds they are, of great learning,
squabbling over an empty dish.

---

[42] James McCloskey (2001), *Voices Silenced*, Dublin, Cois Life, p. 36.

[43] *Ibid.*, p. 41.

[44] Cuthbert Mhag Craith (1967) (ed.), *Dán Na mBráthar Mionúr*, vol. i, Dublin, Institute for Advanced Studies, p. 12.

Résumé

Le titre de cet article est extrait d'un discours prononcé par Peter Robinson, Premier ministre d'Irlande du Nord, en juin 2008, lorsqu'il a déclaré son intention de mettre en place une « Académie Unioniste » afin de promouvoir la culture unioniste et a envisagé, par la même occasion, l'établissement d'un organisme pour l'égalité de la culture britannique qui veillerait sur la culture unioniste et qui répondrait aux attaques lancées contre elle : « Il y a eu une guerre culturelle en quelque sorte ici en Irlande du Nord. Nous allons contre-attaquer. Notre mode de vie unioniste ne sera pas relégué dans un tiroir au fond d'un bureau. Nous sommes britanniques et nous comptons bien le rester ». Cet article étudie les dimensions historiques, politiques et idéologiques qui ont donné lieu à cet état de polarisation culturelle en Irlande du Nord. Notre principal sujet d'étude est la politique linguistique d'Irlande du Nord où l'irlandais et l'ulster-scots sont considérés comme les marqueurs emblématiques des allégeances politiques, religieuses et culturelles.

The Ulster-Scots Movement

A Personal Account

Ian ADAMSON

Ullans Academy

In a letter to me dated 5th June 1975, from what was then the U.E.R. des Pays anglophones of the Université Paris III-Sorbonne Nouvelle, Professor René Fréchet thanked me for my book, *The Cruthin*,[1] which had been published the previous year. This initial contact was to be the beginning of a long and productive correspondence between Professor Fréchet and myself, a friendship which lasted until his death in 1992.

In his obituary, Mark Mortimer, who had taught at the British Institute in Paris for some thirty years, was to say that René Fréchet was for many years the voice of Ireland in Paris. This was by no means an exaggeration. Professor of English at the Sorbonne, and the spirit behind the University's Institute of Irish Studies, set up in 1979, Fréchet served as guide and councillor to the increasing number of students engaged in research on Irish themes. His *Histoire de l'Irlande*[2] was only one facet of his numerous activities in the field of Irish Studies. Apart from his love of Irish literature – his translation of the poetical works of Yeats[3] is a model of precision and sensibility – he paid great attention to events in Northern Ireland which he covered in a series of often outspoken articles published in the French Protestant weekly, *Réforme*. An acute knowledge of facts as well as an enduring affection for every aspect of life in the region guided his particular interest in the North. As a young lecturer he had spent two years at Queens' University Belfast. The experience he acquired, and the long-lasting friendships he made at that time gave him an indisputable authority to comment on developments in the political situation there. There is no doubt that it was through him that the point of view of the Ulster Protestant found its most articulate

---

[1] Ian Adamson (1974), *The Cruthin – The Ancient Kindred*, Conlig, Nosmada Books.

[2] René Fréchet, *Histoire de l'Irlande*, Paris, PUF, coll. « Que sais-je ? », 1970.

[3] René Fréchet, *W. B. Yeats, Choix de poèmes*, Paris, Aubier, 1989.

and sympathetic spokesman in France. His convictions and courageous declarations did much to counter-balance the often superficial representations of this community in the mainstream French press.

The Cross-Community Base

I was greatly honoured that he should take an interest in my work. Commenting on my *Identity of Ulster*,[4] published under my own imprint, Pretani Press in 1982. Fréchet was to write:

> What an interesting, curious piece of work this is. Generally, if we are told it is not a question of a war of religion in Ulster, we are told about opposition between Catholics, whom people think of as mostly wishing for the reunification of the island, and Protestants, who want to remain British.
>
> Adamson however, does not militate in favour of the bringing together of two quite distinct communities. He says that their division is artificial, that they are all more or less the descendants of pre-Celtic peoples, and in particular of the Cruthin, who were constantly moving backwards and forwards between Ulster and Scotland, where they were called Picts, a fact that did not prevent their homeland becoming the most Gaelic part of Ireland. "British," as far as he is concerned, takes on a meaning that Ulster people tend to forget. Here are some quotes that it is interesting to place side by side: "'Old British' was displaced in Ireland by Gaelic just as English displaced Gaelic;" "the people of the Shankill Road speak an English which is almost a literal translation of Gaelic;" "the majority of Scottish Gaelic speakers are Protestants."
>
> In fact, Adamson is especially interested in Protestants, but those Protestants who have worked or are working towards reconciliation (could these even be the United Irishmen of the 1790s?), for a co-operative movement, for a kind of popular autonomy or self-management. He shows the paradoxical confusion of antagonistic, partly mythical traditions, and is trying to convince people of the fundamental unity of Ulster.[5]

Throughout the 1980s, Fréchet continued to follow with great interest my involvement specifically in the creation of several community organisations to promote my ideals of mutual respect, common identity, co-operation and self-help. These included the Farset Steps of Columbanus Project. The idea behind the project was to bring together young people from both sides of the community and allow them to follow in the footsteps of the saint from Bangor in the North of Ireland to Reims

---

[4] Ian Adamson (1982), *The Identity of Ulster: The Land, the Language and the People*, Bangor, Pretani Press.

[5] The original text, in French, and still in my possession, was sent to me in the form of a first draft of a projected review of the book. See also the remarks on *The Identity of Ulster* which Fréchet published in "Une solution pour l'Ulster?," *Réforme*, No. 1935, 22 May 1982, p. 12.

and Luxeuil in France, through St Gallen in Switzerland, to Bregenz in Austria, and finally on to Bobbio in Italy. In a country where violence was dividing the people, it was important to point to a shared past. This project became possible thanks in no small measure to the help of my friend Tomás Cardinal Ó Fiaich, whose foreword to the second edition of my book, *Bangor Light of the World*,[6] in 1987 is testimony to his commitment to the cross-community line we saw as so vital.

The links between the North of Ireland and the continent of Europe came to the fore in another project that emerged around the same period. Following a press conference held on 1st July 1986 under the auspices of the Lord Mayor and Lady Mayoress of Belfast, I proposed a link-up between the twin towers, Helen's Tower in Clandeboye, Northern Ireland, and the Ulster Tower at Thiepval in northern France with museum complexes near both. This was achieved by the Somme Association[7] which I established in 1990 with the help of my friend, the Reverend Dr. Ian Paisley. This association was formed to show the part played by Irishmen of all persuasions in the First World War in France, Belgium and the Dardanelles, supported by an international Friends of the Somme organisation.[8] I also initiated through Farset the concept of twinning Londonderry with La Rochelle[9] and promoting the Musée du Désert in the Protestant community in Ireland.[10]

On 13th January 1992 René Fréchet wrote to me to ask if he could translate my book, *The Ulster People*,[11] into French and have it published by the University Press. He had spoken to Paul Brennan, later to become Professor of Irish Studies at the Sorbonne, who was willing to do so. However, Frechet's tragic death on 24th April of that year brought the proposed translation and publication to an abrupt end.

It was at exactly this period that I began to become increasingly involved in the promotion of Ulster-Scots with my establishment of the Ulster-Scots Language Society and the Ulster-Scots or Ullans Academy. Although Fréchet had not lived to see these projects develop, I would like to think that my vision for Ulster-Scots, as an integral part of an

---

[6] Ian Adamson (1987), *Bangor, Light of the World*, Belfast, Pretani Press [1979].

[7] See the site of the Somme Heritage Centre at http://www.irishsoldier.org/

[8] See *Battle Lines: Journal of the Somme Association*, Issue I, 1990.

[9] The shared experience of a besieged Protestantism, with such radically different outcomes, made such a project attractive. For the historical background, see Ian Adamson (1995), *1690, William and the Boyne*, Conlig, Pretani Press.

[10] The Musée du Désert retraces the history of Protestantism in France, and the Cévennes in particular.

[11] Ian Adamson (1991), *The Ulster People: Ancient, Medieval and Modern*, Bangor, Pretani Press.

inclusive culture that stretches across the sectarian divide, would have met with his interest and approval.

The Genesis and (Arrested) Development of the Ulster-Scots Academy

In 1992, the year of Fréchet's death, I published the three-volume Folk Poets of Ulster Series, including the "Country Rhymes" of James Orr, Samuel Thompson and Hugh Porter.[12] In line with the Scots magazine *Lallans*, I suggested the use of "Ullans" as the name of the magazine the Ulster-Scots Language Society first published in 1993. The term appeared particularly useful, not only as a contraction of "Ulster Lallans" but of the word "Uladh," Gaelic for Ulster, or "Ulidia," and "Lallans," Scotch for Lowlands, as well as being an acronym for the Society's aims in its support for the "Ulster-Scots language, literature and Native Speech." I had also suggested the new name for a proposed Ulster-Scots Academy which I founded in June 1992, following a meeting in Vancouver between Professor Robert Gregg and myself. The Academy was to be based on the Friesian Academy of Sciences in the Netherlands, with its three departments of Linguistics and Literature, History and Culture, and Social Sciences,[13] which I had visited in 1978 with a group of community activists from Northern Ireland.

The Academy aimed to fulfil a need for the regulation and standardisation of the language for modern usage. These standards would be initiated on behalf of the Ulster-Scots Community, Protestant and Catholic, Nationalist and Unionist, and would be academically sound. What we didn't need was the development of an artificial dialect which excluded and alienated traditional speakers. Furthermore, the term "Ullans" was not to be restricted to Northern Ireland and the Republic of Ireland, since as a variety of Central or Mid Scots, it is also spoken in south-west Scotland, an area south of the River Nith, including the country of Robert Burns, and in Galloway and Carrick – corresponding

---

[12] J.R.R. Adams & P.S. Robinson (eds.) (1992), *The Country Rhymes of James Orr, The Bard of Ballycarry, 1770-1816*, Bangor, Pretani Press; J.R.R. Adams & P.S. Robinson (eds.) (1992), *The Country Rhymes of Hugh Porter, The Bard of Moneyslane, c. 1780*, Bangor, Pretani Press; J.R.R. Adams & P.S. Robinson (eds.) (1992), *The Country Rhymes of Samuel Thompson, The Bard of Carngranny*, Bangor, Pretani Press.

[13] The Fryske Akademy in Ljouvert (Leeuwarden), Friesland, Netherlands was started before the Second World War by a group of Friesian students who were concerned to sustain the Friesian language. The initial task was the development of a comprehensive Friesian dictionary, including local dictionaries and shorter dictionaries. The Akademy aspires to University status which they feel is essential for the future of the language. I last visited them on 31st October and 1st November, 2002 with the Ulster-Scots Agency.

roughly to the ancient Kingdoms of Rheged and Aeron[14] – where it is known as "Galloway Irish."[15] The Ullans Academy was to be based in Belfast, which was at the epicentre of all three jurisdictions. It was also to be used to explore the relationships with Ulster Gaelic which I have termed "Ulidian," which was formerly spoken in all three areas, and had been first brought to south-west Scotland by the Kreenies or Cruthin of Dalaradia in Antrim.[16]

In December 1992, I facilitated the formation of the Ulster-Scots Language Society in Craigavon House, Belfast and at a meeting of the Society on Friday 28th May, 1993, I suggested that the Ulster-Scots Academy might be required to act as a teaching and resource centre for the newly formed Language Society.

The first formal meeting of the Academy was held at my home on Monday 10th January, 1994. The following month, I asked Mr. Jim Nicholson M.E.P. to raise the issue of an Ullans Academy in the European Parliament at Strasbourg.[17] This was followed up by the Reverend Dr. Ian Paisley M.P.[18] In December 1995, I asked Dr. Paisley to arrange for Members of the U.S.L.S., including myself, to meet the Northern Ireland Office Minister, Michael Ancram, to put forward a comprehensive proposal for a core-funded Academy. The costed and itemised proposal included details of a language development programme and an Ulster-Scots Language Resource Centre. Without any funding being awarded, the Academy managed to complete some aspects of its agenda on a purely voluntary basis.

It was clear to me that it was of fundamental importance to establish a standard version of the language, while at the same time maintaining local variants. To this end, in 1995, I had published, under the imprint of the Ulster-Scots Academic Press from my premises in 12 Main Street, Conlig, County Down, a regional dictionary by James Fenton, *The*

---

[14] Rheged was the Old British Kingdom whose original language was akin to Breton. See Mike McCarthy (2002), "Rheged: An Early Historic Kingdom near the Solway." *Proceedings of the Society of Antiquaries of Scotland*, Volume 132, Edinburgh, Royal Museum of Antiquities of Scotland, pp. 357-381.

[15] Billy Kay (1993), *Scots: The Mither Tongue* [1986], Darvel, Alloway Publishing, p. 162.

[16] John Mac Queen (2005), *St. Nynia* [1990], Edinburgh, Birlinn Ltd. 47. See also Ian Adamson (1998), *Dalaradia, Kingdom of the Cruthin*, Belfast, Pretani Press.

[17] See verbatim report of proceedings, European Parliament, 07/02/1994 – 08/02/1994, pp. 2-276, Nicholson (PPE).

[18] Letter to Sir Patrick Mayhew MP, Secretary of State for Northern Ireland from Dr Ian Paisley, 31st March, 1994.

Hamely Tongue[19] which was the most important record yet produced of current Ulster-Scots speech and which is now in its third edition.

With the establishment of the Ulster-Scots Agency in the Noarth/ Sooth Boord o Leid under the Belfast Agreement of 1998, and the formal recognition of Ulster-Scots as a European Regional Language by the U.K. Government in 1999,[20] I ensured that the implementation of the Academy's Language Development Programme became a Government imperative. On 10th March, 1999, Marjorie ["Mo"] Mowlam, one of Her Majesty's Principal Secretaries of State, issued Order 1999 Number 8591 establishing North-South co-operation bodies. The functions of the Language Body in relation to Ullans and Ulster-Scots cultural issues would be exercised by an Ulster-Scots Agency of the Body. Ullans was to be understood as the variety of the Scots language traditionally found in parts of Northern Ireland and Donegal. Ulster-Scots cultural issues related to the cultural traditions of the part of the population of Northern Ireland and the border counties which were of Scottish origins and the influence of their cultural traditions on others, both within the island of Ireland and in the rest of the world. This document thus allowed a distinction between the language, which is spoken by people of varying ancestry and nationalities, and the cultural traditions, which are an amalgam of Ulster and Scottish traditions, including Highland, Lowland and Hebridean.

In 1998/99 the Government had funded the U.S.L.S. to produce a development plan for the Ulster-Scots language. This "Edmund Report" was produced in July 2000 by consultant John Edmund, its official title being, *A Strategic Plan for the Promotion of the Ulster-Scots Language*.[21] It provided an updated, detailed language development proposal as a model for the work of the Ullans Academy. This report again provided detailed costings for a core-funded Academy. The resourcing of the critical elements of the language development plan was agreed by Government and approved in the 2000-2003 corporate plans for the Ulster-Scots Agency. However, the agreed £1.5m. expenditure on the language plan was never attributed.

---

[19] James Fenton (1995), *The Hamely Tongue: A Personal Record of Ulster-Scots in County Antrim*, Conlig, Ulster-Scots Academic Press.

[20] Gavin Falconer, "Breaking Nature's Social Union. The Autonomy of Scots in Ulster," in John M. Kirk and Dónall P. Ó Baoill (eds.) (2005), *Legislation, Literature and Sociolinguistics, Northern Ireland, the Republic of Ireland and Scotland*, Belfast, Cló Ollscoil na Banríona, pp. 48-59.

[21] The text of John Edmund's report is available as an appendix to Ulster-Scots Academy Implementation Group, *Proposals for an Ulster-Scots Academy: Public Consultation Document*, 2007 available at: http://www.dcalni.gov.uk/public_consul tation_on_proposals_for_an_ulster_scots_academy.pdf (accessed on 3/10/2009).

In September 2002, the Agency held its first formal meeting with the Ullans Academy. It was agreed that the Academy would reconstitute itself as a company limited by guarantee, in order that the existing voluntary programme with the Academy be properly resourced and established. In October 2002, the Minister for Culture, Arts and Leisure, Mr. Michael McGimpsey, responded to the repeated representations from the Ulster-Scots Community for resolute action by Government to promote Ulster-Scots more effectively. His department organised a three-day "Future Search" conference to clear the way forward between statutory bodies, Government and the Ulster-Scots Community. In the context of Ulster-Scots as a recognised European Regional and Minority Language, the Ullans Academy would be modelled on the Friesian Academy in the Netherlands, which I have already mentioned. However, it would also promote the inter-relationships between Ullans and Ulster Gaelic, as well as the study of Ulster English and Northumbrian English in general. This has led to a difference in philosophical approach between those who would see the promotion of Ulster-Scots as something of a political tool in their opposition to the Irish language and my Ullans movement.

Furthermore, the Academy's research would also extend beyond language and literature to historical, cultural and philosophical themes such as the life and works of Frances Hutcheson and C. S. Lewis, and to studies of the history of Ulidia in general, especially Dalriada, Dalaradia, Dal Fiatach, Galloway and Carrick, not forgetting Ellan Vannin, the Isle of Man. The Scotch-Irish would also provide a particular focus on the American dimension, but emigration studies would also be necessary for the countries of the Commonwealth and other countries. Closely associated were the Heirschipe Villages projects, which were proposals to construct living history and traditional craft centres based on 18th century Ulster-Scots villages and towns at the time of the American War of Independence and the French Revolution. This would have many parallels with the leading American attraction at Colonial Williamsburg in Virginia[22] and would be a centre of cultural tourism development.

In 2003, I was instrumental in ensuring that the Joint Declaration of the British and Irish Governments would indicate that the British Government would take steps to encourage support to be made available for an Ulster-Scots Academy.[23] However, differences in philosophy continued. The original Ullans Academy wished to be associated with An Cultúrlann McAdam/Ó Fiaich and the Gaeltacht quarter of West Belfast.

---

[22] See the official site at: http://www.colonialwilliamburg.com (accessed on 3/10/2009).

[23] Letter in my records entitled "Ulster-Scots Academy" from David Trimble MP to Paul Murphy MP, Secretary of State for Northern Ireland, 20th May 2003.

It was envisaged that the Heirschipe Village concept, initiated by the Ullans Academy, with its focus on cultural tourism, should also be developed under the remit of the Ulster-Scots Agency. The Ullans Speakers Association of Ballymoney, County Antrim, the United Ulster History Forum of the Ards Peninsula, County Down and the Monreagh Project, County Donegal, would be encouraged as Friends of the Academy and an Ullans Centre of Academic Excellence would be established between the University of Glasgow, Queen's University, Belfast, and the University of Ulster. Dr Paisley and I travelled to Glasgow University on Saturday 21st June 2008 to facilitate this.

Conclusion

I hope that I have been able to give you some insights into the recent history of the Ulster-Scots or Ullans movement. A certain amount of research has already been done on this question.[24] However, it has given me great pleasure to be here at a location which was of such crucial importance in the development of that movement. As a physician and student of John-Paul Marat, I have been privileged to tell you about my own private and quiet revolution as a "friend of the people." It has also given me the opportunity to thank René Fréchet, Paul Brennan and Wesley Hutchinson, as well as all those who have been involved in Irish Studies in France. I trust that all our efforts to create an Ullans Academy in Belfast will not be in vain.

Résumé

Cet article retrace les origines du mouvement pour la promotion de l'ulster-scots (aussi appelé Ullans) en Irlande. Partant d'un échange épistolaire entretenu avec le professeur René Frechet (Université Sorbonne Nouvelle-Paris III) de mai 1975 jusque sa mort en 1992, l'auteur rappelle les contacts établis avec la Fryske Akademy au Pays-Bas en 1978, la publication de son livre The Identity of Ulster *en 1981, l'inauguration en juillet 1992 de la Ullans Academy et sa publication de la série intitulée* The Folk Poets of Ulster. *Il examine ensuite la mise sur pied de la Ulster-Scots Language Society en 1992 et sa publication de* The Hamely Tongue *de James Fenton en 1995. L'auteur explique ensuite le rôle qu'il a joué dans les négociations précédant l'Accord de Belfast en 1998, qui dans le domaine de la culture, a donné lieu à la*

---

[24] See Wesley Hutchinson (1999), *Espaces de l'imaginaire unioniste nord-irlandais*, Caen, Presses Universitaires. See also Ian Adamson, "The Ullans Academy," in John M. Kirk and Dónall P.Ó Baoill (eds.) (2005), *Legislation, Literature and Sociolinguistics: Northern Ireland, the Republic of Ireland and Scotland*, Belfast, Cló Ollscoil na Banríona, pp. 65-68, and Frank Ferguson (ed.) (2008), *Ulster-Scots Writing – An Anthology*, Dublin, Four Courts Press.

création de la Ulster-Scots Agency. Enfin, il fait remarquer l'heureuse coïncidence qui a voulu que le débat sur l'ulster-scots reprenne à la Sorbonne Nouvelle, espace neutre, tel que Fréchet et ses successeurs l'ont voulu.

Ulster-Scots Revival or Ullans Twilight?

States in Play in Contemporary Ulster-Scots Literature

Frank FERGUSON

Institute of Ulster-Scots Studies, University of Ulster

The Ulster-Scots Literary Tradition

James Fenton's speaker laments in his prose poem 'Lint (A pooer mines)' the disappearance of that once quintessential feature of Antrim countryside, the flax-dam. They are he says filled in, buried and forgotten, those that do survive are so overgrown that they have become ghosts and worthless shadows of themselves – "a' by."[1] Such declarations of passing and loss are articulated alongside the potential of the writer's memory to elegise, to recall and reinstate the object of desire through the spoken and written word. In these texts there exists indeterminacy, much like the weather of the bogs and townlands of Fenton's native mid-Antrim. It is indeterminacy at play between the past and present, between memory and poetry, between the potential of language to memorialise and enshrine the past and the potential of language to say new things. It might also be said that there is a wider indeterminacy over the nature and interpretation of the meaning of Ulster-Scots in Northern Ireland today. The sense of uncertainty between coming and going in contemporary Ulster-Scots writing could be said to mirror the cultural debates created in Northern Ireland in the wake of the Good Friday and St Andrew's Agreements after Ulster-Scots dialect, culture and heritage, under the new parity of esteem animus, were woven into the fabric of post-Agreement Northern Ireland. This has precipitated much heated debate and has proved itself a rich area to analyse the multifaceted nature of culture war that exists within the north of Ireland, while perhaps not adding greatly to the linguistic or literary knowledge of Ulster-

---

[1]   James Fenton (2000), *Thonner an Thon*, Newtownards, Ullans, p. 65.

Scots in the wider community.[2] In this essay I wish to explore two writers who have been involved in the Ulster-Scots language movement. However, I do not wish to examine their works in order to condemn them for the alleged crimes of "inventing traditions" or for fomenting a new literary Unionism.[3] I will suggest that Philip Robinson and James Fenton write from the perspective of an Ulster-Scots literary tradition. It is a tradition that is, and indeed always has been, aware of its hybrid and marginalised status; drawing as it does inspiration from Lowland Scots vernacular literary traditions within an Irish location. This situation engenders the examination of many cultural, political and linguistic ambiguities. It is a literature at play and in play between national, regional and local allegiances where issues of linguistic, cultural, political, religious and poetic identity are expressed and some resolution to personal and national uncertainties sought. Their work is also derived from a tradition that has adapted itself very well to dealing in double meanings through highly developed comic and satirical modes that often manifest themselves, although this is often a masquerade, in sentimentalism and nostalgia.

In the first part of this essay I will provide an introduction to the Ulster-Scots literary tradition that informs the work of Robinson and Fenton. In the second part of this essay I will examine some of James Fenton's poetry and Philip Robinson's trilogy of novels, *Wake the Tribe o' Dan* (1998), *The Backstreets o the Claw* (2000) and *The Man Frae The Ministry* (2005) and his collection of poems *Alang tha Shore* (2005). I will suggest these texts offer highly sophisticated readings of their cultural and linguistic predicaments. These writers, I will argue, operate in a dialectic between their sense of a receding Ulster-Scots Twilight and a confident, if modest, cultural revival.

The Ulster-Scots literary tradition has evolved over the past three hundred years.[4] The proximity of Scotland to Ireland has always made migration and settlement relatively straightforward and people, culture and texts have travelled freely and creatively between the islands. Substantial Scottish settlement in Ireland throughout the 17th century, particularly in the province of Ulster had a pronounced effect on Irish

---

[2] Cahal McCall (2002), "Political Transformation and the Reinvention of the Ulster-Scots Identity and Culture," in *Identities: Global Studies in Culture and Power*; Vol. 9, No. 2, pp. 197-218; p. 197.

[3] See Gavin Falconer (2005), "Breaking Nature's Social Union – the Autonomy of Scots in Ulster," in John M. Kirk and Donall P. O. Baoill (eds.), *Legislation, Literature and Sociolinguistics: Northern Ireland, the Republic of Ireland, and Scotland*, Belfast, Queen's University Press, pp. 58-59.

[4] See Frank Ferguson (2008), "Introduction," *Ulster Scots Writing: An Anthology*, Dublin, Four Courts, pp. 1-22.

culture in a number of ways. As well as altering the demographic, religious and political complexion of the island, the migration of a sizeable number of Scots speakers also modified the linguistic character of Ireland. This resulted in a rich overlapping trilingual mix of Irish, English and Scots speakers. In addition to the creation of Scots-speaking language communities, Irish literature was also influenced by the migration of Scottish vernacular literature to Ireland. This literary cross pollination may be a less well known product of the processes of the Scottish diaspora in Ireland but it can be argued that the style and generic forms of the vernacular Scots revival of the 18th century in Scotland migrated to Ireland, aided and abetted by an Irish print industry that was unhindered by copyright restrictions and keen to capitalize on producing popular works that would sell. Furthermore, while these texts were closely associated with Scots settlers and their descendants, it was not exclusively the preserve of those groups – just as in England Scottish vernacular poetry became a popular mode of literary expression and fashionable beyond the Scottish community. J.R.R. Adams has noted that Belfast presses in particular pirated a number of Scottish texts in the 18th century that included the works of David Lindsay, Alexander Montgomery, Blind Harry and Allan Ramsay and it is unlikely that these were read solely by Ulster-Scots.[5] The popularity of Robert Burns has often been cited as the major inspiration for the development of Ulster-Scots literature in Ireland.[6] While Burns was a major, if not predominant, inspiration to Ulster-Scots poets, the publication of Scots poetry (by Irish writers) can be traced back, at least in the medium of print, to the early part of the 18th century to several broadsheets and miscellanies.[7] For example, William Starrat. a surveyor from the Strabane/Lifford border. had a poem addressed to Allan Ramsay published in Ramsay's collected poems, and Starrat may also have had poems published in a section of 'Scotch Poems' in the *Ulster Miscellany* (1753).[8] There was also a small, but nevertheless significant printing of

---

[5] J.R.R. Adams (1987), *The Printed Word and the Common Man: Popular Culture in Ulster 1700-1900*, Belfast, Institute of Irish Studies, pp. 72-73.

[6] John Hewitt (2004), *Rhyming Weavers and Other Country Poets of Antrim and Down* [1974], Belfast, Blackstaff, new edition, p. 1. See also Liam McIlvanney (2003), *Burns the Radical: Poetry and Politics in Late Eighteenth-Century Scotland*, East Linton, Tuckwell, p. 223. For a revaluation of Robert Burns influence in Ulster writing see Frank Ferguson and Andrew Holmes (eds.) (2009), *Revising Robert Burns and Ulster: Literature, Religion, Politics c. 1770-1920*, Dublin, Four Courts.

[7] Wesley Guard Lyttle's (1894), *Betsy Gray or Hearts of Down: A Tale of Ninety-Eight*, Bangor, and the series of novels published by Archibald McIlroy, are staples of this tradition. See Frank Ferguson (ed.) (2008), *Ulster-Scots Writing, An Anthology*, Dublin, Four Courts, pp. 17-19.

[8] For further particulars of this poem, see Alexander Kinghorn and Alexander Law (eds.) (1974), *The Works of Allan Ramsay*, 6 vols, Edinburgh, vi, p. 68. *The Ulster*

materials in Scots in Dublin in the 18th century. *Jemmy Carson's Collections*, first published in 1744, contains a number of comic poems and prose pieces and its droll description of a Presbyterian sailor's unwilling "celebration" of the Eucharist in Christ-Church Cathedral in "The North Country-man's Description of Christ-Church" has aroused speculation that this was penned by Jonathan Swift.[9]

Publication of Scots infused poetry and prose continued well into the 20th century in the north of Ireland, with a fondness from the latter half of the 19th century for Kailyard style novels that adapted themselves to the concerns of an Irish setting.[10] However, despite this broad corpus of novels, poetry and newspaper material in the public domain, the figure of the Ulster Scot, especially the Presbyterian Ulster Scot has often endured a difficult time in Irish letters. In Sydney Owenson's, *The Wild Irish Girl* (1806), a disconsolate southern Milesian describes Ulster as "a Scottish colony" where "Scotch dialect, Scotch manners, Scotch modes, and the Scottish character almost universally prevail."[11] However, the Ulster-Scots literary tradition responded with numerous affirmative examples of Ulster Scottish cultural identity. The Strabane novelist and memoirist John Gamble described the mingling of Scottish and Irish traits as a positive phenomenon that fused the best parts of national identities together into a "third character."[12] Such hybridising tendencies have created much to be admired in a number of creative and sophisticated literary texts. Their sense of being betwixt and between states and identities demonstrates a sound capability in negotiating personal and national identities through the adroit manipulation of language. In the early 19th century, the Antrim poet, Samuel Thomson, wrote about being Irish on the outside and Scottish within.

> I love my native land, no doubt,
> Attach'd to her thro' thick and thin,

Miscellany (n.p., 1753?); see also Michael Griffin and Breandán Mac Suibhne (2006), "Da's boat; or, can the submarine speak? *A voyage to O'Brazeel* (1752) and other glimpses of the Irish Atlantis," *Field Day Review*, Vol. 2, p. 113.

[9] Jemmy Carson's Collections: being a revival of his own labours and lucubrations, for thirty years past; with pieces upon different subjects, by several hands (1744), Dublin. See also Kenneth Milne, (2000), "Restoration and Reorganisation 1660-1830," in *Christ Church Cathedral, Dublin, A History*, Dublin, Four Courts, pp. 255-298; p. 263.

[10] See my Introduction, *Ulster-Scots Writing An Anthology, op. cit.*, pp. 19-22.

[11] Sydney Owenson (1806, 1999), *The Wild Irish Girl*, Oxford, Oxford World Classics, p. 198.

[12] John Gamble (1819), *Views of society and manners in the north of Ireland in a series of letters written in the year 1819*, London, p. iv.

Yet tho' I'm Irish all without,
I'm every item Scotch within.[13]

The acceptance of cultural hybridity and the play between allegiances were phenomena readily accepted by these writers. They were
able to switch registers, finding easy movement between classical,
vernacular and emerging Romantic modes.[14] Literature became a means
to record their lives in traumatic times of change and conflict, rather
than as a retreat to simplistic stereotypical stage Scots-Irishry, or a
slavish imitation of Scottish literary models. Situated as they were
between overlapping cultural and linguistic polities, they were acutely
attuned to the potential of language to weave and play between differing
power blocs and mentalities. This ability further manifested itself in a
combative satirical tendency, one that inherited the Scottish vernacular
traditions of flyting and abusive mock elegy – genres that provided
many means for a poet to communicate to two audiences at once.[15] The
first audience was made up of those receptive to the nuances and covert
barbs of the literary forms; the second readership was removed from the
culture, but believing with a certain amount of condescension that they
were enjoying the productions of their social inferiors. Ironically, these
"lesser" poets were often well read and cognisant of the patronising
attitude of the latter section of their readership, and in some cases were
vitriolic in response. The poet Samuel Thomson, for example, demonstrates familiarity with numerous references to Scottish, English and
Irish poets and texts, as well as to a number of classical writers in translation. In Thomson's "Epistle to Robert Burns:"

HOMER I've read an' VIRGIL too,
With HORACE, MILTON, YOUNG and GAY,
Auld SPENCER, POPE and DRYDEN thro',
Sweet THOMSON, SHENSTONE, GOLDSMITH, GRAY.[16]

---

[13] Samuel Thomson (1806), "To Captain M'Dougall, Castle Upton: with a copy of the
author's poems," in *Simple poems on a few subjects*, Belfast, p. 87.

[14] See Tom Paulin (2004), 'Foreword' to *Rhyming Weavers, op. cit.*, pp. vi-vii.

[15] For an introduction to the satirical and combative tradition of flyting see Roderick
Watson (2007), *The Literature of Scotland: The Middle Ages to the Nineteenth Century*, second edition, Houndsmills, Palgrave Macmillan, pp. 59-60; Murray Pittock
(2008), *Scottish and Irish Romanticism*, Oxford, Oxford University Press, p. 156.
For examples from Ulster writing, see *Ulster-Scots Writing an Anthology, op. cit.*,
pp. 20-21.

[16] Samuel Thomson (1793), *Poems on Different Subjects, Partly in the Scottish
Dialect*, Belfast, p. 86. For a further discussion of Thomson's reading see Jennifer
Orr, "Before, and Beyond: Samuel Thomson and the Poetics of Ulster-Scots Identity," in Ferguson and Holmes (eds.), *Revising Robert Burns and Ulster*, pp. 106-
126.

Hugh Porter, who enjoyed the sporadic support of upper class Angli-can patronage, composed several poems that severely berated his patron Thomas Tighe.[17] While it has been often said that these were poets with a strong sense of place as well as "customs, textures and cadences of local life," they were also writers well versed in the intricacies and textures of poetry.[18] Their awareness of using combinations of Scots language and generic forms, themselves the vehicles for dissent and cultural revival in Scotland, made for satisfyingly complex Irish poetry, which could be deployed for powerful political, philosophical and literary statements in the hands of an able poet. Samuel Thomson's "To A Hedgehog," a poem as much about the failure of the '98 as it is an eco-critical homily on the endangered Irish hedgehog, borrows much from Robert Fergusson and Robert Burns' transformation of the "Stan-dard Habbie" stanza form into a vehicle for profound personal, philoso-phical and national deliberation. In this sardonic reinterpretation of William Broome's "To a Coquette," Thomson addresses the fate of the "rougher subject," the hedgehog:

> Thou grimest far o' gruesome tykes,
> Grubbing thy food by thorny dykes,
> Gudefaith *thou* dinna want for *pikes*,
> Baith sharp an' rauckle;
> Thou looks (L–d save's) array'd in spikes,
> A creepin heckle![19]

While there is much pleasure to be had by the earthy mouthmusic of the rhymes in this stanza, this deliberately obfuscating comic brio does not fully camouflage the fact that the hedgehog carries the same weap-ons (pikes) as the United Irishman. Many commentators have been keen to perceive Thomson's writing as part of a school of weaver poets, noting the use of "heckle" (a flax comb) as indicative of the language of the working practices of the linen industry being carried over into local poetry. However, the connotation of the word with a soldier's cockade would seem as appropriate in this instance, adding significance in Thomson's desire to urge caution and seek safety for adherents to the cause, as well as suggesting that the envisaging of these poets as a

---

[17] For example see "Written the Next Morning After Having Dined and Supped with the Rev. Messers. T. and B.," (1813), *Poetical attempts, by Hugh Porter, a county of Down weaver*, Belfast, p. 124.

[18] Tom Paulin, "Foreword" to *Rhyming Weavers, op. cit.*, p. x.

[19] Samuel Thomson (1799), *New Poems*. For a reading of this poem see Frank Fergu-son, "'The Third Character': the Articulation of Scottish Identities in Two Irish Writ-ers," in Frank Ferguson and James McConnel (eds.) (2009), *Ireland and Scotland in the Nineteenth Century*, Dublin, Four Courts, pp. 62-76.

homogeneous, weaving fraternity may be misleading and damaging to their craft and reputations.

Despite the potential for Ulster-Scots writing to add much to the canons of Irish and Scottish literature, there has been a disinclination to examine the work of many of these writers. Even those who were aware of their writing gave them scant praise or exposition. They were deemed sources for social historians, rather than texts to enter Irish or Scottish national literary canons.[20] Seminal studies such as Terence Brown's *Northern Voices* dismissed much of planters' literature of the 18th century as being composed of "prayer-book and sermon, Bible and psalter."[21] There have, since then, been many revisions of this view, with focus placed on the particular literary culture of northerners.[22]

John Hewitt's pioneering study into the poetry of the eighteenth and nineteenth centuries in Ulster, *Rhyming Weavers and Other Poets of Antrim and Down* (1974), suggested that many materials remained under-explored in northern Irish libraries and archives, and he went further than most in praising the literary abilities of the some of the poets whom he had unearthed. Although, even Hewitt can be criticised for some of his responses to the works he recovered, declaring that in the often truncated selection of poems he included in his anthology one would find "little or no highly creative imagination."[23] More recent work on Ulster poets' experimentation with and development of Scottish verse traditions in particular has suggested much more creativity exists in these writers than previous generations have allowed for.[24]

While literary commentators have often ignored the Ulster-Scots literary canon or dismissed it as a pale imitation of Scottish poets, a linguistic debate has smouldered that often has served to obscure study of the Scots language in Ireland in quibbling over whether it is a language or a dialect or if it exists at all. The result has been a standoff between native speakers who perceive themselves as the sole preservers and upholders of the language and those who criticise their position. As

[20] D. H. Akenson and W. H. Crawford (1977), *Local Poets and Social History: James Orr, Bard of Ballycarry*, Belfast, PRONI.

[21] Terence Brown (1975), *Northern Voices: Poets from Ulster*, Dublin, Gill & Macmillan, p. 6.

[22] Tom Paulin (1991), "Northern Protestant Oratory and Writing 1791-1985," in Seamus Deane (ed.) (1990), *The Field Day Anthology of Irish writing*, 5 vols, Derry, Field Day Theatre Company, Vol. iii, p. 314.

[23] *Rhyming Weavers, op. cit.*, p. 127.

[24] Liam McIlvanney has noted James Orr's innovations in the traditional Christis Kirk stanza in his poem "Donegore Hill" in "Across the narrow sea: the language, literature and politics of Ulster Scots," in Liam McIlvanney and Ray Ryan (eds.) (2005), *Ireland and Scotland: Culture and Society, 1700-2000*, Dublin, Four Courts, p. 205.

opinions have polarised, meaningful debate has been suppressed and this has precipitated the foundation of a belief in the cult of the "native speaker." This cult has germinated within and outside the Ulster-Scots community and has been used by insiders to create a linguistic territory for themselves from which activists and enthusiasts can agitate for recognition and also, intriguingly, often well-meaning attempts have been made to safeguard the sanctity of the "native speaker" of Ulster-Scots by "outsiders." This guardianship, on occasion much more stringent in tone than that of the language enthusiasts, has attempted to segregate native speakers from literary dabblers and entrepreneurs who have used such resources as the *Concise Ulster Dictionary* to add an element of Doric zest to their poetry and prose. This stance is laudable in one sense as it protects the Ulster-Scots from becoming little more than a set of obscure archaisms that may embellish the lexicon of the professional northern Irish poet.[25] However, these interventions prevent innovation, creativity and experiment and construct an unhelpful *cordon sanitaire* between Ulster-Scots as spoken language and Ulster-Scots as literary language, further displacing the language, diminishing the literary tradition and underestimating the extent to which writers in Ulster have engaged with Scotland's linguistic inheritance and literary traditions.

Contemporary Ulster-Scots Writing: Philip Robinson and James Fenton

In the mid 1990s concerns were raised about the survival of Ulster-Scots language and literature.[26] Since that time there have been a number of attempts to safeguard and indeed to foster and promote the language, culture and heritage. At present, one could be relatively positive and suggest writing in Ulster-Scots appears to be in quite a healthy state. Recent years have seen its resurgence in the popular and academic press and its profile raised in the public consciousness of Northern Ireland (albeit with varying rates of success). As well as *Ulster-Scots Writing an Anthology*, Ulster-Scots has also featured in some, though not all, recent major anthologies of Irish literature. Andrew Carpenter's *Verse in English from Eighteenth Century Ireland* (1998) contains works by weaver poets and other writers in Scots. Tom Paulin's *Faber Book of Vernacular Verse* (1990) includes several poets from the tradition, and

---

[25] Edna Longley, "Poetry in the wars" (1986, 1991), in *The Field Day Anthology of Irish Writing*, Vol. iii, *op. cit.*, pp. 648-654; p. 651.

[26] Ivan Herbison (1997), "'The Rest is Silence': Some remarks on the disappearance of Ulster-Scots poetry," in *Cultural Traditions in Northern Ireland. Varieties of Scottishness*, Belfast, Institute of Irish Studies, Queen's University Belfast, pp. 129-145.

Paulin has continued his interest by contributing the foreword for the recent new edition of John Hewitt's *Rhyming Weavers* (2004). Such revisions to Ulster-Scots canon in Irish canonicity go some way to compensate the omission of Ulster-Scots writing from literary histories such as Seamus Deane's *Short History of Irish Literature* and from "definitive" modern anthologies such as *The Field Day Anthology*.[27]

Much of the success of Ulster-Scots literature's resurgence could be credited to the Ulster-Scots language movement. Activists have been very industrious in the last fifteen years and initiated the publishing of new and familiar writers in the tradition. In 1992, Ian Adamson published the works of Samuel Thomson, James Orr and Hugh Porter in three separate volumes in *The Folk Poets of Ulster Series*. In the same year, the Ulster-Scots Language Society was established to promote the study and use of Ulster-Scots. This body produces a journal entitled *Ullans* (an alternative name to define the Ulster-Scots language, i.e. a combination of Ulster and *Lallans*), described as the language of 100,000 native speakers.[28] Philip Robinson and James Fenton have both been prominent in the preservation of Ulster-Scots as a written and spoken language. In 1995 Fenton produced *The Hamely Tongue: A Personal Record of Ulster-Scots in County Antrim Speech*, while in 1997 Robinson published *Ulster-Scots: A Grammar of the Traditional Written and Spoken Language*.[29] Alongside the reproduction of classic texts, the Ulster-Scots movement have also published new works, such as Philip Robinson's trilogy of novels *Wake the Tribe o Dan* (1998), *The Back Streets o the Claw* (2000), and *The Man frae the Ministrie* (2005), and James Fenton's collection of poems and prose, *Thonner and Thon* (2000).

Despite the proliferation of Ulster-Scots literature, critical readings of contemporary Ulster-Scots literature have tended to find them inferior to their 18th and 19th century counterparts. Liam McIlvanney's otherwise excellent survey essay claimed:

> [...] contemporary Ullans writing may yet produce important work. As things stand, however it is difficult to avoid a sense of bathos when comparing today's Ullans writers with the best of their vernacular predecessors.[30]

---

[27] *Ibid.*, p. 141.

[28] *Ullans*, 6, Summer 1998, p. 67.

[29] James Fenton (1995), *The Hamely Tongue: A Personal Record of Ulster-Scots in County Antrim Speech*, Newtownards, Ullans; Philip Robinson (1997), *Ulster-Scots: a Grammar of the Traditional Written and Spoken Language*, Belfast, Ullans Press.

[30] Liam McIlvanney, 'Across the narrow sea: the language, literature and politics of Ulster Scots,' in Liam McIlvanney and Ray Ryan (eds.), *Ireland and Scotland: Culture and Society, 1700-2000, op. cit.*, p. 222.

And Ullans poetry, especially, has been lambasted as bearing "the dismal imprint of the Scottish Kailyard" lacking the ambition, technical resource and accomplishment of its Scottish and Irish counterparts.[31] Read in relation to modern Scottish counterparts, the Ullans project is deemed to fall far short. On one hand, one could claim that in the main much of the recent work by those poets claiming to write in Ulster-Scots was not written as serious art but as enthusiastic determination to publicize and foster awareness of a minority language. It is unfair therefore to compare the work of these poets with the art texts of professional academic writers and poets. However, the short-sighted way in which Ulster-Scots has been examined has at times appeared more a hasty diagnosis that is not fully aware of the complexity of the Ullans texts. These readings view Ulster-Scots falling into somewhat reductive categorisations of heavy and light Ulster-Scots. One should consider Manfred Gorläch's finer rendering of types of Scots into at least five categories that range from the representation of living dialect, the modernist experimentation in synthetic forms of Scots, the deployment of ideal Scots for the purposes of institutional standardization, urban Scots for humorous writing or social criticism and the literary use of a minimal Scots.[32] Indeed in Robinson's novels alone these categories all appear to manifest themselves.

While one might agree that there is a Kailyard mode at work in much of Ullans writing, it is one that is conversant with Scottish and Irish forms of the Kailyard, as well as Scottish and Irish attempts to subvert and deconstruct the genre.[33] As much as the texts conform to the staples of the provincial Ulster and Scottish novel, they also borrow much from a satirical approach that incorporates Flann O Brien's modernism of the *Third Policeman* in *Back Streets o the Claw* and other narrative experimentation.[34] How seriously does Philip Robinson stray into Kailyard with his novels? The opening paragraph of *Back Streets o the Claw* – "ten thousand chimneys in wee rows, running this road and that. Every

---

[31] *Ibid.*

[32] Manfred Gorläch (2002), *A Textual History of Scots*, Heidelberg, Universitätsverlag Winter, p. 137.

[33] For reassessments of Kailyard writing see Douglas Gifford, Sarah Dunnigan, Alan MacGillivray (eds.) (2002), *Scottish Literature in English and Scots*, Edinburgh, Edinburgh University Press, pp. 486-488; Robert Crawford, (2007), *Scotland's Books: The Penguin History of Scottish Literature*, London, Penguin, pp. 512-514; Norman Vance, "'Kailyard' stories in Ulster: Northern fiction after Carleton," in Frank Ferguson and Andrew Holmes (eds.) (2009), *Revising Robert Burns and Ulster: Literature, Religion, Politics c. 1770-1920*, Dublin, Four Courts, pp. 148-164.

[34] I am grateful to Philip Robinson for a discussion on the writing of fiction in which he stated that *The Third Policeman* had inspired the ending of *The Back Streets o the Claw*.

reeking lum-pot was proof – a living, breathing proof – of warm hearts and warm hearths below" – does conform to the genre, drawing its reader's attention to a mawkishly short-sighted Ulster-Scots sentimentality. However, it is also arguable, in a novel in which its Jack M'Lean, the main character, will be killed by persons unnamed and unknown, that it is an oblique form of Troubles narrative, or at least a novel that uses the prism of Ulster-Scots language to examine the nature of a Northern Ireland sense of identity.[35] The prefatory extract from James Orr's "Donegore Hill," itself a caustic satire on broken covenants of the Antrim United Irishmen and human infidelity in general, can be interpreted as both a mourning for the loss of faith and identity and also as a statement on the loss of linguistic and community solidarity.

Robinson's fictions borrow from the Kailyard school's emotionalism because their overt sentimentality permits the exploration of emotional attachment to place and language that is pertinent to Robinson's argument about the dislocation of potential Ulster-Scots from their heritage, culture and history. While the novels appear to exist in an uneasily acknowledged present, the gaze of the novel, like the Kailyard, is often cast a generation backwards. In *Wake the Tribe O Dan* the nostalgia for the past centres on whether Betsy Sloan will take on her role as the 'carlin', or titular head of the secret society of the Knights of Gibraltar Pass. This association, mostly an amalgam of Orange and Masonic ritual and practice, provides the social cohesion in the community of Drumcrum. Robinson has been criticised for drawing heavily on the symbolism of British Israelitism in his depiction of the Knights, with some perceiving a conspiracy afoot, an allegation which he has refuted.[36] While the choice of an actual belief system may lead to confusion, the utilization of these symbols, in my opinion, is for satirical effect. It permits Robinson to examine the cultural inheritance of Ulster-Scots at a time of transition when those who can lay the strongest claim to the linguistic and cultural heritage are questioning the utility of such things. It also allows Robinson to explore the processes through which outsiders, whether individuals or government institutions approach the learning of and regeneration of culture. Incidentally, it is worth remembering that the majority of those connected to the Knights and also to the local Presbyterian Church are not necessarily committed believers, they are often practitioners because they were born into or married into the community, not because of any ideological or theological impetus. Robinson's satirizing of such a community makes him more a heir of radical United Irishmen Presbyterian poets Samuel Thomson and James

---

[35] Philip Robinson (2000), *The Back Streets o the Claw*, Belfast, Ullans, p. 7.

[36] See Aodán Mac Póilin, (1999) 'Language Identity and Politics in Northern Ireland,' *Ulster Folklife*, Vol. 45, pp. 108-132.

Orr, than it does an ultra-unionist, crypto-British Israelite. This rootless community may perhaps be at the heart of the double meaning of waking of the tribe of Dan. In one sense Robinson is conducting a wake for the vanishing of traditional ways of acting and thinking, that is part of the Kailyard strategy for expressing longing for the vanished community. Conversely this might also be read as a call to reawaken and to raise the consciousness of the community. Yet Robinson's novel may be asking also what exactly is the tribe of Dan being asked to wake up for? Beset with institutional demands to construct a theme park version of the past, his fictitious 'locals' must negotiate a number of compromises with their own sense of history and language.

Much of the humour is derived from locals providing a government agency with a forged Ulster Scots culture, transmitted through a highly stylised Ullans dialect. The novel raises the spectre of an Ulster-Scots language school whose children speak in medieval Scots.[37] The world that is evoked in Drumcrum, literally the hill of the Cruthin, can be read as an allegory of the uncertainties of Ulster-Scots in the late 20th century, and conceivably also a reworking of the Unionist metanarrative in the face of a postmodern, postindustrial and postimperial United Kingdom. The people of the Cruithin, the prehistoric tribe envisioned by Ian Adamson and others as the forbears of the Unionist community in northern Ireland, appear to be living in the fragments of a culture, not really committed to church or knights hall, but placed into situations where they must choose to maintain, or lose their culture.

It is perhaps difficult to see if Robinson provides solutions to the dilemmas of Northern Ireland, as much as he attempts to chart the disappearance of Ulster-Scots language, and gauge the arc of the Scots diaspora in Ireland and beyond. However, the novels act as readers for Ulster-Scots language, with Ulster-Scots words, grammar and traditional literature being deployed throughout the texts. The trilogy acts as a primer in Ulster-Scots, with *Wake the Tribe O Dan* especially providing a paratextual support in a glossary. This novel's use of prefatory poems acts as a para-anthology of Ulster-Scots writing that underlines the archives of materials available to the language from the medieval to the contemporary period. These extracts simultaneously authenticate the novel, inscribing its textual kinship to past texts and underscore the potential for development. This is the only novel to contain a glossary, which acts both as a tool to enable interpretation and to manage and measure the distance between native speaker and non-native speaker. Later novels do not include glossaries, an act that suggests that readers who engage with the novels have become proficient in adapting to a

---

[37] Philip Robinson (1998), *Wake the Tribe o' Dan*, Newtownards, Ullans Press, p. 137.

prose which moves from the Kailyard tradition of spoken word in the vernacular and the authorial voice in 'standard' English to a situation in which the vernacular is found in dialogue and prose. This attempt to construct a perfect reader (of Ulster-Scots) proposes that language survival is not only possible but that new readers not born into the community can be created. Such attempts at packaging the mentality of the community as exercised through its speech patterns and collective memory also provide a means to journey to that community. Although one wonders if more populist and contemporary forms might have been considered to engage the reader. Robinson is perhaps too conscientious to replicate the Kailyard to bring the reader into full sympathy with the characters and does not do enough in his choice of Protestant secret society iconography to distance the novels from the charges that have been levelled at him. Robinson's novels examine the often fraught interaction between cultural applicant and governmental patronage and the texts address the relationship of individuals and groups to the Northern Irish state and the misunderstandings that occur between the two groups and the dependency culture that arises. The examination of individuals pitted against language and cultural planners makes both a plea for the inclusion of Ulster-Scots in the structure of the state and draws attention to the difficulties of preserving and sustaining a speech community in the face of demographic, political and cultural change.

Robinson, as a poet, works within the flyting tradition of Scots vernacular literature and often links this with the vocabulary of dissent in the Presbyterian mould. He also compares the Ulster-Scots movement's experience to Eastern Bloc dissidence against Soviet repression.[38] While this is an approach that wavers at times into pastiche there is a strong impression of his feeling genuinely victimized and seeking to counteract government intransigence against Ulster-Scots writers with traditional satirical verbal assaults couched in folk verse and apparently prosaic poetry linked to nature, the land and sense of place. Robinson's poem 'Thocht Polis' describes the debate between language enthusiasts and officialdom over the exact nature of Ulster-Scots language as a wrangle over what colour the Flet-Earth society believe a Friesian cow is.[39] On the face of it this collapses a complex discussion into a childish riddle. Such transitions are part of the literary heritage of Ulster-Scots, where political and philosophical discussion often came camouflaged in coun-

---

[38] See "Alba an Albania," in Philip Robinson (2005), *Alang tha Shore*, Newtownards, Ullans, p. 12.

[39] *Ibid.*, p. 9.

try rhyming.[40] Such regressions to the schoolyard call attention to the unfair situation that language enthusiasts feel themselves placed in, being the butt of jokes and establishment attempts to limit their demands for language rights. It is officialdom that is the flat-earther, and it is officialdom that is the language bigot; what better way to illustrate their objections to the language than by depicting them as begrudgers and bureaucrats? Also the comic nature of the poem may act to dispel the somewhat militant mood that the poem ends with, its audience being charged to get set for war and "fear no noise."

If Philip Robinson represents the comic mode of contemporary Ulster-Scots writing, James Fenton may be described as its elegist. Like Robinson he is engaged in expressing a landscape in his verse whose topography is created through a dense vernacular that announces its Ulster-Scottishness through the singularity of its aural and written signs. Fenton's collection *Thonner and Thon*, whose title could be loosely translated as a declaration of location and indication: (*thonner*) yonder/over there's the thing (*thon*), stands as an experiment for how Ulster-Scots can be fashioned in its contemporary sense as a literary language, and how Ulster-Scots can be used by a poet to locate a personal space composed of memory, topography and lyric. Fenton, as Liam McIlvanney has noticed, mines in his poetry. In the vernacular sense he mines, he remembers, and mines in the Heaneyesque sense, in that he explores landscape and memory. Fenton knows the topography of boggy ground and the *moss* of his county Antrim is where much of the poems are set. These watery lands are recorded in a series of poems that deal with the childhood memories and nature closely associated with his sense of place. Water like Ulster-Scots speaks in a variety of ways in the poems. There is a sense of foreignness in the poems, of travelling into a thoughtworld at once Irish and simultaneously somewhere else, where familiar birdsong is defamilarized by calling them by their Ulster-Scots names and the watery landscape blurs and smudges time and space. A world torn between being attuned to native and natural sounds: wind through sallies, gurgling brooks and birdsong; to the transfixing sense of quiet and cessation that permeates the verse. The dialectic of waking and sleeping is also at play within Fenton's verse. In "Dailygan" the twilight that encapsulates the speaker leaves him or her in a sense of stasis, of being incapable of staying or going.[41] Such unstable rootedness, seems at odds with the sense of movement and animation exhibited in the first verse in the darkness of the natural

---

[40] For example Mathew Meek's (1811), *The Tale of the Butterhorn*, published in Belfast, likened Presbyterian acceptance of crown assistance to a dog lulled by thieves.

[41] *Thonner an Thon, op. cit.*, p. 1.

setting. Even the sense of *quaitness* may hold double meanings, the ever-surrounding bog may be quiet around the speaker and may be quite around him also. The sense of light retreating with connotations of final resting place is complicated with the transition (or remembrance) in the second stanza of the woman cooking in the house at twilight at harvest time, such reveries of agricultural and domestic labour are articulated only to be consumed by a fascination with the "gleekin' ee" (blinking eye, l. 14) of the light failing and the inability ever to reside in the past or future where one can neither stay or leave (l. 16).

The fascination with twilight also suggests that Fenton is writing his version of the Ulster-Scots Twilight, commemorating the language, and applying one final time to the page before it will vanish. His poems are very much attuned to memory and commemoration, and like the rhyming weavers, in whose traditions he claims to belong, he records the natural cycle of the year and the traditional work patterns associated with rural life. Indeed his fascination with Ulster-Scots fayre in its *pratas* and *neeps* echoes the Ulster and Scottish vernacular shared obsession with the utilization of folk cuisine to articulate national and regional identity. Although Fenton mocks this somewhat in the poem "A' it taks" with his inventory of local sights and smells that also includes the smell of freshly baked supermarket bread.[42]

While one can see a strong relationship between Fenton's work and the rhyming weavers, his work also appears informed by the developments within wider Scottish and Irish poetry of the 20th century and he steps aside from the limitations of the traditional Ulster-Scots vernacular verse forms and the ubiquitous alternate line rhyming quatrain of popular poetry. He appears to follow on from Kavanagh, Hewitt, Heaney and other northern Irish poets and simultaneously to incorporate the vision of the Scottish Renaissance within his work, and in particularly Hugh MacDiarmid's deft short lyric especially appears adapted to Fenton's Ulster-Scots. The reported observation of natural phenomena as a metaphorical statement about the psyche of the speaker, in terse free verse stanzas, is applied to County Antrim to great effect.

What is more pronounced in Fenton is how his choice of word blurs between meanings in Ulster-Scots and English. While this may be seen as an accidental occurrence and language purists would point out that a non Ulster-Scot speaker might lose many of the hidden meanings in the poems by surmising that it is only English transcribed into a County Antrim accent. His creation of his own orthography to propel Ulster-Scots away from 'standard' English also emphasizes the difference and proximity between the two speech systems. This is language in the half-

---

[42] *Thonner an Thon, op. cit.*, p. 47.

light, oscillating between states, and revelling in the creative force that might be found in the indeterminate spaces of language and a putatively vanishing identity. It is also a powerful indicator of hybridity of how Scots vernacular can travel and be absorbed into an Irish setting, out of which multiple meanings can be created. Fenton suggests possibilities for Ulster-Scots as literary language, with much capability for invention and improvisation, shimmering between sound and meanings in a manner that relates as much to jazz as it does to writing across two literary traditions.

It is perhaps difficult to ascertain if Fenton's and Robinson's work is a rearguard action, an elegy by the last of the rhyming weavers, or a more nuanced evocation of a speech community uncertain if it is imperilled or is edging towards revival or reinvention. Ulster-Scots writing at the present juncture can be said to be moving back and forth between states. While the focus by political commentators has tended to speculate on Ulster-Scots effectiveness or otherwise as a cultural platform to reconfigure Unionist identities, more critical exploration remains to be carried out on the literature created by the contemporary Ulster-Scots movement. This literature written ostensibly in a 'minority' language, which some have declared a DIY language for Orangemen, would seem to be articulating statements about Irish politics, culture and literature that the "majority" might want to consider listening to.

Résumé

On identifie souvent la littérature Ulster-Scots en Irlande du Nord comme étroitement associée aux tentatives unionistes et loyalistes de construire et promouvoir un héritage culturel britannique susceptible de rivaliser avec la culture gaélique nationaliste et républicaine. Cet article suggère que cette interprétation a souvent ignoré les traditions radicales de la littérature Ulster-Scots ainsi que les préoccupations thématiques et culturelles des écrivains contemporains. Il montre que les œuvres du poète James Fenton et du romancier Philip Robinson se situent dans la continuité des traditions de la littérature Ulster-Scots tout en développant et en jouant avec ces traditions. Au lieu d'être de simples agents culturels du loyalisme ou de l'unionisme, leurs œuvres respectives présentent des réflexions personnelles sur la vie et la société du nord de l'Irlande. En effet, leurs écrits, à travers leur adaptation de l'ulster-scots à des fins littéraires, leur improvisation linguistique subtile, et leur critique satirique de plusieurs stratégies culturelles nord-irlandaises, proposent des lectures pertinentes des tensions sociales, culturelles et créatives dans la province.

The Turn to Rights in the Language Question

Diarmait MAC GIOLLA CHRÍOST

Cardiff University

During the last few years the politics of the two most widely spoken Celtic languages, Irish and Welsh, have been defined by a series of language rights campaigns. In Wales this takes the form of a campaign, led largely by Cymdeithas yr Iaith Gymraeg [the Welsh Language Society], for a new Welsh language act that would replace the Welsh Language Act of 1993 and which would establish specific rights for Welsh language speakers. The prospects of this campaign will improve if proposed transfer of legislative competence with regard to the Welsh language from the United Kingdom Parliament in Westminster to the Welsh Assembly in Cardiff Bay goes ahead, as is likely.[1] For the Irish language, campaigning has been divided between specific interests in Northern Ireland and the Republic of Ireland. In the north of Ireland the focal point has been the campaign Acht [Act] to get the Northern Ireland Assembly to agree to introduce an Irish language act founded upon a rights-based approach.[2] The Acht campaign has, thus far, failed following the negative decision of the minister with responsibility for the Irish language in the government of the Northern Ireland Assembly.[3] In the south a campaign, styled Stádas [Status], ended in success as Irish became the 21st official language of EU in June 2005,[4] thereby building upon the rights established for Irish speakers through the Official Languages Act 2003. This shift towards a discourse centred on language rights is not unique to the Celtic languages but reflects a much broader

---

[1] BBC News/Wales, "Welsh language legal bid starts" http://news.bbc.co.uk/1/hi/wales/7863542.stm (accessed 02/02/2009).

[2] See, for example: http://www.pobal.org/english/irishlanguageact.php (accessed 12/05/2009).

[3] BBC News/Northern Ireland "Poots opposes move on Irish act" http://news.bbc.co.uk/1/hi/northern_ireland/7046117.stm 16th October 2007.

[4] Valerie Robinson, "Stadas campaign ends in success as EU minister embrace Irish." *The Irish Times* 14th June 2005.

trend. A global phenomenon is at work here and two of its main pillars are the Declaration on the Rights of Persons belonging to National, Ethnic, Religious and Linguistic Minorities adopted by the General Assembly of the United Nations Organization in 1992 and the Universal Declaration of Linguistic Rights signed in Barcelona in 1996 by a wide range of organisations sympathetic to the case of minoritised or lesser-used languages.[5] The current dominance of the public discourse in this arena by linguistic human rights contrasts with previous eras, defined by other cultural shifts. Prior to the turn to rights, the last such significant shift of such similar significance occurred during the 1960s. In this case the counter-culture politics of 1960s western European and north American society directly informed the appearance and development of groups such as Cearta Sibhialta na Gaeltachta [Gaeltacht Civil Rights] (1969) in the Republic of Ireland, Cymdeithas yr Iaith (1962) in Wales, and the Shaw's Road Gaeltacht (1969) in Belfast in Northern Ireland. Noting such patterns does not, of course, explain them, much less analyse the significance of such shifts. For some actors such shifts will be no more than a tactical, opportunistic or even fashionable reflection of the predominant form or style of political rhetoric at that time. However, despite the motivations of the actors involved, the implications of these shifts can be profound.

What Are Human Rights?

It is necessary at this point to remind ourselves what we mean by human rights in general. According to the *Stanford Encyclopedia of Philosophy* they are to be defined as follows:

> Human rights are political norms dealing mainly with how people should be treated by their governments and institutions. They *are not ordinary moral norms applying mainly to interpersonal conduct* (such as prohibitions of lying and violence). As Thomas Pogge puts it, "to engage human rights, conduct must be in some sense official." [...] But we must be careful here since some rights, such as rights against racial and sexual discrimination are primarily concerned to regulate private behavior. [...] Still, governments are directed in two ways by rights against discrimination. They forbid governments to discriminate in their actions and policies, and they impose duties on governments to prohibit and discourage both private and public forms of discrimination.[6]

---

[5] See, for example: http://www.eblul.org/ (accessed 12/05/2009).

[6] James Nickel "Human Rights", *The Stanford Encyclopedia of Philosophy (Fall 2008 Edition)*, Edward N. Zalta (ed.), URL = http://plato.stanford.edu/archives/fall2008/entries/rights-human/.

According to the *Oxford Companion to Philosophy* they are defined as follows:

> In their strongest sense, rights are justified claims to the protection of persons' important interests. When the rights are effective, this protection is provided as something that is owed to persons for their own sakes. The upholding of rights is thus essential for human dignity. [...] Legal rights, to be justified, must ultimately have moral justification.[7]

Historically, international law did not recognise, much less confer, rights and protections on individual human beings. Instead, it was exclusively concerned with the rights and duties of states and the relationships between them. Individuals who today might be considered to be the victims of human rights abuses had, at that time, no set of values nor any organisation to which they could address their complaints. As is noted in the *Stanford Encyclopedia of Philosophy*, they could 'appeal to heaven, and invoke standards of natural justice, but there were no international organizations working to formulate and enforce legal rights of individuals'.[8] In the period between the First and the Second World Wars (c. 1918-1939), the League of Nations enjoyed limited success in protecting the rights of national minorities in post Treaty of Versailles Europe. This all came crashing down with the advent of the Second World War. The impact upon public opinion of the discovery of the shocking brutalities perpetrated by the Nazi regime during the course of their occupation of much of Europe led directly to a very determined effort on the part of the United States of America, and its Allies, in particular to create a new organisation, replacing the League of Nations, with a particular responsibility for promoting and protecting human rights internationally, and thereby contributing to the prevention of future conflicts. Thus, the United Nations was created in the immediate aftermath of the war in 1945. In its preamble, the founding Charter of the United Nations set out a series of fundamental aims regarding the prevention of war, the recognition of human rights, including the following:

> To save succeeding generations from the scourge of war, which twice in our lifetime has brought untold sorrow to mankind, and

---

[7] Ted Honderich (ed.) (1995), *The Oxford Companion to Philosophy*, Oxford, Oxford University Press, p. 776.

[8] James Nickel, "Human Rights", in Edward N. Zalta (ed.), *The Stanford Encyclopedia of Philosophy* (Fall 2008 Edition), available at: http://plato.stanford.edu/archives/fall2008/entries/rights-human/.

To reaffirm faith in fundamental human rights, in the dignity and worth of the human person, in the equal rights of men and women and of nations large and small [...][9]

In 1948 the United Nations published its Universal Declaration of Human Rights, an international bill of rights. It was similar to its principal historical antecedents namely the French Declaration of the Rights of Man and of the Citizen (1789) and the United States of America's Bill of Rights (1791), but whereas these documents were only to apply to the Republic of France and the United States of America, the United Nations' declaration was to apply internationally, to all citizens of all states. However, the Universal Declaration of Human Rights is not a binding treaty but rather is a set of recommended norms. That said, despite its non-binding status very many of its norms currently form a part of various, widely-ratified United Nations' human rights treaties, conventions and agreements. Thus, the impact of the Universal Declaration of Human Rights has been far-reaching and, invariably, it is the central point of reference for popular conceptions of what is meant by human rights.

In the European context, the idea of linguistic human rights became common currency during the early 1990s as the European Union sought to both expand and deepen. That is to say the European Union set about the twin goals of granting membership to new countries (especially amongst the post-Soviet Union countries of mid and eastern Europe) and to more closely integrating the political, economic and social relations between its member states. A greater regard for the diversity that comprises the European linguistic identity was accepted as a part of the moral fabric or public good ethos of the new Europe. Thus, the Council of Europe European Charter for Regional or Minority Languages (1992) was adopted as a means of affording some degree of protection to the smaller languages of the continent.[10] Since then the variety and extent of legislation in the area of language rights in different parts of Europe has developed enormously.[11] The turn to language rights in Wales and in Ireland ought to be set in this context.

Also, a further, final point to bear in mind at this stage is that the principal features of linguistic human rights, as with human rights in general, are as follows. They are concerned with the relationship be-

---

[9] UN Charter available at http://www.un.org/aboutun/charter/preamble.shtml (accessed 10/05/2009).

[10] For the text, refer to http://conventions.coe.int/treaty/en/Treaties/Html/148.htm (accessed 17/05/2009).

[11] A very useful starting point for exploring this is the website of the organisation "Mercator. Linguistic Rights and Legislation" found at http://www.ciemen.org/mercator/Menu_nou/index.cfm?lg=gb (accessed 17/05/2009).

tween individual human beings and their government or state. In this relationship the government is by far the more powerful actor and therefore the individual requires protection in the form of rights, or norms, that determine how the relationship ought to operate. While political, it is essential that these rights be justified in moral terms. There must be an inherent public good or well-being. A moral principle must be at stake, not merely political self-interest.

Linguistic Human Rights and the State

The political rationale for the contemporary turn to linguistic human rights in Wales and Ireland relates to the specific challenges faced by Irish and Welsh in the three jurisdictions. In the Republic of Ireland that is the failure to effectively and practically realise Irish as the 'national and first official language' in accordance with its constitutional status and the continuing decline of the language in the Gaeltacht (the officially designated Irish-speaking territories of Ireland). In the case of the Welsh language, the issue is the failure of institutions to fulfil their statutory duties under the Welsh Language Act of 1993 and the continuing decline of the Bro Gymraeg (the traditional Welsh-speaking heartland). For the Irish language in Northern Ireland, the challenge has been, and remains, to enable political agreement and power-sharing in Northern Ireland thereby steering ever further from the threat of endemic political violence.

The case of Northern Ireland is particularly instructive in the clarity of the movement in the discourse from civil rights to human rights – from the origins of the Irish republicans' long war against the state in the late 1960s until the sharing of political power between republicans and unionists by the second half of the 1990s. Here, the argument for Irish language rights emerged along with the emergence of the wider agenda regarding human rights in general. Moreover, this agenda is not innocent of politics. It would be a mistake to assume that human rights are universal in the sense that they are timeless, reflecting humanitarian values which are pertinent to human society under any given historical circumstances. This is not the case, they are not transhistorical. Quite simply, specific human rights arise from and are a response to localised and specific contemporary problems.

One argument for human rights is that they comprise a means of holding the state to account. That is to say that rights have addressees upon which duties or responsibilities are imposed. Contrary to popular misconception, rights, as such, are addressed primarily to the state and not to some, other international body such as the United Nations or the European Commission. Human rights are very much addressed to the citizen's state. When, for example, a case is brought by a citizen against an institution of the state the expectation is that another institution of the state will arrive at a judgement on the matter. In short, were an Irish Language Act introduced in Northern Ireland then the linguistic rights of the Irish-speakers there would be addressed (and therefore protected by) the government of the Northern Ireland Assembly in the first place. Further, as Northern Ireland remains a constituent part of the United Kingdom, the British government would also be an addressee. International organisations and other states are addressees of secondary importance.

The campaign to introduce an Irish language act for Northern Ireland has revealed some substantial tensions in the new political arrangement. The campaign has been highly politicised from the start as support for it was only garnered from within the Irish republican and nationalist political family. Some of the evidence presented during the consultative process conducted by the Department of Culture, Arts and Leisure [DCAL] on behalf of the government of Northern Ireland showed that the some people were of the view that a rights-based approach was necessary because the goodwill of the institutions of the state in Northern Ireland could not be depended upon. For example:

> The other legislative models described in the DCAL consultation document are not appropriate for the north of Ireland because they depend on agreement and goodwill within all of the public bodies. There is hostility to the Irish language in the north and this is why a strong, rights-based Irish Language Act is needed.[12]

There are two, very different but equally substantial, problems at work here. In the first place, the failure to elicit political support which transcends the most basic political divisions in Northern Ireland undermines the moral argument for the introduction of rights for Irish-speakers. Secondly, the lack of trust in the institutions of the state implies a profound failure of governance in the most general sense. The local population have democratically elected their representatives to those institutions and yet the institutions remain untrustworthy. This implies that these institutions are in some profound sense ungovernable through local democracy. This explains the rhetorical shift from civil rights to human rights. The two terms presume different types of addressees – the national, on the one hand, and the international, on the other. For example:

> [...] human rights *exist as moral and/or legal rights*. A human right can exist as a shared norm of actual human moralities, as a justified moral norm supported by strong reasons, as a legal right at the national level (here it

---

12 Submission 99 http://www.dcalni.gov.uk/submission_99.pdf (accessed 10/05/2009).

might be referred to as a "civil" or "constitutional" right), or as a legal right within international law.[13]

It could be argued that the implication of this is quite far-reaching. In historical terms the moral justification for the protection of Welsh and Irish has been that of 'freedom' – an unarguable public good, and that this was best realised via nationalism. The political logic of this was quite straightforward in that each nation, defined at least in part by its national language, ought to be sovereign. The failure of this project is best exemplified in Ireland where political independence from the British Empire in the first quarter of the 20th century was quickly followed by the constitutional elevation of Irish as 'the national and first official language'.[14] But, in practical terms this status actually contributed little to the vitality of the Irish language as a popular, spoken vernacular. In fact, its continued decline in the Republic of Ireland during the greater part of the 20th century was quite remorseless. The Official Languages Act of 2003 marks a very significant change of direction. In fact, it is a very clear break with the past in that it is not based upon the premise of the national revival of the Irish language. Instead, the act provides protection for Irish-speakers as a minority in the state. An effect of the act is, therefore, to minoritise the Irish language and to accept English as the normative language.

Linguistic Human Rights and the Nation

A very significant tension for language activists who advocate a rights' based approach is that human rights largely relate to the rights of people as individuals and not as a group or community. The notion of community or group rights is problematic. For example, the Universal Declaration of Human Rights does not include group rights. More recent declarations, conventions and treaties do, and among the group rights recognised are the protection of ethnic groups against genocide, rights to freedom of association, freedom of assembly, freedom of religion, and freedom from discrimination.[15] Some rights are especially significant for linguistic groups or communities. For example, the United Nations' International Convenant on Civil and Political Rights (1966) enshrines the following right:

> In those States in which ethnic, religious or linguistic minorities exist, persons belonging to such minorities shall not be denied the right, in commu-

---

[13] James Nickel, "Human Rights", *op. cit.*

[14] *Bunreacht na hÉireann* [Irish Constitution] 1937.

[15] Will Kymlicka (1989), *Liberalism, Community, and Culture*, Oxford, Clarendon Press.

nity with the other members of their group, to enjoy their own culture, to profess and practice their own religion, or to use their own language.[16]

The key phrase here is 'in community with the other members of their group'. This right to use a given language is contextually specific, with that context being defined by the particular minority, membership of that minority and also, that minority being, in some sense, in community. In the case of both the Irish and the Welsh languages this causes a number of difficulties. In particular, the notion of community implies the occupation of a discrete space by a particular social group. For example, a nation might be said to be a community which ideally occupies its own space in the form of a 'state'. Clearly, for linguistic minorities within nations and within states asserting ownership to their own exclusive and discrete space is problematic.

In the Irish context, while the Gaeltacht of the Republic of Ireland fulfils such a function in theory there have been many difficulties in realising it in practice. Notwithstanding the creation of the Gaeltacht as a statutory geographical territory in various parts of the Irish state with the express aim of protecting the Irish-speaking community therein, the Anglicisation of the Gaeltacht during the 20th century has been relentless. Even during periods of significant community-based political activism centred on the language, such as the protests spearheaded by Cearta Sibhialta na Gaeltachta during the 1960s and 1970s, the end results have been to rework the institutional infrastructure *viz* the creation of Bord na Gaeilge [Irish Language Board] (1978) and Údarás na Gaeltachta [Irish Language Authority] (1981) rather than to halt, much less reverse, long-term demographic decline. Recently, the Irish government has taken a number of steps aimed at making the Gaeltacht a more effective language planning tool. These steps include the placing of linguistic conditions on the new housing developments in the Gaeltacht areas through the Planning and Development Act 2000. The conditions have been subject to challenge by developers as a restriction on their trade. They have also been criticised by Irish language activists in that they are binding for a limited period of time only. Moreover, the results of the latest sociological surveys of Irish language knowledge, behaviours and attitudes show that Irish-speakers are themselves already in a minority throughout much of the Gaeltacht.[17] It is for this reason that the boundaries of the Gaeltacht, it would appear,[18] are to be re-

---

[16] UN International Covenant on Civil and Political Rights, available at: http://www.un.org/millennium/law/iv-4.htm (accessed 10/05/2009).

[17] See, for example, Diarmait Mac Giolla Chríost (2005), *The Irish Language in Ireland from Goídel to Globalisation*, London, Routledge.

[18] It is widely anticipated that one of the outcomes of the lengthy discussions led by the Irish government on the formulation of a long-term strategy for the Irish language in

drawn, thereby much reducing its territorial extent. The implication is that there is very limited scope indeed for exclusive, discrete spaces for minority languages in any state, even one in which the minority language is also a national and first official language.

In Wales, the rural Welsh-speaking heartland, popularly imagined as the Bro Gymraeg, enjoys none of the limited protections afforded to the Gaeltacht. The resulting vulnerability has been ruthlessly exposed during the last quarter of the 20th century as increasing English-speaking migration to the Bro Gymraeg has caused the Welsh language to be a minority language in many parts of the Bro Gymraeg for the first time ever. Some[19] argue that the continuity of such spaces is absolutely essential to the vitality of vulnerable, minoritised languages but, defending them in a much more robust manner is fraught with challenges. Not least, there are real problems with regard to such a community appearing to behave as an illiberal minority. The remark by Plaid Cymru [The Party of Wales – the main nationalist political party in Wales] councillor Seimon Glyn that English-speaking migrants were a 'drain on Welsh-speaking communities'[20] has the unfortunate potential to be read in such a manner. The ensuing controversy reached the floor of the United Kingdom parliament in Westminster where the issue was the subject of a quite divisive debate on 'racism in Welsh politics'. Some members of the Labour Party [the main socialist party in the United Kingdom, and historically the dominant political party in Wales] in Wales made a number of very trenchant remarks regarding the language issue. For example, Wayne David, the Member of Parliament for Caerphilly, asserted that; 'We have seen the racist remarks of Seimon Glyn and the comments of Simon Brooks. What unites their views is an intolerance of English people and those who speak the English language'.[21] Don Touhig, another Labour Party Member of Parliament and, at that time, the Parliamentary Under-Secretary of State for Wales, stated that;

---

the Republic of Ireland will be to substantially change the boundaries of the Gaeltacht, first defined by statute in 1956. The publication of this strategy document is overdue.

[19] In Wales, for example, the creation of the Welsh language group 'Cymuned [Community]' in 2001 was a direct response to the threat to 'y Fro Gymraeg' as that part of Wales where the Welsh language is regarded as being the normal language of everyday life in local communities. See http://www.cymuned.net (accessed 15/05/2009).

[20] His remarks were very widely reported by news outlets in Wales at the time and for some time subsequently, including on BBC News, e.g. http://news.bbc.co.uk/1/hi/wales/2009393.stm (accessed 15/05/2009).

[21] House of Commons Hansard Debates for 7th May 2002 http://www.publications.parliament.uk/pa/cm200102/cmhansrd/vo020507/halltext/20507h05.htm (accessed 10/05/2009).

'Language extremists want to restrict the movement of English speakers, whether or not those English speakers are Welsh-born'.[22] Raising the spectre of racism had considerable impact upon the public discourse and while Cymuned, currently, is still active as a campaigning organisation, much of its energy appears to have been dissipated, partly as a result of this rancorous debate.

Conclusion

Some commentators have argued that the turn to rights is transformational and that the assertion of linguistic human rights plays a crucial role in changing the general relations of power.[23] It is the case that a rights agenda may indeed contribute to the transformation of the place of a minoritised language in a given society. The recognition of a set of rights can form a positive part of a jigsaw of actions that, together, may help the process of reviving a threatened language – a process understood by many linguists as reversing language shift.[24] Linguistic human rights can enable institutional support to be given to minoritised languages. The simple fact of the institutionalisation of a minority language to that extent may positively impact upon the attitudes of the speakers and non-speakers of that language. This, in turn, may positively add to the prestige or status of the language and therefore positively impact upon its vitality.

That said, there are a number of challenges for the Irish and the Welsh languages in their own particular contexts. In the Irish context the linguistic human rights agenda works counter to reversing language shift in some subtle ways. For example, this agenda conceives of the Irish language as a minority language. It can be argued, with some force, that this is a backward step in that the status of the Irish language in the Republic of Ireland is somewhat reduced as a result. Irish was defined as the national and first official language under the Irish constitution of 1937 and related to this was a determination by the state to generally revive the language as the common means of communication and everyday life throughout Irish society. It could be said that the recognition of language rights for Irish-speakers as a distinct minority group in the Irish state represents a negative change in the power relationship between the state and Irish-speakers. Thus, while Bunreacht na hÉireann (1937) confers national status upon Irish, the Official Languages Act

---

[22]   *Ibid.*

[23]   Caoimhghin Ó Croidheáin (2006), *Language from Below: The Irish Language, Ideology and Power in 20th Century Ireland*, Oxford, Peter Lang.

[24]   Joshua Fishman (2001), *Reversing Language Shift*, Clevedon, Multilingual Matters Ltd.

(2003) minoritises the language. But, the irony is that this change has been, in reality, essential to the relationship between Irish-speakers and the institutions of the Irish state in practically enforcing the delivery of public services in Irish for the first time. Thus, the transformation at work here is one which empowers Irish-speakers as individual members of a minority but which disempowers the Irish language as the national language. Very crudely speaking, it is a choice between pragmatism and aspiration.

It is to avoid such enforcement on the part of public institutions that the Unionist [that is, pro-British] political parties of Northern Ireland have been wholly resistant to an Irish language act but, of course, in this case Irish is neither recognised as the national language nor as a minority language by the Northern Ireland Assembly. Rather, it was the government of the United Kingdom that conferred recognition upon Irish in Northern Ireland with regard to the European Charter for Regional or Minority Languages (1992). The British government committed to this as a part of the historic political settlement reached in 1998, bringing to an end the violent political conflict described variously as the troubles or the long war. The conclusion of the long war appears, for many, to have coincided with the outbreak of a culture war, in which the Irish language is the central issue.[25] In this particular context the recognition of language rights would signify a transformation, but that would be to presume a major change in the attitudes of Unionist politicians, and also indeed a similar such change on the part of very many members of the largely Protestant constituency that they represent. Such a transformation is not, at present, a likely prospect.

Given the antipathy of Unionism to the Irish language but the necessity of sharing power with the political parties of Irish nationalism and republicanism (whether the Social Democratic and Labour Party or Sinn Féin), it might be informative to Unionist politicians to note that the human rights agenda in general is largely concerned with the recognition of basic minima.[26] Aspirations tend to be very limited. Human rights are minimal standards, concerned with the 'lower limits on tolerable human conduct rather than great aspirations and exalted ideals'.[27] The practical significance of this is that, as minimal standards, there is scope for very considerable latitude indeed for decision-making at national and local levels of government to interpret the practical implications of legislation and to develop the policies that will determine the

---

[25] See, for example, *Derry Journal*, "Durkan anger at 'war against Irish'," 9th October 2007   and   http://www.bbc.co.uk/blogs/thereporters/markdevenport/2008/07/ culture_wars.html (accessed 17/05/2009).

[26] James Nickel, "Human Rights", *op. cit.*

[27] *Ibid.*

behaviours of public institutions. Beyond minimum standards as defined by any set of linguistic human rights, one could expect very considerable variation in the impact of rights upon the myriad relationships between individual speakers and state institutions.

The recognition of linguistic human rights and their practical implementation is an activity that entails, often, considerable costs. For minoritised languages, the principal cost, almost without exception, is that of translation. The impact on public and, especially, democratic institutions can be far-reaching. The discussions in meetings may require instantaneous translation, minutes may require careful drafting in two or more languages, documents with legal implications will require specialised attention, and so on. It may well be the case that the state is either unwilling or unable to make new resources available to meet such costs and that, as a result, the effective implementation of new linguistic human rights will mean that fewer resources are available for the implementation of existing rights, and other duties, in other areas. In this way there is a balance to be drawn between the competing merits of different rights. Thus, the case has to be made for meeting the costs of linguistic human rights. This has been a significant problem for the Acht campaign in Northern Ireland. One of the more straightforward objections to the introduction of an Irish language act was that of cost.[28] It is worth quoting from the Minister's statement in some detail:

> Those opposed to legislation raised a number of concerns including the significant resource consequences of implementing legislation [...]. Turning to the issue of costs, in 2006/07 Northern Ireland Civil Service Departments and the Northern Ireland Office incurred expenditure of £20.62 million on a range of Irish Language projects and Irish Language translations. This figure includes £10.3 million from the Department of Education for Irish medium education. This does not include expenditure incurred by the Northern Ireland Court Service or Local Councils on Irish translations and linguistic diversity projects. Nor does it include the resources (salaries and running costs) deployed by the various departments in arranging the commitments associated with the £20.62 million annual expenditure. Members will appreciate that it is difficult to estimate the cost and resourcing issues that could arise from Irish Language legislation. For example a "rights based" framework would likely have greater cost than a "language scheme" framework. Equally, it is difficult to estimate the cost and resourcing requirements of a "language scheme" framework without clarity of the content and extent of a typical "language scheme." Officials in my Department undertook a high level exercise to estimate the possible cost of implementing the indicative

---

28   Edwin Poots (2007) *A Statement by Edwin Poots MLA, Minister of Culture, Arts and Leisure, to the Northern Ireland Assembly on the proposal to introduce Irish Language legislation* 16th October 2007: http://www.dcalni.gov.uk/minister_s _statement.pdf (accessed 20/05/2009).

legislation framework set out in the 13 March 2007 consultation document, i.e. a "language scheme" framework. For the purposes of this exercise, these estimates are based on the assumption that the legislation would be applied across all NICS [Northern Ireland Civil Service] Departments and the NIO [Northern Ireland Office] within the financial year 2008/09 and have drawn upon, where possible, estimates based on the experiences in Wales and the Republic of Ireland. For example if Northern Ireland were to have an Irish Language Commissioner's Office similar to that in the Republic of Ireland the annual running costs would be approximately £500,000. The cost of the translation service for the Houses of the Oireachtas are [sic – 'is'] approximately £600,000 per annum compared to £1.28 million in the National Assembly of Wales. It is estimated that almost £200,000 per annum would be required to provide simultaneous translation in Irish for the Court Service, and a similar amount for Tribunals. In respect of the 11 NICS Departments and NIO it is estimated that in 2008-09 if each were to deploy two dedicated staff members fluent in Irish for the purpose of developing Irish Language schemes, monitoring their implementation, giving advice and arranging translations the annual costs would be approximately £927,000. The printing and design of forms to facilitate Irish Language schemes within the 11 NICS departments could cost approximately £309,000, and advertising costs could be in the region of £931,000, based on a 20% up-lift to take account of the increased advertising costs for Irish. It is important to stress that these costs are broad estimates mainly in respect of the 11 NICS departments. These departments account for 22,973 civil servants as opposed to the 111,128 employed in the wider public sector including for example Local Government, Health Trusts, Education and Library Boards and various NDPB's [non-departmental public bodies]. If this exercise to estimate the cost of implementing a "language scheme" approach within the 11 NICS departments were to be extrapolated across the wider public sector, and if, for example, the agreed language schemes required public bodies to provide bilingual services, the costs, in this scenario, would clearly be very significant. Members will be aware of the current pressures on public expenditure in Northern Ireland. In light of this, it is highly debatable if our community is prepared to contemplate the level of expenditure that would be required to introduce even a modest form of Irish Language legislation at this time. Mr Speaker, there will always be competing priorities for public expenditure, however, can the additional potential cost be considered as a sufficiently high priority in comparison to the need for investment in infrastructure, health, and other vital public services? Furthermore, bearing in mind the current expenditure of approximately £20.62 million per annum on Irish language projects and Irish language translations, I very much doubt if the legislative route is necessarily the most cost effective way to achieve outcomes in terms of enhancing and protecting the development of the Irish language.[29]

---

[29] *Ibid.*, pp. 3-5.

If real, the costs are substantial but the detail could easily be challenged. It is widely understood that public institutions in Northern Ireland are not especially well-disposed to the Irish language. As they were responsible for making the estimations of cost it is not surprising that the results reflect rather negatively on the case regarding legislation on the Irish language.

The Minister's reference to Wales is pertinent, but not quite, perhaps, for the reason assumed by him. Rationalising the costs of translation in respect of the Welsh Language Act (1993) has been expressed as a matter of increasing concern in some surprising quarters.[30] Similar concerns are regularly raised in the Republic of Ireland with regard to Irish. Clearly, even in relatively consensual cases, there is a balance to be struck between rights and costs. In the case of the Irish language in Northern Ireland there is, for language activists who remain convinced of the appropriateness of an Irish language act, a need to develop a more robust position on costs and their moral justification in terms of public good. This particular problem serves to highlight a very simple point with regard to linguistic human rights. Linguistic minorities suffer the tyranny of crude majoritarianism in democracies, even under power-sharing. And, while majorities can only govern morally with the consensus of minorities, minorities must struggle in order to exist. A minority group, including a linguistic minority, is charged with determining the nature of that struggle – it must make its case and do so continually. And the pervasiveness of language in society means that such a struggle is total. But, equally, the state and its institutions must be themselves sufficiently robust to accommodate that struggle and to respond positively to difference, to diversity and to dissension. Here is the transformative moment – the struggle, in and of itself.

Résumé

Pendant les années 1990, la langue a pris une part essentielle dans les préoccupations de la défense des droits de l'homme au niveau international. Au même moment, la rhétorique des droits linguistiques est devenue un leitmotiv du discours des militants qui œuvraient en faveur des langues minoritaires. Pour certains commentateurs, ce déplacement vers un discours des droits de l'homme a des implications profondes. Dans le contexte irlandais, par exemple, la lutte pour les droits linguistiques est porteuse de transformations à venir car cette prise de position modifie le jeu des rapports de force existants. Dans cet article, Dr Mac Giolla Chríost passe au crible les implications de ce déplacement du débat sur le terrain des droits de l'homme notamment

---

[30]   BBC News/Wales, "Welsh Assembly in translation row," http://news.bbc.co.uk/1/hi/
       wales/873167.stm (accessed 20/05/2009).

en ce qui concerne le gallois et l'irlandais. Au-delà du discours des militants et des gouvernements, l'auteur pose un certain nombre de questions philosophiques fondamentales dans un contexte linguistique, historique et politique. Qu'est-ce qu'un droit ? Quels sont les enjeux de pouvoir dans le recours aux droits ? Enfin, en replaçant ces questions philosophiques dans la réalité empirique de la sociologie linguistique du gallois et de l'irlandais, il pose une question directe : dans quelle mesure le recours à une logique des droits de l'homme peut-il transformer une société ?

PART II

IRISH IN THE EDUCATION SYSTEM

"I Got Second in Latin, Greek, and English, and Eleventh in French"

Attitudes to Language(s) in the Correspondence of Daniel O'Connell (1775-1847)

Grace NEVILLE

University College Cork

At first sight, the birthplace of Daniel O'Connell, Carhan outside Cahersiveen in Iveragh, South-West Kerry (not Derrynane as some people wrongly believe), seems an unremarkable place. Even today, there is no village there, no hamlet in sight: Carhan is just a crossroads, near a tumbledown cottage where O'Connell was reputedly born. And yet, from this apparent *non-lieu*, one of Ireland's few truly international statesmen emerged. In his lifetime, O'Connell was already well known from Russia to South America, and from Egypt to Australia. His concerns throughout the half century of his public life were those of the intellectual, the visionary, the citizen of the world. He campaigned for the rights not just of Catholics but of slaves, women, workers and Jews everywhere. To quote the then President of Ireland, Mary Robinson, in a tribute she addressed to O'Connell in the Reform Club in London (a club of which he had been a member) to mark the 150th anniversary of his death, on 15 May 1997:

> The iron logic of his conviction that there was no border to the universality of justice and right meant for him that he had no choice but to stand up and be counted whether it was for Jews in Britain, African slaves in America or the rent-racked peasants of the villages of India.[1]

He read Voltaire and Rousseau, Bossuet and Boileau, corresponded with Jeremy Bentham, met l'Abbé Grégoire, was influenced by Tom Paine and was a friend of William Godwin and Mary Wollstonecraft. He was visited in his Derrynane home by a succession of continental European luminaries, including the young Charles de Montalembert. Such

---

[1] Mary Robinson, 'Daniel O'Connell: A Tribute', *History Ireland*, Winter 1997, p. 31.

visits continue: on his well documented visit to Ireland in 1969, the hero of France's Liberation, General Charles de Gaulle, insisted on visiting the home of Ireland's Liberator in Derrynane, explaining that his grandmother, Josephine Marie de Gaulle, had written an impassioned, romantic biography of O'Connell.[2] Balzac himself is reputed to have gone so far as to state that he would have liked to have met three men only in his century: Napoleon, Cuvier and O'Connell.[3] In the House of Commons, in 1844, renowned Whig historian, Thomas B. Macaulay, had this to say about O'Connell:

> Go where you will upon the Continent, dine at any *table d'hôte* […], enter any conveyance, from the moment your speech betrays you to be an Englishman, the very first question you are asked – whether by the merchants or manufacturers in the towns in the heart of France, or by the peasants, or by the class who are the yeomen, the first question asked is, What has become of Mr. O'Connell? [*'Oh, oh'*]. Let those who will deny this assertion take the trouble to cross the Channel, and they will soon be convinced of its truth. Let them only turn over the French journals.[4]

O'Connell's death in Genoa, on his way to Rome, in 1847, was world news. In Paris, a memorial service was held for him in Notre Dame Cathedral. In New York, a parade to mark his death attracted thousands. From O'Connell's own rich and voluminous correspondence, with its impossibly wide range of topics spanning the public and private spheres through fifty-five years from 1792 until his death in 1847, this paper will focus on his attitudes to language and to languages.[5]

O'Connell is widely hailed as one of the most powerful wordsmiths of Irish politics ever. His reputation needs no rehearsing here. It is so well established that it seeps from reportage into folklore: a constellation of well-known examples of his oratorical brilliance in both Irish and English are drawn almost certainly not from his life but from international medieval *exempla*.[6] But such was the strength of O'Connell's

---

[2]   Pierre Joannon (1991), *L'Hiver du Connétable: Charles de Gaulle et l'Irlande*, Paris, Artus.

[3]   See J. J. Lee in Maurice O'Connell (ed.) (1991), *Daniel O'Connell: Political Pioneer*, Dublin, Institute of Public Administration, p. 4.

[4]   Hansard (ed.), *The Parliamentary Debates*, 3rd series, Vol. lxxii, House of Commons, 19/02/1844, 'State of Ireland, Adjourned Debate', col. 1185-1186.

[5]   Maurice R. O'Connell (ed.) (1972-1980), *The Correspondence of Daniel O'Connell*, Vol. i (1792-1814), Vol. ii (1815-1823), Vol. iii (1823-1828), Vol. iv (1829-1832), Vol. v (1833-1836), Vol. vi (1837-1840), Vol. vii (1841-1845), Vol. viii (1846-1847). Dublin, Irish University Press for the Irish Manuscripts Commission, henceforward referred to in this chapter as *C*. Details such as the writer and place of writing are added where deemed relevant.

[6]   See Ríonach Ní Ogáin (1984), *An Rí gan Choróin: Dónall Ó Conaill sa Bhéaloideas*. Dublin, An Clochomhar Teoranta.

reputation for oratory that, like some irresistible centripetal force, it drew to itself these anecdotes anyhow. His powers of oratory explained his hold on the Irish people who, according to eye-witness Jean-Jacques Prévost, were "électrisé par ses discours:"[7]

> L'empire de M. O'Connell sur le peuple tient réellement de la fascination et du prodige. Pendant cinq heures, le libérateur fit presque seul tous les frais du meeting, tantôt plaisantant tantôt familièrement, tantôt s'indignant, tantôt discutant avec gravité et éloquence, prenant tous les tons, s'interrompant parfois au milieu de sa dialectique pour décrocher un trait sur quelqu'un de ses adversaires, et, pendant cinq heures, l'attention de l'auditoire ne se lassa pas un moment. Toutes les têtes étaient tendues avidement vers le grand orateur, tous les yeux étaient attachés sur lui et ne le quittaient pas. Certes, M. O'Connell est toujours le roi, l'idole de ce peuple.[8]

Interestingly, O'Connell's contrasting soubriquets in English and Irish, *the Liberator* and *an Counseiléir* (the counsellor or advisor), reflect his dual words *and* action nature: the former highlighting action and the latter stressing language.

Already as a twenty-one year old law student in London, O'Connell shows his keen awareness of the power of linguistic excellence as a tool for changing the world:

> Though I am extremely anxious to become a greater lawyer, law makes little more than the principal part of my study. I read with attention history, rhetoric, philosophy, and sometimes poetry. While I apply myself to the English language, I endeavour to unite purity of diction to the harmony and arrangement of phraseology (*C.*, letter 20, 1796, from London).

So flexible were his language skills that he was at ease addressing the Houses of Parliament in Westminster as he was addressing the hundreds of thousands of largely illiterate Irish peasants who attended his 'monster meetings'. His linguistic stamina was legendary: one letter here refers to a speech lasting five hours, confirming Prévost's commentary *supra* (see *C.*, letter 2062, 1834). His edited correspondence runs to eight volumes, with the original letters scattered throughout the world in almost one hundred libraries and private collections from University College Cork to Harvard, Oxford to Chicago, and Amsterdam to North Carolina, with the bulk of them in University College Dublin and the National Library, Dublin.[9] Even this, however, does not capture all his extant letters. By the editor's own admission, O'Connell's letters have often been shortened or even omitted:

---

[7] Jean-Joseph Prévost (1846), *Un tour en Irlande*. Paris, Amyot, p. 14.

[8] *Ibid.*

[9] His editor, Maurice O'Connell, lists 96 sources.

Fully 4,000 letters to and from O'Connell have been transcribed. Of these about 3,500 – all that are considered significant – are being published. These have been pruned of unimportant and repetitious matter [...] O'Connell's 'public letters' have been omitted from this collection. These include correspondence with newspapers, committees and other bodies – letters written in the knowledge that they would be published or receive public circulation [...] A large part of O'Connell's letters to his wife, of which 660 are extant, consist of expressions of love and affection to the extent that makes tiresome reading. Consequently about a fifth of these have been omitted while those published have been pruned of the more tedious repetition.[10]

Just as his fame and his concerns far transcended national boundaries, his correspondence similarly reveals a world at once international and multilingual. His letters are peppered with references to Cuba and China, Capetown and Caracas, St. Petersburg and Syria, Haiti and Egypt. Some of these letters written to him are in French. Correspondents contact him from exotic locations like Bogota and Quito; his children write to him from France, Italy and South America. In this context, the following is not unusual – from his son, Morgan, who gives his address as 'Mons. M. O'Connell, Cadet dans le 4e régiment de chevaux légers à Vicenza'

I write to my mother today also and will write to her again from Lyons, Turin, and Milan but don't intend to write again to you till I reach Vicenza (*C.*, letter 1034, 1823).

O'Connell had a command of three languages, English, Irish and French, and had a good working knowledge of Latin. His fluency in French is attested *inter alia* by Prévost in a rare scene from the intimacy of the elderly O'Connell's study at his Dublin home on Merrion Square in the mid-1840s:

Je trouvai M. O'Connell dans son cabinet, entouré d'un amas de livres, de journaux, de papiers épars, jusque sur le plancher [...] Il me parla aussi, et en très-bon [sic] français, des affaires générales de l'Europe, et de la politique particulière de la France.[11]

The two-year period he had spent in Flanders and France in his midteens (bookended by periods of study in Cork and London) was intensely formative in many ways. After arriving in Ostend with his younger brother late in 1790, he first attended schools in Liege and then Louvain. From January 1791 to August 1792 he studied in St Omer, and in Douai from August 1792 to January 1793, after which the brothers

---

[10] *C.*, Vol. i, pp. vii-viii.
[11] Prévost, *op. cit.*, pp. 9-11.

fled to London at the height of *la Terreur*. His French education, for him as for generations of boys from well-off Catholic Kerry families before him, was in English-style public schools... albeit in another country and (in the case of his school in Douai) run by the Benedictines. The mission of his school in St Omer,[12] for instance, was:

> to produce the complete public man, whose eloquence was based on sound learning and a thorough grasp of the techniques of exposition and persuasion.[13]

In one of his earliest letters home, sent from St Omer at the age of fifteen to his Derrynane uncle, Muiris a' Chaipín, who was financing the continental education of his favourite nephew and possible heir, the young O'Connell has this to say:

> In this college are taught the Latin and Greek authors, French, English, and geography [...] We have composed for the second time since I came here. I got second in Latin, Greek and English, and eleventh in French (*C.*, letter 1, 1792).

This poor performance in French is later explained away: it's all the school's fault:

> I have learned other particulars relative to the college of Douai since my last left this which are that French is paid no great attention to there, nay, almost totally neglected (*C.*, letter 3, 1792, from St Omer, France).

Over forty years later again, in any case, O'Connell rewrites his school record:

> At St. Omer, I was first in the first class and got premiums in everything; so far from being idle there, I shook my constitution by intense application (*C.*, letter 2474a, 1837).

Independent evidence elsewhere confirms this account of his formidable work ethic that was to stay with him all his life: this is how, years later, a former schoolmate from their St Omer days remembers the O'Connell brothers:

> I recollect there were two brothers, one very studious, and the other something like myself, very wild (*C.*, letter 1079, 1824).

O'Connell's earliest letters home, written from France in his mid-teens, thus encapsulate everything that was to come: his competitive nature, his self-confidence, his strong work ethic, his eagerness and his

---

[12] See Louis Cavrois (1867), *O'Connell et le collège anglais à Saint-Omer*. Arras, Rousseau-Leroy, 2nd edition.

[13] Oliver MacDonagh (1991), *O'Connell: The Life of Daniel O'Connell 1775-1847*. London, Weidenfeld and Nicolson, p. 23.

ability to please, his ability to treat his audience as his linguistic and intellectual equals (even if they were not), with language – his avowed linguistic proficiency at least in Latin and Greek – used as the vehicle for this potent mixture.

His schools in France provided a grounding in the classics with unseen translation from Latin to Greek as part of the menu of exercises taken by the young teenager:

> As the Easter *examen* [sic] in just over, our studies begin again on another footing, instead of the books I mentioned before we now read Mignot's harangues, Cicero and Caesar, those are our Latin authors, though they are read over without any study beforehand, Caesar is given us chiefly to turn into Greek; our Greek authors are Demosthenes, Homer, and Xenophon's Anabasis; our French one is Dagaso's speeches (*C.*, letter 2, 1792, from St Omer).

O'Connell clearly saw the value of these classics as exercises in rhetoric, an area in which he would excel throughout his political career:

> We study at present Rhetoric and logic. For the Rhetoric we read and get by heart Cicero's orations, *Orationes Collectae*, Bossuet's funeral orations and Boileau's art of poetry. The last two are French authors (*C.*, letter 7, 1793, from London).

Beyond language competence, this familiarity with the classics enabled him to relate to similarly educated former public school boys – his colleagues in Westminster and in the London and Dublin law courts, as remarks such as the following make clear: one correspondent refers to 'the anecdotes of Themistocles, Aristides, Pulfio and Varenes' (*C.*, letter 1463, 1828), while another remarks: 'Now that you are enjoying the *otium cum dignitate* and can say with *Caesar – veni, vidi, vici* [...]' (*C.*, letter 1706, 1830). In other words, knowledge of the Greek and Latin classics gives them a shared language, the in-language of the powerful.

Throughout his life, it is clear that for O'Connell, a civilised, reputable person was, by definition, someone who could function in a number of languages (excluding Irish, however, of which more later). In the education he plans for his sons studying in Clongowes,[14] for instance, languages – especially classical languages – feature prominently. Indeed, here as elsewhere, his intense interest in his children's welfare, academic and otherwise, translates into constant attempts to fashion them in his own image and experience. For his sons, he wishes:

---

[14] Jesuit school founded in 1814, O'Connell was closely involved as legal advisor in the negotiations leading up to the founding of Clongowes.

the acquisition of much classical learning, a solid formation in the classics, especially in Greek, being in my opinion of great value to real education. I would wish them also to acquire the French language (*C.*, letter 508, 1815).

I sent quite a library for my Danny, and a Latin and Greek grammar for my poor John (*C.*, letter 1033, 1823).

Latin and Greek were, of course, professional tools useful if not necessary for any young man intent on making a career in the Catholic Church, as is evident from a letter from O'Connell regarding a local Kerry boy:

I believe I did not tell you that Dr Murray received Charles [Connor] very kindly. He found, however, that he was not sufficiently prepared in Latin and Greek, and Charles goes to Tralee to devote himself for a few months to those languages. He will then get on the establishment at Maynooth (*C.*, letter 1112, 1824, to his wife).

This lack of emphasis on modern languages for boys was, of course, part of the culture of the day, and is highlighted by a priest from Clongowes in a letter to O'Connell about a boy whose fees he was also paying:

Alexander is now growing very big and it would be much more useful to him to attend solely to an English education than to spend his time in the elements of languages of which he will never know much (*C.*, letter 1067, 1823).

In a letter of instructions written to his wife in 1823 on their sons' education, O'Connell widens horizons by adding law, history, mathematics and chemistry, to languages (*C.*, letter 990, 1823). In other words, proficiency in specific languages represented just part of the overall formation that would mould his boys into successful adults.

For girls, however, everything was different... though curiously the same. Though never openly flagged as such, their education was also structured in order to prepare them for their adult careers: as wives in Dublin's upper middle classes.[15] In this context, therefore, they were not expected to understand or to study Latin. O'Connell forwards his wife a letter written to her in Latin from a Mr Magee:

which I opened. You must get one of your sons to translate the Latin for you as your husband is not at home. What an odd idea, darling, to write Latin to a lady! (*C.*, letter 1945b, 1832).

---

[15] On at least one occasion, Mary refuses to accede to her husband's request that the family move to Derrynane: the house there was damp, she protested and, in any case, where was she supposed to find suitable husbands for her girls in South West Kerry? That the O'Connell daughters did indeed marry into Ireland's upper classes is evident from their married names e.g. Hely-Hutchinson!

For his daughters, O'Connell prioritises excellence in modern languages, especially French, a concern reinforced by Mary:

> Ellen is equally anxious for a reply to her letter written on Saturday. How do you like her first attempt in French? I should like to know if she understands the language and how you approve of Miss G's [sic] instruction in English and writing (*C.*, letter 620, 1816, from his wife).

In response, he teasingly suggests that his daughter's written French is so excellent that her governess must have helped her:

> I got my sweet Nell's French letter yesterday. It was so perfectly well written that *of course* Miss Gaghran assisted in the language. It is impossible Ellen could have written it without aid and in fact is an excellent specimen of Miss Gaghran's own knowledge of the true genius of the language (*C.*, letter 619, 1816, to his wife).

His wife is anxious to claim all credit for their talented daughter:

> All our darlings here are quite well, Ellen is in great spirits at your approbation of her French letter. Miss G declares Ellen deserves all the merit. She only assisted her in two words (*C.*, letter 622, 1816).

His avowed linguistic ambitions in modern languages for his daughters are high and reveal his academic judgement of each of them:

> Tell my Nell that her father expects she will learn Spanish and German as well as French and Italian. I hope the summer after next to take them and you to Italy. If the rents come in, you may depend on it. Tell my Kate I will be satisfied with her being a French and Italian scholar. As to my Betty I will not yet decide (*C.*, letter 959, 1822, to his wife).

However, not all females are by definition adept at modern languages: class and social standing can outweigh gender. O'Connell's own wife and cousin, his beloved Mary, daughter of an impoverished Tralee doctor and not the beneficiary of the kind of hot-housing O'Connell could provide for his young daughters, knew little or no French. Even her children and their governess could speak better French. Her letters convey her anxiety around this whole topic. Here, for instance, she appears (understandably?) anxious to avoid succumbing to pressure to come up to speed by becoming the pupil of her young daughter:

> Ellen is very anxious that I should become a pupil of hers to begin my French grammar. I fear she would rather be an impatient governess for, when she is deputed by Miss G to hear the little ones their lessons, she can't bear to have them miss a word (*C.*, letter 717, 1817).

Mary appears never to have really broken through this linguistic barrier, even during the almost two years she spent in France with six of her children (in an attempt to salvage the family finances which were spiralling out of control).[16] Her continuing linguistic anxiety and lack of confidence is relayed by their young son, Daniel, writing to his father from Tours in 1823:

> I speak French better than *Old Woman Mod Mary*. Sometimes she tells me to speak to the maids for her so as to bring wood, and things of that kind, though she speaks it very well and is picking up like me herself. It's Mod that I say my lesson to and she takes a great deal of pains with me (*C.*, letter 998, 1823).

While her stay in France may have improved her oral French, Mary appears never to have mastered written French. When O'Connell's uncle, the Comte de France, wishes to alert his nephew to the catastrophic state of the Liberator's finances, the older man writes in French so that Mary cannot understand (*C.*, letter 776, 1819). Mary, however, does make it known that she understands the purpose of this linguistic stratagem: to exclude her deliberately from bad news (*C.*, letter 782, 1819). Her inability to read French stayed with her apparently all her life: writing to her in Dublin from London in 1829, O'Connell requests: 'Darling, let me have by post the little French papers regularly. You do not read them and they interest me'.

The roles of gender and class in linguistic competence intersect in O'Connell's references to his family maidservants who accompanied his family to France:

> Tell me something too of Hannah and Julia. How do they get on with the French servants? I think poor Hannah must often be at a loss how to get on at all. I should be glad to see her attempting to make herself understood by a person who knew nothing of English! (*C.*, letter 964, 1822, to his daughter in Pau).

In other words, none of the three adults who accompanied six of his seven children on their two-year sojourn in France (his wife and two servants) could function in French. Far from being worried, however, O'Connell knew that he could rely on his children to help their elders in language matters: writing to his wife in Tours, he suggests:

> Darling, as soon as you receive this, call with Ellen as an interpreter to the house of the banker Boulanger Cartion. Let her tell him from me that I am extremely grateful to him for his great kindness in preventing soldiers or officers from being billeted on my family (*C.*, letter 1005, 1823).

---

[16] See Grace Neville, 'I hate France with a mortal hatred: Daniel O'Connell and France', in Eamon Maher and Grace Neville (eds.) (2004), *France-Ireland: Anatomy of a Relationship*. Frankfurt, Peter Lang, pp. 241-257.

He could even occasionally allow himself some mild amusement at the adults' linguistic shortcomings since he knew that all three adults could rely on the linguistic competence he had arranged for his children.

For O'Connell, factors other than gender and class could also play a role in determining levels of linguistic competence. Intellectual ability was one of these. Witness, in this letter to his wife in Bordeaux, his reluctance to impose languages other than English on one of his sons:

> I wish you would retard his [Danny's] speaking French in order not to inter-fere with his English (*C.*, letter 959, 1822).

Such was his confidence in his other children's intellectual abilities, however, that he had no such qualms or concerns about any of them, male or female.

All his life, thus, his image of a cultured person, beginning (and end-ing?) with himself, was of someone who commanded several languages. By definition, therefore, anyone who fails here is 'not one of us', a *homo rusticus*, a laughing stock. In a description of an event at Dublin Castle, he tries to amuse his wife (as was his wont, perhaps out of guilt at having forced her into financial exile in France):

> A college lad, tall and strong in his cap and gown, got his share of the wine and distinguished himself afterwards by translating his Connaught dialect of broken English into worse Latin to everybody he could get to listen to him [...] my worthy collegian fell in with the Committee and got talking his bad Latin. I never saw a more vulgar hound (*C.*, letter 983, 1822).

The 'college lad' ridiculed here was presumably a native speaker of Irish: underneath his 'broken English' lay his mother tongue, Irish. Whereas O'Connell's parents spoke English, he acquired fluent Irish from his monolingual Irish-speaking foster parents with whom he lived until the age of four. His alleged indifference, if not hostility, towards Irish has long been dissected by historians, politicians and even charac-ters in plays: witness Máire's steely determination, in Brian Friel's masterpiece, *Translations*, to abandon Irish for the newer language, her decision is strengthened by invoking authority figures such as her mother but especially O'Connell whose pragmatism she shares:

> We should all be learning to speak English. That's what my mother says. That's what I say. That's what Dan O'Connell said last month in Ennis. He said the sooner we all learn to speak English the better [...] I'm talking about the Liberator. And what he said was this: "The old language is a bar-rier to progress." He said that last month. And he's right. I don't want

Greek. I don't want Latin. I want English. I want to be able to speak English because I'm going to America as soon as the harvest's all saved.[17]

The (in)famous phrase attributed to O'Connell: 'I can witness without a sigh the gradual disuse of the Irish', has entered popular historiography where, along with the Catholic church and the national schools, he is cast as the scapegoat responsible for the demise of Irish. The correspondence under discussion here reveals no animosity towards Irish on O'Connell's part, however: in fact, little or nothing is said about it anywhere in these seven volumes. Attempts by one of O'Connell's sons to learn Irish warrant just a fleeting, non-committal reference. The most extensive letter focusing on Irish here is penned not by O'Connell himself but by a correspondent, a priest who was an Irish scholar working on the London mission. He is concerned that copies of the Protestant bible in Irish are being widely distributed, at not inconsiderable expense, throughout Ireland and even in London among the Irish poor, by proselytisers: 'a more dangerous scheme could not be devised', he warns (*C.*, letter 1136, 1824).[18] In other words, the Irish language is being targeted as a conduit for non-Catholic material – a strategy that could be very successful especially among the poor, given their attachment to the Irish language, according to the letter-writer. So high is its status for many of them that it is far beyond price:

> A respectable clergyman in the County Tipperary told me that he offered a poor labourer in his parish 10 guineas for an old manuscript which he indignantly refused though he was at the same time in the greatest indigence (*C.*, letter 1136, 1824).

The lengths to which these proselytisers are prepared to go in order to bring their religion to unsuspecting Irish speakers are recounted:

> I have heard that 2 Protestant clergymen and 2 Methodist preachers have learned the Irish merely for the purpose of preaching to the poor Irish here in their own language (*C.*, letter 1136, 1824).

In other words, the Irish language becomes the *locus* of religious subversion, a means to an inauspicious end. No response from O'Connell to this letter features in the correspondence but the tone of the letter suggests that the letter-writer presupposes that O'Connell would be of one mind with him. From his letters, O'Connell's overall lack of enthusiasm for Irish and his corresponding emphasis on English

---

[17]   Brian Friel (1981), *Translations*. London, Faber, pp. 25-26. I am grateful to Professor Martine Pelletier for reminding me of this reference; see also Richard Pine (1990), *Friel and Ireland's Drama*. London, Routledge.

[18]   See Irene Whelan (2005), *The Bible War in Ireland: The 'Second Reformation' and the Polarization of Protestant-Catholic Relations 1800-40*. Madison, University of Wisconsin Press.

could be interpreted as part of his pragmatic, 'modernising' agenda, on a par with his enthusiasm expressed in these letters for the modernising of his beloved Iveragh, with the building of new roads and, indeed, the building of a lighthouse on Skellig Michael. There is no nostalgia here for a 'golden' past, no harking back to times when people were 'poor but happy'. His boundless energy is focused on the future, on modernity, on international issues. Irish plays no part there. Here though not always elsewhere, Mary agrees with her husband: witness her (doomed!) search for an English-speaking wet nurse on Valentia Island: the possibility that her babies might drink in the Irish language along with their wet nurse's milk could not be countenanced! Writing to her from London, O'Connell teases her for her English pronunciation with its interference from Irish: she says 'asso-she-ation', (*C.*, letter 1173, 1825), a pronunciation still typical in the traditional Kerry accent to this day. He reassures her, however, that this is also how upper class Londoners pronounce this word. Perhaps this is a back-handed compliment to her and to his fellow county men and women in his beloved Kerry: their country accent reminds him of his fellow parliamentarians in Westminster. Or could it be playful homage to his fellow parliamentarians implying that they sound like Kerry peasants: the ultimate compliment! That said, O'Connell himself, a fluent Irish speaker, occasionally in his letters appears to be thinking in Irish while writing in English, as may be the case in the following auto-correction:

> I hope to carry Scott's last novel. That is an Irish phrase: I mean his next (*C.*, letter 1065, 1823).[19]

The role of English as the written language of Irish speakers is evident elsewhere in the correspondence when an Irish speaker writes in English, the language in which he would have learned to write, whereas French speakers write to O'Connell in their first language, French.

One of the most interesting elements in these letters is O'Connell's constant weaving, on almost every page, of phrases, idioms and quotations culled from languages other than English. Many of these are from Latin and refer to legal matters. Some are quite standard: *bona fide* (*C.*, letter 1189, 1825), *sine die* (*C.*, letter 520, 1815), *sine qua non* (*C.*, letters 234, 1809 and 1291, 1826), *nisi prius* (*C.*, letter 523, 1815), *ipse loquitur* (*C.*, letter 1798, 1831), *quem vult perdere* (*C.*, letter 1861, 1831); others are more esoteric: *quieta movere* (*C.*, letter 1108, 1824). Latin quotations from the classics of his schooldays also surface. Latin maxims abound. French, too, is a constant presence, for instance in references to diplomatic and court life: *levee* (*C.*, letter 1081, 1824),

---

[19] My thanks to an Dochtúir Seán Ó Súilleabháin, Department of Modern Irish, University College Cork, for his help with this statement.

protégés (*C.*, letters 328, 1811 and 1396, 1827), *carte blanche* (*C.*, letter 2416, 1837). Other French terms such as *éclat* are used arguably because they have more *éclat* in French! However, some terms are more problematic: *tête-à-tête* (*C.*, letter 996, 1823), *salle-à-manger* (*C.*, letter 999, 1823), "an *élève* of Stanley" (*C.*, letter 2123, 1834), a *morceau* of news (*C.*, letter 1126, 1824): one wonders why French terms are used here in preference to perfectly adequate English ones. O'Connell's frequent use of the throwaway remark, "nous verrons," lends an oral quality to his writing (*C.*, letters 2046, 1834, letter 1724, 1830 and letter 1718, 1830), as does the flourish, "n'importe" (*C.*, letter 1718, 1830). Very often, he incorporates sayings from other sources in his letters: "'le pauvre homme'!!! as the French say" (*C.*, letter 2553, 1838), "'aux ordres' as they say in France" (*C.*, letter 3124, 1845), "the French proverb, 'qui s'excuse, s'accuse'" (*C.*, letter 3102, 1844) and "it would be, according to Talleyrand's phrase, 'le commencement de la fin'" (*C.*, letter 1979, 1833). This lends a multi-voiced quality to his letters. One of the most intriguing aspects of this macaronic tendency can be found in his letters to Mary:

> I am weary of being absent from you and I feel the Swiss *malade du pays* as they call it (*C.*, letter 1184, 1825 from London).

Given that Mary did not understand written French, why not write 'homesickness'?[20] Similarly, elsewhere he writes to her of 'Mr Coleman's maxim "beaucoup de piété, beaucoup de gaieté"' (*C.*, letter 475, 1814). Could it be that these French and Latin phrases are so fossilised that they no longer belong to any specific language but to a kind of *lingua franca* understood even by monoglots like Mary? At all events, his use of a composite language neatly mirrors his intellectual life in which his concerns were similarly composite and international.

O'Connell continues to fascinate: his latest biography, recently published and concentrating on the first five decades of his life, *King Dan: The Rise of Daniel O'Connell 1775-1829*, by Trinity College Dublin historian, Patrick M. Geoghegan, featured twice in an *Irish Times* item on the best books of 2008.[21] In it, University College Dublin historian, Mary E. Daly, had this to say of it: 'O'Connell's colourful early life – high spending, constant debt, duelling, womanising and involvement with the United Irishmen – is worthy of a historical novel', while for Trinity College Dublin historian, Micheál O Siochrú: 'the story of his life, replete with monstrous egos, unfeasibly large personal debts and

---

[20]   In any case, the Swiss do not call it 'malade du pays': O'Connell gets it wrong: it should read *mal du pays*.

[21]   Patrick M. Geoghegan (2008), *King Dan: The Rise of Daniel O'Connell 1775-1829*. Dublin, Gill and Macmillan.

tangled love lives, would resonate with any modern reader'.[22] In this whirlwind of a life, attitudes to language and to languages form admittedly but a small element. Nonetheless, I would argue that here, as elsewhere, O'Connell quite literally has much to say.

Résumé

Daniel O'Connell, un des plus grands orateurs de l'histoire de l'Irlande, était à l'aise en plusieurs langues dont le gaélique, l'anglais et le français qu'il apprit à l'école en France où il étudia également le latin et le grec. On voit dans sa correspondance que pour lui, l'homme civilisé était quelqu'un qui maîtrisait plusieurs langues, y compris les langues classiques ; en revanche, pour la femme, il exigeait plutôt les langues modernes, le français et l'italien, par exemple. Sa correspondance volumineuse accorde peu d'attention au gaélique malgré les accusations dirigées contre lui quant au rôle qu'il aurait joué dans son déclin. Son emploi constant d'éléments tirés d'autres langues est à l'image de sa vie intellectuelle, également composite et internationale.

---

[22] *The Irish Times* (weekend review supplement), 22/11/ 2008, p. 10.

The Campaign for the Recognition of the Irish Language in National Schools (1878-1904)

Adeline TISSIER-MOSTON

Université Sorbonne Nouvelle-Paris 3

The system of National Education, which was set up in Ireland by the British authorities in 1831, was generally welcomed by the population, especially the Catholics, as it was meant to provide instruction to the children of the poorest classes without the fear of proselytism. In the decades preceding the implementation of the national system, education in Ireland had been left in charge of a series of societies which, one by one, had lost the confidence of the Catholic majority as they used their schools to try and spread the influence of the Protestant religion in Ireland. Primary sources from the period and subsequent discussions of the national system tend to focus heavily on the religious aspects of the question: the revolutionary concept of educating both Protestant and Catholic children in the same classrooms; separating religious instruction from other lessons with one day a week being set apart for it; and lastly the gradual failure of the original ideal as the church authorities rebelled against the system and eventually took over in most schools, making the national system de facto a denominational one. The religious quarrel which dominated the national system almost from its very beginnings tended to obscure the question of the actual educational and cultural impact of the schools. The national system, mainly because it offered so many safeguards against religious corruption, quickly spread over the entire country. After a few decades, the majority of the children of the poorer classes were being educated within the national system, and this means the influence of the schools should not be underestimated. It is therefore of significant importance that the Irish language was not, for most of the 19th century, officially recognised within the national system. Textbooks were written specially for the new schools (since the non-denominationalism of the system in effect prohibited the use of already existing books) and they were written entirely in English.

The lessons themselves, throughout the country, were conducted in the English language.

From early on in the history of the schools, there was evidence that, in some areas, the impact of the new system remained limited because of the existence of a language barrier between pupils and teachers. In 1837, a Select Committee reported to Parliament on the new plan for education in Ireland. One of the many people who gave evidence to the Committee was Reverend Norman McLeod, Moderator of the Scottish Presbyterian General Assembly. He had visited Ireland in 1833 in order to establish the potential for converting the native Irish by using their own language or one close to it:

> I was extremely anxious, and required to ascertain this point, how far licentiates belonging to the Church of Scotland speaking the Gaelic language, or the dialect that is spoken in the Highlands, could be useful as missionaries in those districts in Ireland where the Irish is spoken; whether our Scotch Gaelic could be understood by the Irish.[1]

In August 1833, the Reverend McLeod visited a National School near Westport in County Mayo: "My great object was, as all the children spoke Irish, that I might know how the teaching them English answered."[2] He discovered a school in a state of "great confusion" with a slightly "eccentric" teacher. He asked for the most advanced class to read English to him and eventually managed to get a few boys to read one of Aesop's Fables to him. The boys read "very distinctly." However, it soon became obvious that they did not understand a word of what they were reading:

> When they had read the fable, I asked them to close the book, and to give me the substance of the meaning of what they had read in English; and the boys looked at me, and seemed not to understand it; and I said to the teacher, "they do not seem to understand my strong Highland accent; will you tell them what I wish them to do; to give me the meaning in their own way?" and he laughed very heartily, and said, "they cannot do it; to be sure they cannot do it;" and when I asked, "Why?," he said, "They have no English; they are Irish boys, those, and they have no English" [...] and I said, "Do you understand the Irish so well as to explain to them?" and he said he had no Irish; The boys had no English and he had no Irish; and I then simply asked the man, "And pray, what is the good of this teaching? They are learn-

---

[1] *Report of the Select Committee on the New Plan of Education in Ireland; together with the minutes of evidence, and an appendix and index*, H.C., 1837, VIII, pt II, p. 106.

[2] *Ibid.*, p. 108.

ing to read what they do not understand, and which you do not explain to them;" and he said, "Indeed, Sir, I do not know."[3]

McLeod carried on to provide further evidence that "the only effectual method that can be taken is to instruct them through the medium of their own language."[4]

The situation described here appears both amusing and discouraging and shows that the British authorities received evidence from the very beginning of the national system of the existence of monoglot Irish boys and girls in many parts of the country. Closer to home for the Commissioners of National Education, the reports submitted each year by their own inspectors often mentioned the issue of Irish speaking children within the schools. Their reports pinpointed for the Commissioners the areas where the Irish language was still widely spoken and often identified the language barrier as the cause of the mediocrity they encountered in many of those schools. Thus Dr Newell, General Inspector for the County of Cork, considered that the lack of knowledge of children in the national school of Trafask was explained by the fact that "most of those present spoke Irish, and a short time since heard no other language"[5] and that "English [was] almost a foreign language to them."[6] A similar situation was to be found in many other villages in the area. Most inspectors met with this type of schools during their tours of inspection, and they were more frequent in Counties where the Irish language was widely spoken, such as Donegal, Galway, Cork or Waterford. In those counties, every single report contained a reference to the linguistic question. In 1857, Patrick Joseph Keenan raised the issue during a tour of Donegal: "Only two of the children of the first class could point out a horse – thus showing the ignorance of English – although there was a horse within a few yards of the class upon the road."[7] Patrick Joseph Keenan was the only inspector to be truly concerned about the linguistic problems in national schools. Other inspectors were merely pointing out facts without expressing an opinion or suggesting solutions. Keenan, in his reports between 1855 and 1858, gave a large portion of his general comments about his tours of inspection over to the place of the Irish and English languages in national schools. In his mind, there was no doubt

---

[3] *Ibid.*, p. 111.

[4] *Idem.*

[5] *Twenty-First Report of the Commissioners of National Education in Ireland, for the year 1854*, H.C., 1854-55, XXIII, Vol. II, p. 136.

[6] *Idem.*

[7] *Twenty-Fourth Report of the Commissioners of National Education in Ireland, for the year 1857*, H.C., 1859, session 1, VII, p. 143.

that the national system played an important role in the decline of the Irish language:

> There are three things which the National System is effecting, which are not at all gratifying to our patriotism. We are quietly but certainly destroying the national legend, national music, and national language of the country. [...] The Census Returns show that upwards of a million and a half, or 23.3 per cent of the population, spoke Irish in the year 1851. The National System is every day diminishing this number. Even in places where all social communication is carried on in Irish, and where, in short, few or none of the adult population know a word of English, the language of the National Schools, the books, the teaching, etc, are entirely English.[8]

However, Keenan remained an enthusiastic supporter of the national education system and became Resident Commissioner to the Board of National Education in Dublin a few years after the publication of those reports. In the 1850s, as an inspector, he did attempt to convince the Commissioners of National Education of the benefits of a bilingual education. In the schools he inspected, he conducted a few experiments, questioning the children in English and then in Irish. The difference he noted was astounding: "Children who were quite stupid whilst being examined in English only, exhibited the greatest vivacity and intellectual sharpness, when undergoing a rational examination in their own tongue."[9] These observations led him to recommend a bilingual education as a means to ensure that Irish-speaking children would benefit truly from the national system and obtain a sound knowledge of the English language. Keenan was in no way attempting to protect the Irish language but was merely anxious to optimise the effects of the national system throughout the country.

None of these appeals or pieces of evidence seem to have made any impact on the Board of National Education who met regularly in their Dublin headquarters. It is possible that they were too preoccupied with the fierce religious battle which raged over the national system almost from the outset. It was only when a religious compromise had been reached with the principal denominations that there was enough interest in the linguistic and cultural cause for it to be addressed.

In July 1878, the Council of the Society for the Preservation of the Irish Language presented a "Memorial" to the Board of National Education, asking for the Irish language to be placed on the results programme of the national schools. This system of payment by results had been introduced by the newly appointed Resident Commissioner, Patrick

---

[8]   *Twenty-Second Report [...], for the year 1855*, H.C., 1856, XXVII, Vol. II, pp. 73-74.

[9]   *Twenty-Fourth Report [...], for the year 1857, op. cit.*, p. 146.

Joseph Keenan, in 1872. It had been one of the recommendations of the Powis Commission, which published an extensive study of national education in 1870 and a similar system was already in place in England since 1862. The idea was that all children in Irish national schools be examined annually by an inspector in reading, writing, and arithmetic, and that a fixed sum would be paid for each child who passed in each subject, providing that the child had attended school regularly during the year.[10] Part of a teacher's salary would therefore be dependent on the results of his or her pupils. The main benefits of the new system were a significant rise in the number and regularity of attendances in the schools as well as an incitation to teachers to push their pupils to higher levels of education than before.[11]

The system also further limited the freedom of individual teachers and brought in a new cramming ethos in many classrooms. The compulsory subjects were reading, writing, spelling, grammar, geography and arithmetic for each class, plus agricultural theory for older boys in rural schools and needlework for girls in all schools. The Commissioners' report for 1875 also listed 21 extra subjects that would also receive result payments, including geometry, algebra, botany, Latin, Greek, French and cookery. The Memorial from the Society for the Preservation of the Irish Language (SPIL) is the equivalent of a modern day petition and ran to four pages, stating the reasons why the Irish language should be given a better place within the national system. The main argument of the memorial was based on an extensive quote from "a Head Inspector" from 1855 showing the effect the national system was having on the Irish language:

> The Census Returns show that upwards of a million and a half, or 23.3 per cent of the population, spoke Irish in the year 1851. The National System is every day diminishing this number. Even in places where all social communication is carried on in Irish, and where, in short, few or none of the adult population know a word of English, the language of the National Schools, the books, the teaching, etc., are entirely English. [...] The shrewdest people in the world are those who are bilingual [...] But the most stupid children I have ever met with are those who were learning English whilst endeavouring to forget Irish. It is hard to conceive any more difficult school exercise than to begin our first alphabet, [...] and first attempt at reading, in a language of which we know nothing, and all this without the means of reference to, or comparison with, a word of our mother tongue. Yet this is the

---

[10] Donald Akenson (1970), *The Irish Education Experiment, The National System of Education in the Nineteenth Century*, London, Routledge and Kegan Paul, p. 317.

[11] *Ibid.*, p. 321 & p. 323.

ordeal Irish speaking children have to pass through, and the natural result is that the English which they acquire is very imperfect.[12]

This "Head Inspector," having spent some time in County Donegal in 1854, had come to the conclusion that Irish should be taught grammatically in the schools, and that English should be taught to Irish speakers through the medium of the Irish language, which would result in a better education for those people and a better grasp of the English language on their part. This extract from an inspector's report carried all the more weight when the reader learnt that the Head Inspector was none other than Patrick Joseph Keenan, who at the time of the SPIL appeal was Resident Commissioner of National Education in Ireland. In fact, his 1850s reports would often come back to haunt him in the last quarter of the 19th century, as they were seized upon by nationalists and revivalists as an unassailable argument in favour of the introduction of Irish lessons and/or a bilingual system in national schools. The Council of the Society followed their long quote by stressing the fact that Latin, Greek and French were part of the results programme and remarked on the irony of a national system that did not teach the national language: "We may [...] be permitted to observe that any system of national education must be regarded as incomplete, that does not provide for the teaching of the nation's language; and therefore an opportunity should be afforded all Irishmen of having their children taught their native tongue."[13] The theme of the alliance between language and country ran throughout the memorial:

> It is the language of Ireland, and the best suited to the natural genius of the countrymen of Scotus Erigena, the "perfervidum ingenium Scotorum," the best calculated to preserve the traditions and idiosyncrasies of the nation, being cast in that Celtic or intellectual mould which rendered the country so singularly famous in former times, and thus enabled her to become the leader of civilisation in Western Europe.[14]

The other major argument used by SPIL was the value put on Celtic as a subject by scholars throughout Europe, noting for instance that the University of Oxford had recently established a chair for the study of Celtic. The Memorial insisted on the Irish language as a flourishing literary language, with many books being published in the language as well as famous works being translated into Irish (most recently the *Illiad*). Irish was thus presented as a language which was worth saving for its cultural richness. This particular argument would be used extensively by the Gaelic League some years later and was a reply to the

---

[12]   H.C., 1878, LX., p. 496.

[13]   *Idem.*

[14]   *Ibid.*, p. 497.

common belief held by many English speakers that the Irish language was merely the dialect of ignorant peasants. This belief was being passed on to Irish children through the schoolbooks used in national schools, with remarks such as this one from a geography lesson in the *Third Book of Lessons*: "Various languages are spoken by the nations of Europe, besides our own English. Even in some parts of Ireland, a different language is spoken, viz. Irish; though all who learn to read, learn English, and prefer speaking it."[15] SPIL was also keen to present the Irish language as a living language and provided Census figures to show that around 200,000 persons under the age of 20 were Irish-speakers at the time, with a concentration of Irish speakers in Munster, Connaught, Donegal and the West of Ulster. SPIL harked back to the fact that French, Greek and Latin were then taught in Irish national schools and had been placed on the Results Programme. They used the Commissioners' latest report to show that only 963 pupils had gained a pass in those three languages combined in 1876, a figure which seemed minute compared to the potential of almost 200,000 students for Irish. Finally, SPIL showed how the teaching of Irish in national schools would be easily introduced, with over 2,000 teachers "able and willing to teach [it], provided it be placed on the Results Programme"[16] as well as by the introduction of a couple of Irish lesson books published by the Society itself. In fact, the memorial stated that some teachers had already established Irish classes in connection with their schools and the list of all such classes was enclosed with the memorial. Finally, the SPIL ventured to hope that Irish would receive the same treatment as Scottish Gaelic, whose teaching had just been recognised in the Highland schools.[17] The real power of the Memorial, however, was not the appeal to Patrick Keenan or the Census figures in favour of Irish but the sheer number of people who signed it, and, even more importantly, the number of religious and lay dignitaries who added their names to the list, 1,500 in total.[18] The members of the Society included several Members of Parliament and its President was the Archbishop of Tuam, one of the first and most vehement Catholic antagonists of the national system. Two other Archbishops, including the Primate of all Ireland, also signed the Memorial, in addition to twelve Bishops, the Lord Mayor of Dublin

---

[15] *Third Book of Lessons for the Use of Schools* (1853), Dublin, p. 142.

[16] H.C., 1878, LX., p. 497.

[17] This recognition had come from the Education Department "within the past few weeks" according to the Memorial, *ibid.* p. 497.

[18] The campaign led by the SPIL was in fact, according to Ó Buachalla, "worthy in its sophistication, of a political party of the modern era" due to its extent and comprehensiveness. See Séamas Ó Buachalla, "Educational Policy and the Role of the Irish Language from 1831 to 1981," *European Journal of Education*, Vol. 19, No. 1, 1984, pp. 75-92, p. 77.

and forty-one Members of Parliament. And the list went on with 94
signatories from Trinity College Dublin, various members of the Catholic University, three pages of lesser clergymen as well as 596 signatures
which were mentioned but not printed in the document sent to the
Commissioners. The support received by the SPIL memorial was beyond the resistance of the Commissioners of National Education and
Irish was introduced as a subject in the Results Programme almost
immediately (1879), even though they still refused to see that the teaching of Irish was a necessity:

> Whilst convinced of the fact that in the national schools English was the
> universal and familiar language of teachers and pupils, and that, in the in-
> struction of the pupils, no difficulty existed even in the counties in which
> the Irish language is, to any extent, spoken, the Commissioners, however,
> felt that they were bound to defer to the representations of a memorial so
> influentially promoted, and accordingly they resolved to place the Irish lan-
> guage as a philological subject on the programme of extra branches.[19]

This 'confession' was not made until five years later, in a long letter
from the Commissioners of National Education to the Chief Secretary
for Ireland. In 1884 a memorial was sent to the Irish Executive by the
Council of the Gaelic Union, requesting that Irish be used as a means for
the teaching of English[20] in Irish-speaking districts and that the Irish
language become part of the ordinary curriculum of the national schools.
The Chief Secretary forwarded the memorial to the Commissioners with
a letter requesting further information on the status of the Irish language
in the national system, past and present. The Commissioners' reply,
which included the above "confession," was thorough and damning.
According to them, Irish had been consciously excluded from the national system at its outset when "the anxiety of the promoters of the
National System was to encourage the cultivation of the English language and to make English the language of the schools."[21] This time, the
memorial was not backed by powerful dignitaries, but merely the fanci-
ful demands of an "archaeological society," and the Commissioners
refuted all the arguments put forward in favour of the Irish language.

---

[19] *Copy of Correspondence between the Irish Executive and the Commissioners of
National Education in Ireland, with respect to the Teaching of Irish in the National
Schools*, H.C., 1884, LXI, p. 628. "Extra branches" was the name given to subjects
taught in addition to the main curriculum in National Schools. Irish was therefore
given the same status as, for example, Latin or Greek and given a slight advantage
over French.

[20] The idea was to help monoglot Irish speakers cope better in the classroom through
the introduction of Irish translations and vocabulary lists, giving them a known reference in their attempt to learn the English language and avoiding situations like the
one described by McLeod in Westport in 1833.

[21] *Copy of Correspondence, op. cit.*, p. 625.

The Commissioners refused to see the Irish language as a living language (they went to great lengths to refute the census figures quoted by the Gaelic Union):

> In a country where all the interests, social, commercial, and political combine to favour the acquisition of the English language by the people, it would certainly be neither natural nor rational to impose upon the children who know English an obligation to study Irish also, simply because they have to any extent, great or small, a colloquial knowledge of the Irish. If accordingly the Irish language is to be cultivated at all by such children, it must be as a philological accomplishment, when age and capacity fit them for it, like the acquisition of Latin, Greek, or French.[22]

The Gaelic Union memorial, like most appeals in favour of the Irish language in the last quarter of the 19th century, leant heavily on the reports of Patrick Keenan in the 1850s: it quoted the exact passage quoted in the SPIL memorial but also added extracts from the evidence given by Keenan before a Royal Commission in 1868 as well as references to his reports on language teaching in the Island of Malta in 1878. The Irish Executive therefore requested the Resident Commissioner, now Sir Patrick Keenan, to provide an opinion on the teaching of the Irish language in national schools. Keenan replied that the situation in Malta, where all the natives speak Maltese, bore no resemblance to the current situation of Donegal, which he considered to be "entirely different from the Donegal of 1855."[23] So although he had recommended that Maltese be the language of the schools in Malta, he no longer believed that Irish should be the language of the national schools anywhere in Ireland. The conclusion of this exchange of correspondence between the Irish Executive and the Commissioners of National Education was a letter from the Chief Secretary for Ireland to the Secretaries of the Gaelic Union stating that "after careful consideration [...] I feel bound to express my concurrence in the view expressed by [the Commissioners], that they have reached a limit to the steps which, in the public interests, could wisely be taken in respect to the cultivation of the Irish language in the primary schools, and I am not prepared to urge upon them to take any further steps in the matter."[24]

This answer from the Chief Secretary seemed final and might have sealed the fate of the Irish language. However, the Gaelic Union was soon taken over by men who would not take no for an answer as far as the language question went and by the time it had been engulfed in the newly formed Gaelic League, in 1893, the language movement in

---

[22] *Ibid.*, p. 624.

[23] *Ibid.*, p. 633.

[24] *Ibid.*, p. 636.

Ireland had taken on another dimension. The Gaelic League made the introduction of the Irish language in national education a priority in its first decades. After claiming in 1893 that "no language has ever been kept alive by mere book-teaching,"[25] the League rapidly changed tack and threw itself heart and soul in the teaching of the Irish language to the Irish population, setting up weekly classes throughout the country and Summer Colleges in the Gaelic West. This marked an early change in policy for the Gaelic League, which had initially been set up as a preservation society but soon became a revivalist organisation. The leaders of the League soon realised that the problem had to be tackled at its root and that the survival and revival of the language would only be possible with its inclusion in the national system. The Leaguers had learnt from previous demands and their reception by the British authorities regarding Irish in the schools. Douglas Hyde, founder and president of the Gaelic League, had indeed been a member of SPIL and then of the Gaelic Union. The League, through meetings, rallies and publications throughout the country, succeeded in awakening the conscience of the Irish people and in making them realise what giving up their native language would imply. Once the idea had taken root, it became obvious to most people that the Irish language should have a role to play in the education of Irish children. Thus the League could rely on immense popular support throughout their long battle with the Commissioners of National Education and this proved crucial on several occasions: the reply of the Commissioners to requests concerning the Irish language had usually been that there was no demand for it, an argument annihilated by the Gaelic League. In its early years, the League concentrated on raising the profile of the Irish language, by opening branches throughout the country and having their main members appear in public whenever possible. *The Gaelic Journal*, initially run by the Gaelic Union then taken over by the League, faithfully reported what was then called "news of the movement." As a result, anything to do with the promotion of the Irish language in national schools was given place of honour. Thus, the July edition of 1893, only a few months after the foundation of the Gaelic League, reported a speech by one of their supporters before the Congress of Irish National Teachers, urging the Irish-speaking teachers to help save the language: "Let us, teachers in Irish-speaking districts, do our duty by our grand old language, and we may hope that at no distant day our schools may give other O'Currys, O'Donovans, and Joyces to Irish literature."[26] The attendance of some leaders of the League at the National Teachers' Congress became a

---

[25] Eoin MacNeill, "A Plea and a Plan for the extension of the movement to preserve and spread the Irish language," *Gaelic Journal*, Vol. IV, No. 44, March 1893, p. 178.

[26] *Gaelic Journal*, Volume IV, July 1893, p. 187.

regular feature and the *Gaelic Journal* reported John McNeill's presence at the 1894 Congress, at which a resolution advocating the teaching of Irish in the schools was passed,[27] while the edition of March 1895 contained the optimistic and encouraging idea that national teachers "will save the Irish language."[28] In May 1896, the Journal again reported that the National Teachers' Congress had passed a resolution in favour of teaching the Irish language.[29] One of the Gaelic League's strategies was a constant lobbying of politicians regarding all aspects of the Irish language and particularly its place in the system of national education. In May 1896, when an election campaign was underway, the *Gaelic Journal* urged its readers to lobby their candidates on the question of bilingual instruction for Irish-speaking children in national schools.[30] And in July of the same year, the Journal published a number of letters and addresses to politicians concerning the reduction of marks given for Irish in the Intermediate examinations (secondary education) as well as a list of Irish MPs who had voted in favour of and against the Irish language in parliament (an early use of the name-and-shame strategy). The Journal also published letters that had been sent to teachers who were listed as Irish speakers but were not teaching the language in their schools.[31]

These examples show the relentless fashion in which the Gaelic League attempted to rescue the Irish language in national schools. Unlike their predecessors, they were not satisfied with an occasional petition and their tenacity as well as the growing support they received were what paid dividends in the end. Even so, it was to be a long battle for the Gaelic League and results for the Irish language in national education did not appear until the turn of the century. From 1899, the League began inundating the public with pamphlets, and five of the first ten pamphlets, published between 1899 and 1901, dealt with national education and the Irish language. These were pamphlets No. 2, "The Case for Bilingual Education in the Irish-speaking Districts," No. 3, "Irish in the Schools," No. 5, "Parliament and the Teaching of Irish: the Irish language debate in the House of Commons, on Friday, 21st July 1900," No. 8, "Bilingual Education" and No. 9, "The Future of Irish in the National Schools." The pamphlets were all well researched and well written, often by dignitaries of the League such as the Archbishop of Dublin, Patrick O'Hickey, John McNeill and the young Patrick Pearse.

---

[27] *Gaelic Journal*, Volume V, No. 2, May 1894, p. 193.
[28] *Ibid.*, No. 12, March 1895, p. 254.
[29] *Gaelic Journal.*, Volume VII, No. 1, May 1896, p. 34.
[30] *Id.*
[31] *Gaelic Journal*, Volume VII, No. 3, July 1896, p. 98.

The arguments used in favour of the Irish language were similar to those used by SPIL and the Gaelic Union, with added anecdotes, figures and quotations, but again it was the sheer volume of publications which carried the League through. By 1900, Irish was allowed to be taught during school hours, though attendance of classes were still optional and inspectors still had to approve the standards of the pupils in the other required subjects. In 1902, 51% of the National Schools were allowed to teach Irish. In 1900 also, results fees in general were abolished but the League succeeded in maintaining the ten shillings grant which was given to schools that taught Irish outside school hours.[32]

Once the Irish language had entered the general curriculum of national schools, the Leaguers concentrated on the remaining Irish-speaking districts, which they believed deserved special treatment. The campaign for bilingual education in the Gaeltacht was officially launched at the first Oireachtas in June 1899 and the League canvassed schools throughout the country, published pamphlets and lobbied the Commissioners and the Irish Executive until the Bilingual Programme was introduced in the Irish-speaking districts in 1904.

The irony is that the Commissioners finally caved in for reasons of their own as well as under pressure from the League. It seems that the new programme was essentially implemented, not to preserve the Irish language, but to ensure that the children of the Gaeltacht received a basic primary education, that is to say a grasp of arithmetic and elementary English. The argument first put to the Commissioners by Patrick Joseph Keenan, that teaching English through the medium of English to Irish-speaking children virtually prevented the children from learning anything at all, an argument that was quoted and reiterated countless times, by SPIL and the Gaelic Union in their memorials, and by the Gaelic League in a number of pamphlets, speeches and articles, this argument at last hit home with the Commissioners, some 50 years down the line.

Résumé

Le système d'Éducation nationale en Irlande mis en place en 1831 a dès le départ privilégié la langue anglaise et a plus ou moins ignoré l'existence même de la langue irlandaise. Cependant, les parents irlandais à travers le pays, surtout les parents catholiques, ont accueilli le système à bras ouverts car il proposait, enfin, pour leurs enfants un système d'éducation à un coût raisonnable sans menace de prosélytisme. Ce n'est qu'à la fin du XIXe que l'aspect anti-irlandais du sys-

---

[32] Colmán Ó hUallacháin (1994), *The Irish and Irish, a Sociolinguistic Analysis of the Relationship Between a People and their Language*, Dublin, Assisi Press, p. 123.

tème a été soulevé. Cet article étudie les approches utilisées par plusieurs organismes qui militaient en faveur de la langue irlandaise afin d'obliger les Commissaires de l'Éducation nationale (dont le siège était à Dublin) de faire figurer la langue irlandaise dans le curriculum. Une attention particulière est accordée ici à la Ligue gaélique qui a fait pression sur les Commissaires et sur le gouvernement britannique en publiant de nombreux tracts et plusieurs articles dans des revues et journaux. Leur campagne a enfin porté ses fruits car la reconnaissance accrue accordée à la langue a suscité la mise en place d'un programme bilingue dans les régions gaélophones (Gaeltacht) à partir de 1904.

Immigrant Pupils and the Irish Language in Republic of Ireland Primary Schools

Patricia FOURNIER-NOËL

Université Sorbonne Nouvelle-Paris 3

Introduction

As enshrined in the Irish Constitution ever since 1922, Irish, as the national language, is the first official language of Ireland, whereas English is equally recognised as another official language,[1] or even, in the words of the 1937 Constitution, as "a second official language."[2] However, there is a gap between this official status of Irish and the fact that English is the native and everyday language of the majority of the Irish population.[3] Primary schools are important in that regard, as they are the sites where Irish is transmitted to the next generation of Irish citizens, more particularly to those coming from an English-speaking background. Has the recent increase in the number of immigrant pupils attending Irish primary schools led schools to clarify the status of the Irish language? The term "immigrant pupils" will be used throughout this paper to refer to all pupils who have an immigrant background, i.e. whose parents immigrated to Ireland. Most of the pupils involved immigrated along with their parents but, among the younger ones, some were

---

[1] *Constitution of the Irish Free State (Saorstát Éireann) Act* (1922), Article 4, http://acts.oireachtas.ie/zza1y1922.1.html, (accessed 20/05/2009).

[2] See article 8 of the 1937 Constitution, still in force today, *Bunreacht na hÉireann*, Dublin, Government of Ireland [1937], http://www.taoiseach.gov.ie/index.asp?docID=243, (accessed 20/05/2009).

[3] According to the 2006 Census, 46.3 percent of Irish nationals (aged 3 and over) could speak Irish, but almost 27 percent of them spoke Irish within the education system only; about 25 percent never spoke Irish; 35 per cent used it less often than weekly; less than 2 per cent spoke Irish both within and outside the education system and about 9 percent used it daily or weekly. These last two categories make up about 5 percent of all Irish nationals. Central Statistics Office (CSO) (2006), *Census*, Dublin, CSO, http://www.cso.ie/census/default.htm (accessed 20/05/2009).

born and raised in Ireland and are not first generation immigrants as such. A significant number of the immigrant pupils enrolled in Irish schools spoke neither English nor Irish, so they were entitled to receive language support. In the majority of schools, where English is the language of instruction,[4] these children have received language support in English only. We can therefore ask ourselves what role the Irish language can play in the exclusion or inclusion of these immigrant children in Irish schools. Inclusion is here used in the sense of children being given the opportunity of participating fully in the education offered by schools, as defined by Niall Crowley, Chief Executive Officer of the Equality Authority at a conference organised in 2004: "Inclusion [...] is about participation by all pupils within this diversity [the diversity of pupils attending schools] in all areas of school life."[5] This paper will focus on the status of Irish in three Roman Catholic primary schools with a significant number of immigrant pupils on roll. Primary schools were selected for two main reasons. Firstly, they are the first contact many immigrant children have with the Irish education system. Secondly, the integration of the curriculum, the fact that all subjects should be interconnected and taught by the same teacher in the same classroom, means that exemption from a part of this curriculum can set immigrant pupils apart from their Irish peers.

Roman Catholic schools were chosen as the object of study because they represent the overwhelming majority of Irish primary schools and also because, given their numbers, immigrant pupils are more likely to attend them than other types of schools.[6] For the purposes of this paper

---

[4] According to the latest figures available on the Department of Education and Science website, there were 3,291 primary schools in the 2006/2007 school year; among which 139 were all-Irish schools, in which instruction takes place through Irish, and 6 Gaeltacht schools, located in areas where Irish is the first language of the community, making up together slightly more than 4 percent of all primary schools. Department of Education and Science (2007), *Primary Schools*, http://www.education.ie (20/05/ 2009).

[5] Irish National Teachers' Organisation (INTO); Equality Authority (2004), *The Inclusive School. Proceedings of the Joint Conference of the Irish National Teachers' Organisation and the Equality Authority, Limerick, 27th March 2004*, Dublin, INTO / Equality Authority, p. 13.

[6] In the school year 2006/2007, 3,026 out of 3,291 primary schools were Roman Catholic, *i.e.*, about 92 percent. The second most numerous group of schools came under the patronage of the Church of Ireland and other Protestant denominations and comprised 196 schools, *i.e.* about 6 percent of all schools. The third group consisted of multi-denominational schools, mostly under the patronage of Educate Together, with 51 schools, or less than 2 percent. Seven of the remaining schools were labelled inter-denominational, eight were classified as "Others/Not stated" and there were two Muslim schools and one Jewish school. Department of Education and Science (2007), *Primary Schools, op. cit.* New schools have opened since 2006, including 17

and in order to protect the anonymity of the three schools visited, they will be referred to as schools A, B and C. All three schools were located in urban or suburban areas. School A was made up of two co-educational schools sharing the same site, a junior school catering for children from junior infants, age 4, to second class, age 7, and a senior school catering for children in the higher classes, from third class, age 8, to sixth class, age 12. Only data collected in the senior school will be used here. School B was a girls' school offering the full range of primary school classes, from junior infants to sixth class, and school C was a boys' school, with classes from second to sixth. All three schools had a proportion of immigrant pupils above the national average. School A senior catered for 153 pupils, seventeen of whom were immigrants who represented about 11 percent of the school population. School B catered for 187 pupils, including 47 immigrants, *i.e.* 25 percent. Finally, School C had 262 pupils, including 39 immigrants or 15 percent of the school population. The national average for children aged five to fourteen, which is close to the age range of primary school children, was about 8 percent, according to the 2006 Census.[7] Finally, all three schools happened to have disadvantaged status, although this was not a criterion used for selection.[8] Each case study lasted from three to four weeks and took place between 2005 and 2007. Each case study included consulting school documents, attending classes in different grades and interviewing the participants involved in the life of the school, *i.e.*, principals, teachers whose classes were observed, pupils from different grades and, in some limited cases, parents. The data is still being analysed and so only preliminary findings will be presented here.

Although the issue of the Irish language was not the core issue in the research project, which focused more generally on the way specific schools adapted to the presence of immigrant pupils, the aim of this paper is to provide an insight into what role the Irish language played in the inclusion or exclusion of immigrant children in the schools visited. This account, therefore, does not aim at being statistically relevant but might help identify what issues the status of Irish raised in these schools. One of the objectives in carrying out these case studies was to see how national guidelines were put into practice in given schools. The most important documents describing the organisation of schools and their

---

Educate Together schools, but this has not changed the statistical predominance of Roman Catholic schools.

[7]   Central Statistics Office (2006), *Census, op. cit.*

[8]   The main criterion used was a sufficient number of immigrant pupils on roll to warrant the provision of English language support classes.

mission are the *Education Act*,[9] passed in 1998, and the *Revised Primary Curriculum*,[10] introduced in 1999. Both these documents contain provisions regarding the status and teaching of Irish in primary schools.

1. Irish in Mainstream Schools

National Guidelines

Part I Section 6 of the Education Act (1998) states the objects of the act. The first provisions concern the right of children and adults to education, as well as the rights of parents. Subsections (i) and (j) in particular deal with national education and language. In that regard, the aim of the act is:

> (i) to contribute to the realisation of national policy and objectives in relation to the extension of bi-lingualism in Irish society and in particular the achievement of a greater use of the Irish language at school and in the community;

> (j) to contribute to the maintenance of Irish as the primary community language in Gaeltacht areas;[11]

Subsection (i) implicitly recognises that Irish is not the first language in Ireland but that bilingualism should be extended and that schools need to promote the use of Irish.

As to schools, their function differs according to their location. Ordinary schools need to: "(f) promote the development of the Irish language and traditions, Irish literature, the arts and other cultural matters."[12] Here, the Irish language is not seen in isolation but is depicted as part of a wider culture, also represented by Irish traditions, literature, arts, etc. Schools located in Gaeltacht areas have a specific mission; they need to "contribute to the maintenance of Irish as the primary community language."[13] The conception of Irish is linked to the idea that if it disappears as a living language in the community, it will disappear completely, whereas in English-medium schools, Irish is presented as part of a heritage to be transmitted.

---

[9] Government of Ireland (1998), *Education Act* http://www.acts.ie/zza51y1998.1.html (accessed 20/05/2009).

[10] Department of Education and Science (DES) (1999), *Revised Primary Curriculum*, Dublin, Stationery Office, http://www.ncca.ie (accessed 20/05/2009).

[11] Government of Ireland (1998), *Education Act, op. cit.*

[12] *Ibid.*

[13] *Ibid.*

The second important document is the *Revised Primary Curriculum* that was introduced in 1999.[14] The introduction to this document refers to the importance of achieving quality in education and the acquisition of literacy and numeracy as the first of its key issues.[15] It then shifts to the need to develop a sense of Irish identity and promote the Irish language: "The curriculum recognises that an experience and a knowledge of Irish are important in enabling the child to begin to define and express his or her sense of national and cultural identity."[16] Irish is here presented not only as an important element of Irish people's cultural identity but also as part of their national identity. In the language section of the introduction, three different kinds of schools are listed according to the respective status of English and Irish in each:

> Schools in which English is the mother-tongue of the children and the principal medium of instruction; schools where Irish is, typically, the language of the home and the medium of instruction in school; and scoileanna lán-Ghaeilge, where Irish may or may not be the language of the home but where it is the medium of instruction in school.[17]

The schools visited fell into the first category. The right to learn both Irish and English is partly justified on the basis of Irish history: "Psychologically, historically and linguistically, an experience of both languages is the right of every Irish child."[18] Moreover, this document mentions that a third language can be learnt as part of the pilot project on modern languages.[19] Thus, the promotion of bilingualism in English and Irish seems to be extended to a foreign European language. However, the schools visited did not offer that possibility.

To return to the teaching of Irish, there are two different curricula according to the status of the language in the school. In the majority of schools, where English is the medium of instruction, the use of Irish is to be encouraged partly by making its learning and use enjoyable.[20] As to the curriculum for English, the emphasis is put on the traditional skills of speaking, reading and writing.[21] Although the time devoted to the second language has been reduced from 4.5 hours a week to

---

[14] Department of Education and Science (DES) (1999), *Revised Primary Curriculum, op. cit.*

[15] *Ibid.*, Vol. 23, p. 26.

[16] *Ibid.*, p. 27.

[17] *Ibid.*, p. 43.

[18] *Idem.*

[19] "Modern languages" here refers to European languages.

[20] Department of Education and Science (1999), *Revised Primary Curriculum, op. cit.*, Vol. 23, p. 44.

[21] *Ibid.*, p. 45.

3.5 hours,[22] it is still significant compared to the four hours set aside for the first language and the three hours a week spent on mathematics.[23] Nonetheless, the first language is given precedence over the second in that it is also the medium of instruction of all or most of the subjects taught. The discrepancy between the official high profile status of Irish and the fact that the time devoted to it has been reduced in English-medium schools can have an impact on the way pupils see the language. This is highlighted by the situation of immigrant pupils, many of whom are exempt from learning it.

Exemptions from Learning Irish

Children can be exempted from learning Irish only in specific circumstances. These are set out in a 1996 circular.[24] Exemption is to be granted in exceptional cases only:

> It is a fundamental principle of the primary school curriculum that due allowance should be made for individual pupil differences in ability, interests and circumstances. In accordance with this principle, the primary school programme in Irish is designed to meet the learning needs of a wide variety of pupils. It is taught in a stimulating and activity-centred fashion and the main emphasis is on oral learning and interaction. The question of the need to grant exemption from the learning of Irish should arise only in rare and exceptional circumstances.[25]

The emphasis on oral language and interaction is used as justification of the fact that no pupil should be exempt from Irish if it can be avoided. This puts those who are exempt in a situation where they can be seen as excluded from part of the prescribed curriculum. Pupils may be exempted on six different grounds of which we shall only quote the first four:[26]

---

[22] It is slightly less in the infant classes as the school day is shorter. Department of Education and Science, Inspectorate (2007), *Irish in the Primary School: Promoting the Quality of Learning*, Dublin, Department of Education and Science, p. 19, http://www.education.ie (accessed 20/05/2009).

[23] Department of Education and Science (1999), *Revised Primary Curriculum, op. cit.*, Vol. 23, p. 78.

[24] Department of Education (June 1996), *Circular 12/96 To Boards of Management and Principals of National Schools, Revision of Circular 18/79 on Exemption from the Study of Irish.* 20 May 2009 <http://www.education.ie>. Although this circular pre-dates the *Revised Primary Curriculum* (1999), it was still in force at the time the schools were visited.

[25] *Ibid.*, paragraph 1.

[26] The two remaining grounds are more specific as they relate respectively to children of diplomatic or consular representatives in Ireland and children of political refugees. *Ibid.*, paragraph 1.

(a) up to 11 years of age they have been educated in Northern Ireland or outside Ireland;

(b) pupils formerly enrolled in national schools but who are re-enrolled after spending time abroad, if three years have elapsed in between and the pupil is at least 11 on re-enrolment.[27]

These subsections apply to pupils from Northern Ireland as well as return migrants. The following subparagraphs list additional grounds for exemption: "(c) pupils who have certain learning disabilities; (d) pupils from abroad who have no understanding of English when enrolled."[28] These cover both pupils with special needs and immigrant pupils. Subparagraph 1(d) specifies that immigrant pupils with no prior knowledge of English "would be required to study one language only, Irish or English."[29] In practice, it would be interesting to see if any child has been exempted from learning English, as this document implies is possible. In the schools visited, where English was the dominant language, there was no question of being exempt from it and language support for immigrant pupils was provided solely in English. However, the circular mentions that being exempt from Irish does not mean that the children concerned should not be brought into contact with the language:

> Pupils from the above categories may be allowed to remain in the class during the Irish lesson so that they may have an opportunity to gain a knowledge of spoken Irish and to participate in the learning activities. Alternatively, other suitable arrangements may be made such as allocating school work on other subject areas.[30]

Exemption from Irish therefore means that the pupils who are exempt are not assessed in the language but might still attend Irish classes and be asked to take part in them, although this is not compulsory. In practice, it is up to the class teacher to decide what exempt pupils do during the Irish lesson.

To sum up, exemption from Irish is either linked to having lived abroad or having specific learning difficulties. With regard to immigrant pupils more specifically, Irish is seen as less useful than reaching adequate competence in English in order to access the curriculum. However, the emphasis put on the fact that exemption should be the exception may have a negative impact on how children who are exempt are perceived by others, at least in theory. We can now turn to the status of

---

[27] *Idem.*

[28] *Idem.*

[29] *Ibid.*, subparagraph 1(d).

[30] *Ibid.*, paragraph 1.

Irish in the three schools visited to see if this holds true and if Irish contributed to including immigrant pupils in, or excluding them from, the school community.

2. The Irish Language in Practice in the Schools Studied

Irish Classes

In order to see what a normal school day was like, class observations were carried out in the three schools studied. It is within this framework that Irish classes were observed. In all three schools, a significant number of immigrant children were exempt from Irish.[31] This was particularly true for children who started school in Ireland in the middle and higher grades (from third class onwards), whereas immigrant pupils who had started in the lower grades learnt Irish at the same time as their Irish peers did. For those who enrolled in the middle and higher grades and who had no word of English, learning English was seen as a priority and English language support classes were sometimes organised at the time set out for Irish. As far as possible, English language support teachers tried to withdraw pupils from class at different times during the week so that they did not always miss the same subject. But Irish and religion seemed to be picked more often than other subjects, whereas physical education (PE) and art were seen as important for immigrant children in that they did not require English language skills as much as other subjects and were also popular subjects among all pupils. Therefore, withdrawing immigrant children from class at those times might have been seen as a punishment by them.

However, exemption from Irish varied among immigrant pupils depending on their respective country of origin and length of residence in Ireland. For example, most Nigerian children did Irish, as many of their parents hard arrived at the end of the 1990s and the children now in the higher grades started school in Ireland in the lower grades and so learnt Irish. Also, many of these children had a good command of English. Although it was not the native language of all, the children observed and interviewed were fluent in it. The situation was different for Polish children. Most of the older ones were exempt, as they had arrived more recently and did not speak English prior to enrolment. These differences in immigrant pupils' exemption from Irish, are in line with the findings

---

[31] No list of exempt pupils was consulted during the research visits, so the following figures are based on observation and pupil interviews: in school A senior, among the seventeen immigrant pupils, twelve were interviewed, and six of them were exempt; in school B, there were 47 immigrant pupils, eight were interviewed, among whom three were exempt; and in school C, which had 40 immigrant pupils, ten were interviewed, eight of them were exempt.

of the 2006 Census. Indeed, 45 percent of Nigerian children aged five to nineteen said they spoke Irish,[32] as compared to about 20 percent of Chinese children[33] and ten percent of Polish children.[34] Most of the pupils from the latter groups are likely to be exempt from Irish. However, as is recommended in the circular quoted earlier, children who were exempt from learning Irish often attended Irish classes, which leads us to focus on the way Irish was taught in the schools studied.

The *Revised Primary Curriculum* (1999) recommends a living approach to the language, with an emphasis on oral Irish.[35] This was put into practice in the three schools visited. The pupils were taught to use Irish in real life situations. For instance, in the classes observed, the pupils had to ask other pupils for school items (School A senior, fourth class), be able to describe the weather (School B, junior infants), tell the doctor where their bodies hurt (School C, fourth class), or talk about activities they did at home during their leisure time, such as playing games on their computer (School B, third class). All these oral activities relied on a contemporary and everyday use of the language. However, they often involved repetition. For example, before doing role play in Irish the children rehearsed in groups of two or three. This made it possible for immigrant children to take part. They could practise with other pupils and say their lines when performing the role play they had rehearsed. This was done in a supportive atmosphere since the whole class applauded after each role play.

The teaching of Irish was also based on poems or songs that the children had to learn. These activities were very popular among young children and all eagerly participated in them. Even those who were not necessarily confident in Irish were able to learn by rote and take part. This was especially true in the lower grades, where English and Irish were taught in a similar way. For example, in junior infants (school B), the children learnt poems and rhymes about body parts. This was done both in English and Irish. Immigrant children in that class learnt English and Irish at the same time.

The integration of the curriculum means that Irish could also be used in other subjects than the language classes proper. In the classes observed, Irish was only used in one other subject which was religion.

---

[32] CSO (2008), *Census 2006, Non-Irish Nationals Living in Ireland*, Dublin, Stationery Office, p. 38, 20 May 2009, http://www.cso.ie/census/Census2006Results.htm (accessed 20/05/2009).

[33] *Ibid.*, p. 50.

[34] *Ibid.*, p. 30.

[35] Department of Education and Science (1999), *Revised Primary Curriculum, op. cit.*, Vol. 23, p. 44.

Children sometimes recited prayers in Irish. In the case of immigrant children, this practice could exclude those who are not Catholic from practising Irish or would serve to imply that Irish is the language of Catholic pupils only. But this could apply to the whole range of subjects that are taught. Because the curriculum is integrated, the various subjects can be taught in accordance with the ethos or characteristic spirit of the school, in that case Catholicism. So, this type of potential exclusion of non-Catholic pupils from a particular lesson is not restricted to Irish.

Also, associated with Irish were Irish dancing and Gaelic games. Everyone took part in them. Schools A and C had a special coach coming in for Gaelic football and hurling respectively whereas school A had an Irish dancing teacher whose class was very popular among immigrant and Irish pupils alike.

One of the things that helped immigrant pupils catch up with Irish is the fact that the schools visited were recognised as disadvantaged. This meant that Irish was not seen as a priority compared to numeracy and literacy in English. This was mentioned by several of the teachers, including one fourth class teacher from school C who was speaking about immigrant pupils: "They're learning Irish at the same time as they're learning English, so they're actually good at it. And the others [the other pupils] are so behind that they can catch up. And because it's an inner-city school, Irish is not a priority, it's English and maths."[36] As a result, some of the immigrant children were able to participate. Some of them were actually doing well, as they had already mastered at least two languages, their home language, English, and sometimes a third one. But this seemed to be related to their general level of ability in school. For example, one Nigerian girl who spoke English and had learnt German while she was living in Germany, was also doing well in Irish. But she was doing equally well in all subjects.[37]

However, the use of Irish is not supposed to be limited to the Irish class only. It should be used as a living language during the school day.

Irish in School Life

One of the recommendations relating to the use of Irish as a living language was to have it used by the teachers "as an informal means of communication."[38] All children, including immigrants, were exposed to it then. For example, in all three schools, when teachers called the roll, pupils had to reply in Irish. When a pupil was out, the whole class said

---

[36] School C, fourth class teacher, interview with the author, April 2007.
[37] School A senior, fourth class, class observation, February 2005.
[38] Department of Education and Science (1999), *Revised Primary Curriculum, op. cit.*, Vol. 23, p. 44.

the expected phrase in a chorus ("níl sé/sí anseo"). Besides, basic school rules were also written in Irish in several of the classrooms and each group of pupils at a given table sometimes had an Irish name. In school C, in third class, all tables were given names of colours in Irish.[39] The problem was that Irish was often used for disciplinary purposes. For example, Irish was used to tell the children to be quiet ("ciúnas"), to listen ("éist"), or to sit properly and put their bags away under their tables. Nonetheless, in some cases, it was also used to encourage pupils and congratulate them when they had completed a particular task successfully. A mix of English and Irish was sometimes used by one of the teachers in that circumstance. When a child had done something right, she would ask the class to give her a "bualadh bos," or round of applause, and the whole class clapped.[40] In school A, the principal sometimes spoke Irish to the fifth class teacher in order to discuss a problem so that the children did not understand.[41] This could be seen as an incentive for them to learn Irish and try to understand, but it was also a way of showing that children only had a limited command of Irish. Thus, the use of Irish within the three schools was ambiguous insofar as it was very often used as a disciplinary language rather than as an everyday language, or one that was used positively. This may have an impact on how pupils, immigrants and Irish alike, see the language.

3. Participants' Attitudes to the Irish Language

Teachers' Perception of the Language

Irish did not come up very often in interviews with teachers because they were asked about their general point of view on the school and what they did to cater for immigrant children. But a few remarks are worth mentioning here. As has already been shown, Irish was not seen as a priority because the schools were disadvantaged.[42] The priority was to focus on English and maths. This was highlighted by the fact that there was no remedial teaching available in Irish, whereas it was offered to the pupils who needed it in English and maths.

However, there were differences in the emphasis put on Irish according to the grades pupils were in. For example, the focus on Irish became more important in sixth class because Irish is one of the subjects pupils are tested in when they apply for enrolment in a secondary school.

---

[39] School C, third class, class observation, April 2007.

[40] School B, junior infants, class observation, February 2007.

[41] School A senior, fifth class, class observation, February 2005.

[42] It would be worth seeing whether more advantaged schools display different attitudes towards Irish.

Besides, although in interviews teachers mentioned that Irish was not a priority in their school, in class they encouraged all the pupils to take part in the Irish lesson, including immigrant pupils who were exempt. It remains to be seen what message was actually given to the pupils and what they thought of Irish as a school subject.

Pupils' Point of View with Regard to Irish

Irish was sometimes mentioned in interviews with pupils when asked about what they liked or disliked in school and the first thing that came to mind was the different subjects they had to study. In school A senior, out of the 14 Irish and 12 immigrant pupils interviewed, Irish was never quoted as something they particularly liked. Only six class pupils however, mentioned Irish as something they did not like. Seven of them, both Irish and immigrant pupils, out of the 12 sixth class pupils interviewed did so. One Irish girl said Irish was "difficult and boring," another in the same group interview said she agreed and added "you learn the same thing again and again." Two of their immigrant classmates, one from the Congo, the other from Georgia, said they did not like Irish either, although they were exempt from it. The same happened in the second group interview with pupils from the other sixth class. Two Irish boys said that they did not like Irish because they found it "hard" and one immigrant pupil said he agreed. However, Irish dancing was quoted as something they really liked by two boys from third class, one Irish, one Nigerian, and Gaelic sports were mentioned positively by one fifth class Irish boy.

In school B, out of the 19 pupils interviewed, eight of whom came from an immigrant background, Irish was mentioned as something they particularly liked by two immigrant pupils, one from Bangladesh, the other from Cameroon. On the contrary, it was quoted as something they disliked by three girls, the first Irish, the other two immigrants from Poland who were exempt from it. The Irish girl said: "[Irish] is kind of hard, nobody in class likes Irish."[43] However, most pupils only mentioned Irish when asked what languages they could speak but did not cite it as something they particularly liked or disliked in school.

In school C, 20 pupils were interviewed, ten of them Irish, the other ten immigrants. Among them, only one boy, in sixth class, said he liked learning how to speak Irish. Two fourth class boys said they were not very good at it. One boy, whose parents were from Bulgaria, explained why he did not like Irish: "We're made into speaking it. Most schools do that, make you learn a language. It's OK. It just makes you feel

---

[43]   School B, Irish girl, fourth class, interview with the author, February 2007.

you're three years old when you're, like, nine."[44] However, five boys, two of them immigrants, including the boy from Bulgaria, said they liked hurling and one of them added he liked piping as well.

Thus, in general, Irish did not particularly stand out as something the pupils really liked or really disliked. Although other forms of Irish culture, such as sports, dancing and music, were popular among several of the pupils interviewed. When Irish was actually quoted, it was more often as something negative, partly because pupils found it difficult. Strangely enough, some of the immigrant pupils who were exempt from it also said it was difficult. One possible explanation would be that they were present during Irish classes even if they were exempt from taking Irish tests. In that case, their level of understanding during these classes must have been limited and possibly created a sense of frustration. Another explanation could be that immigrant children who are exempt from Irish repeated what they heard some of their Irish peers say. More-over, Irish was mentioned more often in negative terms among older children. These were also the children who enjoyed school less. Accord-ing to a fifth class teacher in school A senior, pupils in fifth and sixth, the highest grades in Irish primary schools, start to be bored at school.[45] Paradoxically, the Bulgarian pupil who said he did not like Irish did not find it too difficult but frustrating because of the gap between his com-petence in English and what he was required to say in Irish. This gap, which is less apparent in junior and senior infants, widens in the middle years of primary school, which can explain this feeling of frustration. This might also explain why some pupils said Irish was both hard and boring.

Apart from these interviews, the status of Irish was discussed during a debate on education in school A senior. Fifth class pupils were work-ing on a text from their religious education textbook. They were reading the story of a Pakistani girl who did not go to school. The story was used by the teacher to trigger a debate about education and its usefulness and Irish was mentioned by one pupil as something useful, "if you go somewhere where you have to speak Irish."[46] The teacher used this example to ask the class "[if they thought they] should be bothered to learn Irish, because it [was] not of practical use." Just then, the principal came in to speak to him in Irish. When he left, the pupils explained that although they did not all like Irish, it was important to learn it: "I don't like Irish but I think you should learn it because it's our language" (Irish boy 1); "It's our native tongue." (Irish boy 2); "It's our own language"

---

[44] School C, Bulgarian boy, third class, interview with the author, February 2007.

[45] School A senior, fifth class teacher, interview with the author, February 2005.

[46] School A senior, fifth class, class observation, February 2005.

(Irish boy 3); "I want to be a teacher and I didn't have a clue what [the principal] was saying" (Irish girl 1, exempt from Irish); "You should be proud of your language" (Irish girl 2).[47] Only one girl did not agree and said, "We shouldn't learn it, it's extinct."[48] Thus, apart from this girl, there seemed to be a consensus to say that even though not all pupils liked Irish, they had to study it because it was their own language. The reference to Irish as "our native language" from a child who learnt it at school shows the sense of collective ownership attached to the language, although its representation as "native" does not literally reflect reality in this case. This sense of collective ownership of Irish based on history means that children who do not study it are in some way potentially prevented from partaking in this collective identity, which can be problematic for children with special needs but probably more so for immigrant children. The exemption from Irish which aims at helping them spend more time working on subjects that are seen as more fundamental can become a symbol of exclusion.

Irish was also mentioned when pupils were asked what languages they spoke. The overwhelming majority said that they only used Irish within school. Four pupils from school B said that they used Irish outside school, among whom three used it in a family context: one spoke Irish with her grandmother, the other two, one Irish, the other from Cameroon, tried to teach it to a family member who could not speak it. The fourth girl was from Bangladesh and had tried to use it outside school, with mixed results:

> Sometimes I start, I speak Irish when I go outside, sometimes I do. They say "What did you say?," I say, they say, "you call me a bad word?," "no, I speak Irish with you" and they go like, "Irish, I don't know Irish," and I say, "you're Irish people and you don't know," and they go like, "I was supposed to but I didn't go to school and my exams [*sic*]!"[49]

This shows that there is still a paradox in the way Irish is presented. Immigrant children, like their Irish peers, are taught that Irish is the national language but English remains the language used everywhere around them.

Conclusion

On the whole, immigrant pupils who started school in the lower grades learnt English and Irish together. So, in those classes, Irish was not something that set them apart from the rest of the class. On the contrary, children who started school in Ireland in the middle or higher

---

[47] *Idem.*

[48] *Idem.*

[49] School B, Bangladeshi girl, fourth class, interview with the author, February 2007.

classes were often exempt from Irish, although some were encouraged to take part in the Irish lesson nonetheless. Whatever the case, Irish did not seem to have a negative impact on immigrant pupils' inclusion in their respective classes. However, there were two issues that stood out. Firstly, there still seemed to be a discrepancy between the official status of Irish as the national language and its actual status both within schools and outside them. The impact this has on how immigrant pupils perceive the language as they go through the education system would be worth analysing more in depth than is possible based on the limited data collected on the topic within these case studies. It would seem, however, that the older immigrant pupils interviewed were starting to hold negative attitudes to Irish, similar to those of their Irish peers. The definition of Irish as the national language may impact negatively on the attitudes of pupils who have difficulties learning it. Besides, there also seemed to be some confusion as to the reasons for studying the language. On the one hand, it was defined as part of a national heritage; on the other, there was an emphasis on oral language, while at the same time recognising that the opportunities for using it in real life situations were rare. It might, therefore, be useful to define the aims and objectives of learning Irish more clearly and adapt the approach used to teach the language accordingly. Secondly, bilingualism was presented as a desirable goal to be achieved when it applied to speaking English and Irish, at least in theory, but this did not extend to immigrant children's native languages. Many of the teachers interviewed mentioned the fact that immigrant children's native languages were an obstacle to their learning of English, although this is not supported by research on multilingualism.[50] It would therefore seem necessary to ensure that multilingualism is effectively promoted in Irish schools and that languages are not solely perceived in terms of their immediate practical relevance, so that those not seen as directly useful are not rejected as having no value.

Résumé

L'immigration récente, qui est devenue un phénomène relativement important dans les années 1990, a modifié le profil de nombre d'écoles primaires irlandaises. Dès lors que ces écoles ont pour mission de promouvoir la pratique de l'irlandais comme langue nationale, il paraît intéressant de voir ce que cela signifie pour les enfants étrangers en leur sein. Afin d'évaluer le rôle de la langue irlandaise dans l'inclusion ou l'exclusion des enfants étrangers dans les écoles primaires, nous présenterons des données récoltées dans le cadre de trois études de cas d'écoles primaires catholiques.

---

[50] Jim Cummins (2001), "Bilingual Children's Mother Tongue: Why is it Important for Education?," *Sprogforum*, Vol. 19, pp. 15-20.

"It's Only a Language"

The Attitudes and Motivation of Irish-medium Education Students to the Irish Language

Pádraig Ó DUIBHIR

Coláiste Phádraig, Droim Conrach

Introduction

Irish is the first official language of the Republic of Ireland with English being the second. Despite its official status it could be classified as a minority or lesser used language.[1] All students in Ireland are re-quired to study Irish from the age of four/five when they commence primary school until they leave second level education at age 16/17/18. One of the results of this policy is that 1.66 million people, representing 41.9% of the population, responded in the most recent census that they are able to speak Irish[2] (Central Statistics Office, 2007). Most of these (68.5%) never speak Irish or speak it less than once a week. The vast majority of the remainder are those that speak it within the education system. When the census responses are further analysed it emerges that there are only 72,148 daily speakers of Irish outside the education system.[3] Thus the number of daily speakers of Irish is relatively small and thinly dispersed. Education through the medium of Irish has been a feature of the Irish education system since the foundation of the Irish Free State in 1922. The new independent Irish government identified the schools as central to its policy of reversing the language shift from

---

[1] B. Ó Catháin (2001), "Dearcadh an teangeolaí ar chomharthaí sóirt Ghaeilge an lae inniu," in R. Ó hUiginn (ed.), *Léachtaí Cholm Cille XXXI*, Maigh Nuad, An Sagart, pp. 128-149.

[2] Central Statistics Office, (2007), *Census 2006*: Volume 9 – Irish language, Dublin, Stationery Office.

[3] A. Punch (2008), "Census data on the Irish language," in C. Nic Pháidín & S. Ó Cearnaigh (eds.), *A New View of the Irish Language*, Dublin, Cois Life, pp. 43-54.

English back to Irish.[4] Following an initial period where this state-led initiative flourished[5] there were only 10 Irish-medium schools remaining in 1972. A new parent-led movement[6] emerged during the 1970s and there has been sustained growth since then. There are now 139 Irish-medium primary schools in the Republic of Ireland and that number continues to grow each year. Approximately 7.5% of students receive their primary education through the medium of Irish in all-Irish schools (5%) or Gaeltacht (Irish-speaking areas) schools (2.5%).[7] Although students in Irish-medium schools attain satisfactory competency in Irish, they have been criticised for speaking Irish using non target-like forms.[8] This study makes a systematic attempt to explore the attitudes and motivation of students to speaking Irish with greater grammatical accu-

---

[4]   See: M. R. Coady & M. Ó Laoire (2002), "Mismatches in language policy and practice in education: The case of Gaelscoileanna in the Republic of Ireland," Language Policy, 1, pp. 143-158; A. Kelly (2002), *Compulsory Irish: Language and Education in Ireland, 1870s-1970s*. Dublin, Portland, OR, Irish Academic Press; P. Ó Riagáin (2007), "Relationships between attitudes to Irish, social class, religion and national identity in the Republic of Ireland and Northern Ireland," *The International Journal of Bilingual Education and Bilingualism*, 10(4), pp. 369-393.

[5]   J. Coolahan (1981), *Irish Education: Its History and Structure*. Dublin, Institute of Public Administration.

[6]   There was a change in state policy towards the Irish language in the education system in the late 1960s and early 1970s. Some parents were unhappy with the standard of Irish in English-medium schools (see H. Ó Murchú (2008), *More Facts about Irish*. Dublin, Coiste na hÉireann den Bhiúró Eorpach do Theangacha Neamhfhorleathana). They wanted to ensure that their children would achieve a reasonable competence in Irish and this led to the establishment of parent-led Naíonraí, i.e. Irish-medium pre-schools (see M. Mhic Mhathúna (1993), "Staidéar ar roinnt fachtóirí atá ag cabhrú le sealbhú na Gaeilge i naíonraí," unpublished MEd thesis, Trinity College Dublin, and Gaelscoileanna, i.e. all-Irish schools (see H. Ó Murchú (2001), "Irish – The Irish Language in education in the Republic of Ireland," Leeuwarden, Netherlands: Mercator Education: Retrieved from http://www1.fa.knaw.nl/mercator/regionale_dossiers/ PDFs/irish_in_ireland.pdf). In many cases it was the success of the Naíonra in a community that led to parental demand for the establishment of an all-Irish primary school. This new generation of all-Irish schools represented a new direction in Irish represented a new direction in Irish language education (M. Ní Mhurchú (1995). "Research on Canadian Immersion Education and the Relevance of its Findings for Gaelscoileanna in Ireland." *Oideas*, 43, pp. 48-68). The schools resulted from the wishes and desires of parents rather than from state policies (P. Ó Riagáin (1997), *Language Policy and Social Reproduction: Ireland, 1893-1993*, Oxford, Clarendon).

[7]   C. Máirtín, (2006), *Soláthar Múinteoirí do na Bunscoileanna Lán-Ghaeilge: Bunachar Sonraí agus Tuairimíocht Phríomhoidí i Leith Gnéithe den Staid Reatha sa Ghaelscolaíocht*. Baile Átha Cliath, An Chomhairle um Oideachas Gaeltachta agus Gaelscolaíochta.

[8]   C. Nic Pháidín (2003), "'Cén fáth nach?' – Ó chanúint go criól." In R. Ní Mhianáin (ed.), *Idir Lúibíní: Aistí ar an Léitheoireacht agus ar an Litearthacht*. Dublin, Cois Life, pp. 113-130.

racy. The majority of Irish-medium primary schools employ a total early immersion policy for the first year.[9] This is followed by the introduction of English language arts representing almost 15% of the instructional time. The remaining 85% of instruction is through the medium of Irish and this percentage remains the same throughout the students' schooling to the end of second level school. Irish-medium schools differ from immersion schools in other jurisdictions in that the level of instruction in the target language does not decrease below 85%. They differ also in that the vast majority are whole-school immersion centres rather than an immersion track within a majority language school. There are a small number of tracks at second-level. Irish is the language of communication in the school and students are expected to converse in Irish at all times within the school environment including the school playground at break-time. This provides the students with opportunities for output and social interaction through the medium of Irish outside the classroom.

Literature Review

Research studies conducted over many years have consistently shown that immersion students achieve high levels of fluency in the target language and their receptive skills of listening and reading are close to those of native speakers.[10] Their productive skills of speaking and writing however, contain many non target-like forms that appear to

---

[9] M. Ní Bhaoill, & P. Ó Duibhir (2004), *Tús na Léitheoireachta i Scoileanna Gaeltachta agus Lán-Ghaeilge*. Dublin, An Chomhairle um Oideachas Gaeltachta agus Gaelscolaíochta.

[10] See: P Allen, M. Swain, B. Harley & J. Cummins (1990), "Aspects of classroom treatment: Toward a more comprehensive view of second language education," in B. Harley, P. Allen, J. Cummins & M. Swain (eds.), *The Development of Second Language Proficiency*. New York, Cambridge University Press, pp. 57-81; C. Baker & S. P. Jones (1998), *Encyclopaedia of Bilingualism and Bilingual Education*, Clevedon, Multilingual Matters; E. Day & S. M. Shapson (1987). "Assessment of oral communicative skills in early French immersion programmes." *Journal of Multilingual and Multicultural Development*, 8(3), pp. 237-260; B. Harley (1987). *The Development of Second Language Proficiency. Final Report*. Volume II: *Classroom Treatment*, Toronto, Modern Language Centre, Ontario Institute for Studies in Education; B. Harley (1993), "Instructional Strategies and SLA in Early French Immersion." *Studies in Second Language Acquisition*, 15, pp. 245-259; W. Lazaruk (2007), "Linguistic, academic, and cognitive benefits of French immersion." *The Canadian Modern Language Review*, 63(5), pp. 605-628; R. Lyster (1987), "Speaking Immersion," *The Canadian Modern Language Review*, 43(4), pp. 701-717; T. Nadasdi, R. Mougeon & K. Rehner J. Harris (2005), "Learning to speak everyday (Canadian) French." *The Canadian Modern Language Review* 61(4), pp. 543-563; M. Swain (2000), "French immersion research in Canada: Recent contributions to SLA and applied linguistics." *Annual Review of Applied Linguistics*, 20(1), pp. 199-212.

persist over time.[11] The pedagogical approach in early immersion programmes has been identified as an experiential one where the primary focus is on meaning.[12] The students are required to interpret the meaning of the teacher's verbal utterances and the nonverbal clues of the classroom context and it is through this negotiation of meaning that they acquire the second language.[13] While this approach leads to the development of god fluency in the target language and near native-like ability in the receptive skills of reading and writing, it is less successful in developing grammatical accuracy.[14] What appears to be lacking in experiential learning are the analytical strategies for organising learning in a more conscious or explicit way.[15]

---

[11] C. Baker (2001), *Foundations of Bilingual Education and Bilingualism* (3rd ed.), Clevedon, Multilingual Matters; F. Genesee (1985), *Second language learning through immersion: A review of U.S. programs. Review of Educational Research*, 55(4), pp. 541-561; H. Hammerly (1991), *Fluency and Accuracy: Toward Balance in Language Teaching and Learning*, Clevedon, Multilingual Matters; B. Harley (1993), *op. cit.*; M. Kowal & M. Swain (1997), "From semantic to syntactic processing: How can we promote it in the immersion classroom?" in *Immersion Education: International Perspectives*, Cambridge, Cambridge University Press, pp. 284-309; R. Lyster (1987), *op. cit.*; R. Mitchell & F. Myles (1998). *Second Language Learning Theories*. London, Arnold; P. Neil, G. Nig Uidhir, & F. Clarke (2000). *Native English Speakers Immersed in Another Language – A Review of Literature*, Bangor, Department of Education, Northern Ireland; J. Rebuffot (1993). *Le point sur l'immersion au Canada*, Québec, Édiflex; A. Salomone (1992). "Student-teacher interaction in selected French immersion classrooms," in E. B. Bernhardt (ed.), *Life in Language Immersion Classrooms*, Clevedon, Multilingual Matters, pp. 97-109; M. Swain (2005). "The output hypothesis: Theory and research," in E. Hinkel (ed.), *Handbook of Research in Second Language Teaching and Learning*, Mahwah, N.J., Erlbaum, pp. 471-483; M., Swain & S. Lapkin (1982). *Evaluating Bilingual Education: A Canadian Case Study*, Clevedon, Multilingual Matters; M., Swain & S. Lapkin (2008). "Lexical learning through a multitask activity: The role of repetition," in T. W. Fortune & D. J. Tedick (eds.), *Pathways to Multilingualism: Evolving Perspectives on Immersion Education.* Clevedon, Multilingual Matters, pp. 119-132.

[12] B. Harley (1993), *op. cit.*; H. H. Stern (1990). "Analysis and experience as variables in second language pedagogy." In B. Harley, P. Allen, J. Cummins & M. Swain (eds.), *The Development of Second Language Proficiency*, pp. 93-109.

[13] F. Genesee (1985), *op. cit.*

[14] Allen *et al.* (1990), *op. cit.*; B. Harley, J. Cummins, M. Swain, & P. Allen, (1990). "The nature of language proficiency," in B. Harley, P. Allen, J. Cummins & M bridge University Press, pp. 7-25; R., Lyster & H. Mori (2008), "Instructional counterbalance in immersion pedagogy," in T. W. Fortune & D. J. Tedick (eds.), *Pathways to Multilingualism: Evolving Perspectives on Immersion Education.* Clevedon, Multilingual Matters, pp. 133-151; Mac Corraidh, S. (2008), *Ar Thóir an Dea-Chleachtais: The Quest for Best Practice in Irish-medium Primary Schools in Belfast*, Belfast, Cló Ollscoil na Banríona; H. H. Stern (1990), *op. cit.*

[15] N. C. Ellis (1994). "Introduction: Implicit and explicit language teaching," in N. C. Ellis (ed.), *Implicit and Explicit Learning of Languages*, San Diego, CA, Academic Press, pp. 1-31.

Research studies of Irish immersion programmes have been limited in number and scope. Nonetheless, they show that Irish immersion students achieve high levels of fluency and comprehension, levels that considerably exceed those achieved by students taking Irish as a school subject.[16] These advantages are achieved without cost to their literacy skills in English.[17] Similar to other immersion settings, concern has been expressed that the productive skills of speaking and writing acquired by Irish immersion students, do not reach native speaker levels, and their speech includes a range of resistant deviant forms.[18] One reason that students fail to attain grammatical accuracy in their productive skills is that they may lack the motivation to do so.

The Role of Motivation in Second Language Learning

Motivation has been shown to be one of the key variables in individual differences that significantly affect success in second language learning.[19] Much of the research work on motivation was first carried out by Robert Gardner and his colleagues in Canada.[20] A key element of Gardner's social-psychological model[21] was student attitude towards the L2 community. Dörnyei & Skehan[22] suggest that the former makes sense as few learners will master the language of a community with low status. Gardner[23] divided language learner goals into two broad categories, integrative orientation and instrumental orientation. Integrative orientation concerned a positive interpersonal disposition toward the target

[16] J. Harris (1984), *Spoken Irish in Primary Schools: An Analysis of Achievement.* Dublin, Institiúid Teangeolaíochta Éireann; J. Harris, P. Forde, P. Archer, S. Nic Fhearaile & M. O'Gorman (2006), *Irish in Primary Schools: Long-Term National Trends in Achievement,* Dublin, Department of Education and Science.

[17] Department of Education (1991), *Report on the National Survey of English Reading in Irish Primary Schools,* Dublin, The Curriculum Unit; C. Parsons, & F. Liddy (2009), *Learning to Read in Irish and English: A Comparison of Children in Irish-medium, Gaeltacht and English-medium Schools in Ireland,* Dublin, An Chomhairle um Oideachais Gaeltachta agus Gaelscolaíochta.

[18] NCCA (2006), *Language and Literacy in Irish-Medium Primary Schools: Descriptions of Practice,* Dublin, National Council for Curriculum and Assessment.

[19] Z. Dörnyei (2005), *The Psychology of the Language Learner: Individual Differences in Second Language Acquisition,* Mahwah, N.J., Lawrence Erlbaum Associates; Z. Dörnyei (2006), "Individual differences in second language acquisition," *AILA Review, 19,* pp. 42-68; Z. Dörnyei & P. Skehan (2003), "Individual differences in second language learning," in C. Doughty & M. H. Long (eds.), *The Handbook of Second Language Acquisition* Oxford, Blackwell, pp. 589-630.

[20] Z. Dörnyei (2006), *op. cit.*
[21] R. C. Gardner (1985a), *The Attitude/Motivation Test Battery: Technical Report.* Ontario, University of Western Ontario.
[22] Z. Dörnyei & P. Skehan (2003), *op. cit.*
[23] R.C. Gardner (1985a), *op. cit.*

language group and a desire to interact and even become similar to respected members of that group. Instrumental orientation was associated with personal gains that might accrue to an individual such as a better job or higher salary. It was suggested that these categories determine an individual's motivation to learn a second language[24] (Masgoret & Gardner, 2003). It is the former area of integrative motivation that has seen the greatest level of research and is, according to Dörnyei & Skehan, made up of three major components:

(i) integrativeness, subsuming integrative orientation, interest in foreign languages, and attitudes toward the L2 community:

(ii) attitudes towards the learning situation, comprising attitudes toward the teacher and the course;

(iii) motivation, which according to Gardner is made up of motivational intensity, desire to learn the language, and attitudes towards learning the language.[25]

It was these components and their constituent parts that informed the development of Gardner's Attitude/Motivation Test Battery (AMTB).[26] Dörnyei[27] conceived a new approach to L2 motivation which he termed the 'L2 Motivational Self System'. Within this system he equates integrativeness and integrative motivation with an 'Ideal L2 Self'. As he explains: 'If one's ideal self is associated with the mastery of an L2, that is if the person that we would like to become is proficient in the L2, he/she can be described [...] as having an 'integrative' disposition'.[28] L2 motivation according to this model is seen as the desire on the part of the learner to bridge the gap between the actual self and the ideal self. Another facet of this model is the notion of an 'imagined community'.[29] The idealised self can be seen as a member of an imagined community. These developments were incorporated into an adapted and revised version of the AMTB in the present study through the creation of new sub-scales. Gardner's AMTB is a well developed and tested instrument for survey type approaches to student attitude and motivation where the concern is in-school and across-school factors in relation to the target language.

---

[24] A.-M. Masgoret, & R. C. Gardner (2003), "Attitudes, motivation, and second language learning: A meta-analysis of studies conducted by Gardner and associates," *Language Learning, 53*(1), pp. 123-163.

[25] Z. Dörnyei & P. Skehan (2003), *op. cit.*, p. 613.

[26] R.C. Gardner (1985a), *op. cit.*

[27] Z. Dörnyei (2005), *op. cit.*

[28] Z. Dörnyei (2006), *op. cit.*, p. 53.

[29] Z. Dörnyei (2005), *op. cit.*, p. 102.

Design

Eight all-Irish schools were chosen as a purposive sample from a total of 130 such schools in existence in September 2006. The rationale for this selection was to choose schools that would represent the full range of different types of all-Irish school found in the Republic of Ireland against a set of criteria that included school size, geographical location, the number of years in existence, socio-economic status of the students' parents, proximity to a Gaeltacht 'Irish-speaking' heartland community, access to an Irish-medium second level school. 172 students (n=172) from these schools completed an AMTB, the purpose of which was to provide information about the nature and strength of students' attitudes and motivation in relation to Irish. There was a 100% response rate as the questionnaires were administered during class time by the researcher.

There are two parts to the AMTB. Part 1 consists of 57 item-stems or statements. Students were invited to indicate their responses to these items using a five-point Likert-type scale, from 'Strongly disagree' to 'Strongly agree'. Part 2 consisted of four write-in items for the students to complete at the end of the questionnaire. This part collected data on the students' perceptions of the language-learning process itself and the factors that motivate them to speak Irish.

The 57 item-stems in Part 1 are divided into the following scales and sub-scales:

    1. Integrativeness scales

        a. Attitude to Irish speakers (7 items)

        b. Integrative orientation to Irish (4 items)

    2. Motivation scales

        a. Desire to learn Irish (5 items)

        b. Motivational intensity to learn Irish (4 items)

        c. Attitude to learning Irish (8 items)

    3. Other scales

        a. Instrumental orientation to Irish (3 items)

        b. Parental encouragement (7 items)

        c. Irish-ability self-concept (8 items)

        d. All-Irish school scale (11 items)

A quantitative analysis was performed on the students' responses to these items using SPSS (Statistical Package for the Social Sciences). It is beyond the scope of this paper to report on all the student responses to the above scales. The report of the results that follows will concentrate on responses to individual items and scales.

Results

Figure 1 shows the mean scores for the present study compared to the mean scores for the Harris & Murtagh study.[30] (It will be noted that there are only seven scales shown for the Harris & Murtagh (1999) study as scales 8 and 9 were developed for the purposes of the present study.) The maximum positive score is five and the minimum negative score is one, thus a score greater than four can be considered to be strongly positive. When the scores are compared it can be seen that the total scores for the present study are more positive. This is as might be expected as the Irish-medium school students in the present study are being compared with students that were learning Irish as a subject only.

Figure 1 Item mean scale scores for the present study (Irish-medium students) compared to Harris & Murtagh (1999) (Irish as a subject students)

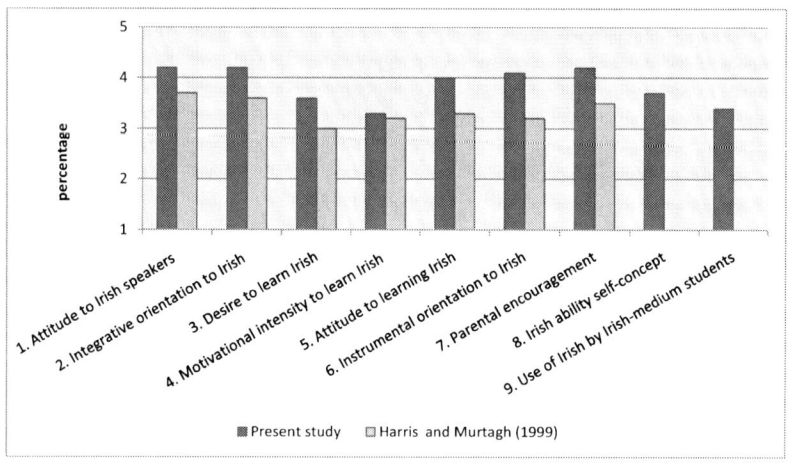

Students' Attitudes to Irish Speakers

The mean score for students' attitudes to Irish speakers sub-scale was very positive at 4.2 as shown in Figure 1 above. Table 1 presents some of the individual items from that scale i.e. items 6, 12 and 25.

---

[30] J. Harris & L. Murtagh (1999), *Teaching and Learning Irish in Primary School: A Review of Research and Development*. Dublin, Institiúid Teangeolaíochta Éireann.

75.4% of students strongly agreed with the statement in item 6 that: The Irish language is an important part of Ireland and the Irish people. A similar percentage 73.7%, strongly agreed with the statement in item 12 that: If Ireland lost the Irish language and the Irish way of life, it would really be a great loss. A high percentage of students also agreed with item 25 that: People in our country who only speak English should try harder to learn the Irish language, 55% of them strongly agree and 28.7% of them slightly agree. It can be seen from these responses that the students in the study have a very positive attitude to Irish speakers.

Table 1 Responses to items 6, 12 and 25 regarding students' attitudes to Irish speakers

	6. The Irish language is an important part of Ireland and the Irish people. (n=171)		12. If Ireland lost the Irish language and the Irish way of life, it would really be a great loss. (n=171)		25. People in our country who only speak English should try harder to learn the Irish language. (n=171)	
	%	CI	%	CI	%	CI
Strongly disagree	1.8	2.0	2.3	2.3	3.5	2.8
Slightly disagree	2.3	2.3	2.3	2.3	2.3	2.3
Neutral	5.3	3.4	8.8	4.4	10.5	4.8
Slightly agree	15.2	5.8	12.9	5.4	28.7	8.0
Strongly agree	75.4	12.9	73.7	12.8	55.0	11.1

CI = Confidence interval.

Students' Perceptions of Their Parents' Attitudes to Irish

Table 2 summarises responses relating to students' perceptions of their parents' attitudes to Irish. 73.2% of students agreed that: My parents try to help me with my Irish. 68.6% of students strongly agreed with item 9 that: My parents think that I should try hard to study Irish at school. A further 16.9% slightly agreed with this statement. 65.9% of students agreed with the statement in item 5 that: My parents feel that because we live in Ireland, I should study Irish. These responses are in keeping with a very positive mean score of 4.2 for the Parental encouragement scale as reported in Figure 1 above.

**Table 2 Responses to items 1, 9 and 5, students' perceptions
of their parents' attitudes to Irish**

	1. My parents try to help me with my Irish. (n=172)		9. My parents think that I should try hard to study Irish at school. (n=172)		5. My parents feel that because we live in Ireland, I should study Irish. (n=170)	
	%	CI	%	CI	%	CI
Strongly disagree	8.1	4.2	0.6	1.2	8.8	4.4
Slightly disagree	4.7	3.2	5.2	3.4	5.9	3.6
Neutral	14.0	5.6	8.7	4.4	19.4	6.6
Slightly agree	36.0	8.9	16.9	6.1	26.5	7.7
Strongly agree	37.2	9.1	68.6	12.3	39.4	9.4

Students' Use of Irish Outside of School and School Activities

Table 3 presents the responses of the students to items relating to their use of Irish outside of school and school activities. 30.4% of students agree with the statement in item 56 that: I often speak Irish outside of school and school activities. A similar number 32.3% disagree with the statement in item 40 that: I would be uncomfortable speaking Irish to my school friends outside of school and school activities. Item 10 reveals that 41.2% of students agreed that: If there was a chance to speak Irish outside school, I would like to try to speak it. Finally 66.9% of students responded positively to item 54 that: If there were Irish-speaking families living near me, I would like to speak Irish to them.

Table 3 Responses to items 56, 40, 10 and 57 regarding students'
use of Irish outside of school and school activities

	56. I often speak Irish outside of school and school activities. (n=171)		40. I would be uncomfortable speaking Irish to my school friends outside of school and school activities. (n=170)		10. If there was a chance to speak Irish outside school, I would like to try to speak it. (n=172)		54. If there were Irish-speaking families living near me, I would like to speak Irish to them. (n=172)	
	%	CI	%	CI	%	CI	%	CI
Strongly disagree	26.9	7.7	19.4	6.6	14	5.6	8.1	4.2
Slightly disagree	19.9	6.7	12.9	5.4	14.5	5.7	9.9	4.7
Neutral	22.8	7.1	27.6	7.9	30.2	8.2	15.1	5.8
Slightly agree	24.6	7.4	22.4	7.1	23.8	7.3	32.6	8.5
Strongly agree	5.8	3.6	17.6	6.3	17.4	6.2	34.3	8.7

The picture that emerges from the analysis presented in Tables 1, 2 and 3 above is that the students in the present study have a very positive attitude to Irish speakers. Their parents also have a positive attitude to Irish and encourage them to work hard at learning Irish. Just under one third (30.4%) of them often speak Irish outside of school and school activities and more of them report that they would like to speak Irish if they had the opportunity.

Students' Perceptions of Their Own and Native Speakers' Irish

Figure 2 shows that there is a substantial gap between those who agree strongly with item 29 that: I would like to be able to speak Irish like a native speaker (43.3%) and those who agree strongly with item 50 that: I speak Irish like a native speaker (4.7%). This indicates that a substantial number of students realise that the variety of Irish they speak is not like that of a native speaker but that their 'ideal self'[31] is associated with the native speaker variety of Irish.

---

[31] Z. Dörnyei (2006), *op. cit.*, p. 53.

**Figure 2 Comparison of responses to Items 29 and 50.
I speak/would like to speak Irish like a native speaker**

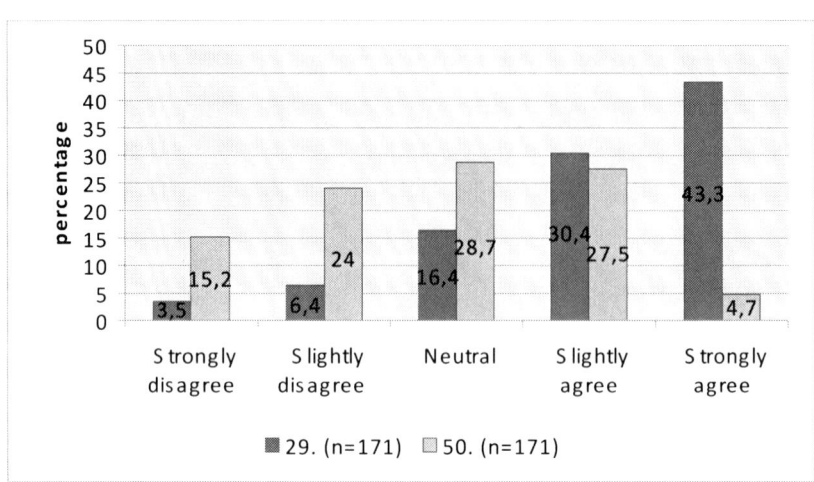

Students' Attitude to Learning Irish and to Speaking Irish Accurately

Table 4 summarises issues pertaining to students' accurate use of Irish. The responses to item 37: I want to learn as much Irish as possible, have been included to illustrate students' general attitude to learning Irish. 80.2% of students agree that they want to learn as much Irish as possible. In response to item 51 however: I know that I make mistakes when I am speaking Irish but it would be too much trouble to correct them, 48% of students agree with this statement with almost 39% disagreeing. It appears then that although four-fifths of students want to learn as much Irish as possible, only two-fifths disagree with the statement that it would be too much trouble to correct the mistakes that they make when they are speaking.

While 51.8% of students agree with item 32 that: It is important for me to speak Irish without mistakes when I am speaking to my friends at school, this figure increases to 81.7% in item 55: It is important for me to speak Irish without mistakes when I am speaking to the teacher. If the "strongly agree" responses for items 32 and 55 are compared it can be seen that the percentages are 23.3% and 53.5% respectively. A Wilcoxon T test revealed that this difference was significant. It appears from this that the students make a greater effort to speak Irish accurately to their teacher than to their peers.

Table 4 Responses to items 37, 51, 32 and 55 concerning students' attitude to learning Irish and to speaking accurately

	37. I want to learn as much Irish as possible. (n=172)		51. I know that I make mistakes when I am speaking Irish but it would be too much trouble to correct them. (n=171)		32. It is important for me to be able to speak Irish without mistakes when I am speaking with my friends at school. (n=169)		55. It is important for me to be able to speak Irish without mistakes when I am speaking with the teacher at school. (n=172)	
	%	CI	%	CI	%	CI	%	CI
Strongly disagree	1.2	1.6	21.7	6.9	12.8	5.4	3.5	2.8
Slightly disagree	4.7	3.2	17.0	6.1	15.7	5.9	4.1	3.0
Neutral	14.0	5.6	14.0	5.6	19.8	6.7	10.6	4.8
Slightly agree	33.7	8.6	31.0	8.3	28.5	8.0	28.2	7.9
Strongly agree	46.5	10.1	17.0	6.1	23.3	7.2	53.5	10.9

Write in Items

We now turn our attention to the analysis of the views expressed by the students in their own words on their experiences of learning Irish and the factors that motivate them to speak Irish. These were their responses to four write-in items in the final section of the student questionnaire. The report below on each item will confine itself to the top six categories of response. All 172 students that completed the questionnaire were asked to respond to the following four items:

The things I like about the way I learn Irish in school …

The things I dislike about the way I learn Irish in school …

I would enjoy the way I learn Irish in school more if …

These are the things that motivate me or make me want to speak Irish...

What the Students Like about the Way They Learn Irish

Table 5 shows that the two most frequent thematic responses, by 10.8% of the students in the case of each theme, were: 'Factors associated with the teacher' and 'Learning their native language.' In the case of the teacher, the factors the students referred to were: the manner in which the teacher helped the students to learn Irish, how he/she explained things, corrected them when they made errors and did so in a kind and humorous way. All of these things made an impact on one-tenth of the students. Similarly just over one in ten students cited the fact that they were learning their native language as one of the things that they like about learning Irish.

Row 3 shows that 9.8% of students responded that they like the fact that they had a good standard of Irish, they like improving it and learning new words and grammar. Almost the same percentage, 9.7%, mentioned learning other subjects through Irish as a thing that they liked. In many cases it was the subject that the students felt that they were good at. 9.2% of students responded that they enjoy speaking Irish and that learning Irish gives them the opportunity to do so. Over 6% of students enjoy activities such as songs, poetry, music and debates.

**Table 5 'Likes': Percentage distribution
of students' responses by thematic category**

	'The things I like about the way we learn Irish at school'	% of responses (n=172)
1	Factors associated with the teacher	10.8%
2	Learning their native language	10.8%
3	Having a good standard of Irish and improving it, learning new words and grammar	9.8%
4	Learning other subjects through Irish	9.7%
5	Speaking Irish	9.2%
6	Activities (songs, poetry, music and debates)	6.7%

What the Students Dislike about the Way They Learn Irish

Although the categories may not be exactly the same it will be seen that some themes were common to both 'likes' and 'dislikes'. Table 6 shows that the aspect that students disliked most about learning Irish was Irish grammar with a response rate of 19%. This was closely followed by Irish sometimes being 'difficult to learn' and 'boring' (18.6%). This contrasts with the 6.2% of students who liked learning Irish (Table 5) because it was fun, enjoyable and easy to learn, and there was the possibility of getting a prize. In Row 3, 14.8% of students disliked learning other subjects through Irish. These first three categories represent the majority of all the 'dislikes' at 52.4%. It is interesting to note that 9.7% of students (Table 5) responded positively to learning other subjects through Irish compared to the negative response of 14.8% for this item. Similarly while 9.8% (Table 5) of students like having a good standard of Irish and improving that standard, learning new words and grammar, it can be seen in Table 6 that 19% of students dislike learning Irish grammar.

The next set of responses in Row 4 is interesting because almost one tenth of students (9.5%) indicated that there was nothing about the way they learned Irish at school that they disliked. 8.6% of students disliked having to speak Irish at all times in school. It will be recalled from Table 5 that a slightly higher percentage of students (9.2%) indicated that they enjoy speaking Irish. The lack of suitable reading material in Irish was cited by 4.8% of students as one of the things that they disliked about learning Irish.

**Table 6 'Dislikes': Percentage distribution
of students' responses by thematic category**

	'The things I dislike about the way we learn Irish at school'	% of responses (n=172)
1	Irish grammar	19.0%
2	Learning Irish is difficult and boring sometimes	18.6%
3	Learning other subjects through Irish	14.8%
4	There is nothing about learning Irish that I do not like	9.5%
5	Having to speak Irish at all times in school	8.6%
6	Lack of books and their suitability	4.8%

The Aspects that Students Would Like to Change about the Way They Learn Irish

Aspects of learning Irish that students would like to change often mirror data in the 'likes' category. It can be seen from the first row in Table 7 that the students would like to learn Irish more through games, debates, sport and music. This was by far the most common response from students with almost one in three students (28.6%) suggesting this type of activity. 7.1% of students would like more books and resources in Irish as some of the books are unsuitable for their age or are uninteresting. A similar percentage, 7.1%, would prefer to have more emphasis on Irish in general and on speaking Irish in particular. Table 5 showed that 9.2% stated that speaking Irish was one of the things that they liked about learning Irish while 8.6% in Table 6 disliked that they had to speak Irish all the time in school.

5.2% of students responded that they would not like to change any-thing. This compares with 9.5% in Table 6 that responded that there was nothing about learning Irish that they did not like. The responses in Rows 5-6 are related in that it appears from the students' responses that they would like to make learning Irish easier. In Row 5 it can be seen that 4.8% of students would like to study other subjects through English. Mathematics was mentioned by a number of students in this context who stated that they did not understand it in Irish sometimes. This theme also emerged in Tables 5 and 6 where 9.7% liked the fact that they study other subjects through Irish in the former and 14.8% disliked it in the latter. Opinion appears to be divided on this issue and it may be the case that some students perceive that they struggle in other subjects due to the fact that they study them through the medium of Irish. In a similar way in Row 6, 4.3% of students wished that learning Irish was easier.

Table 7 'Changes': Percentage distribution of students' responses by thematic category

	'I would enjoy the way we learn Irish more if ...'	% of responses (n=172)
1	Activities: games, debates, sport and music	28.6%
2	Books and resources	7.1%
3	More emphasis on Irish and on speaking Irish	7.1%
4	Do not change anything	5.2%
5	Study other subjects through English	4.8%
6	Make it easier	4.3%

Discussion and Conclusion

The students in the present study were shown to have a very positive attitude and motivation as measured on the nine scales in the AMTB test battery. These positive attitudes also emerged from the write-in items where students viewed other Irish speakers as a motivating factor in speaking Irish. Such attitudes are important not only in supporting the attempts to promote bilingualism in Ireland,[32] but also in maintaining the motivation required to master a second language over a long period.[33] This indicates that students have a very positive attitude to the Irish language itself and would be favourably disposed to integrating with a network of Irish speakers or a native-speaker community.

---

[32] J. Harris & L. Murtagh (1999), *op. cit.*

[33] R. C. Gardner (1985b), *Social Psychology and Second Language Learning: The Role of Attitudes and Motivation*, London, Edward Arnold.

While 73.7% of students agree that they would like to be able to speak Irish like a native speaker (item 29), only 32.2% of students disagreed with item 40 that they would be uncomfortable speaking Irish to their school friends outside of school or school activities (item 40). The complex sociolinguistic reasons why a substantial number of all-Irish school students feel 'uncomfortable' speaking Irish to their school friends outside of school has yet to be explored in any depth. It may be that Irish is perceived as the language of the curriculum but not the language of peer culture. These responses by the students illustrate how difficult it is to extend the use of a minority language learned at school, from the school to the community.[34] It suggests that increasing the number of active bilinguals who use Irish on a daily basis is a complicated undertaking and while producing students competent in the language is necessary in order to extend the use of Irish it is not sufficient.

One theme that emerges from the data and which was also found in the Harris and Murtagh study[35] is that items that require passive support for Irish receive a more positive response from students while those requiring more active support receive a less positive response from students. The lesser effort that a significant number of students make to speak Irish without mistakes when speaking with their peers illustrates this. Further examples of this passive/active distinction were found in items 37 and 51. In item 37, 80.2% of students want to learn as much Irish as possible. Agreement with this statement does not require active support. In item 51 on the other hand, 48% of students admit to making mistakes when they speak Irish but that it would be too much trouble to correct them, illustrating a decrease in agreement when active support is required. This finding has implications for any potential changes in immersion programmes that might seek to remediate students' language errors. Similarly in the write-in items in relation to improving their Irish, 19% of students dislike Irish grammar and a further 18.6% find learning Irish difficult and boring sometimes. This may indicate that students are less willing to expend the effort required to learn to speak Irish with accuracy. The pattern of active/passive support has also been a feature of attitudinal surveys to Irish in Ireland in recent decades where strong support for Irish language policies does not translate into actual language use.[36] The less positive support for items requiring greater effort also support the notion that students make less effort to improve their

---

[34]   C. Baker (2002), "Bilingual education." In R. B. Kaplan (ed.), *The Oxford Handbook of Applied Linguistics*, Oxford, Oxford University Press, pp. 229-242.

[35]   J. Harris & L. Murtagh (1999), *op. cit.*

[36]   P. Ó Riagáin (2008), "Irish-language policy 1922-2007: Balancing Maintenance and Revival." In C. Nic Pháidín & S. Ó Cearnaigh (eds.), *A New View of the Irish Language*, Dublin, Cois Life, pp. 55-65.

target language competence when communicative sufficiency has been reached due to an absence of sociopsychological motivation and pressure from their peers to change and adjust their grammar.[37]

The students responded in the questionnaire that they monitor their output more critically when they speak to the teacher than when they speak to their friends. This type of 'pushed output' has been shown to be effective in shifting learners from semantic to syntactic processing.[38] Teachers could seek to maximise the opportunities for the production of 'pushed output' by setting tasks for students which involve the preparation of oral presentations and materials for real audiences. These tasks require students to reflect on what they want to say and teachers can assist them in choosing the most appropriate language forms. Tasks such as these could also enable the teacher to integrate language and content objectives more effectively.

Résumé

Cet article présente les résultats d'une étude quantitative sur les attitudes et la motivation de 172 élèves irlandais de CM2 en immersion gaélophone à l'égard de l'irlandais. L'étude utilise une version modifiée et adaptée du « Attitude/Motivation Test Battery ». Les données démontrent que l'attitude et la motivation des élèves sont très positives envers l'apprentissage de la langue irlandaise. Ces attitudes sont importantes si l'on veut maintenir la motivation requise pour acquérir une seconde langue sur une longue durée. Les éléments qui s'appuient de manière passive sur la langue irlandaise ont reçu une réponse plus positive de la part des élèves que ceux qui nécessitent un engagement plus actif. Les conséquences de ces résultats pour la pédagogie sont également étudiées.

---

[37] E. Day, & S. Shapson (1996), *Studies in Immersion Education*. Clevedon, Multilingual Matters.

[38] M. Kowal & M. Swain (1997), *op. cit.*; M. Swain (2005), *op. cit.*

PART III

LESSER-USED LANGUAGES AND THE STATE

L'irlandais peut-il seulement être une langue ?

Ronan BARRÉ

Université Rennes 2

La question un tant soit peu sibylline posée dans le titre de cet article renvoie en fait directement à la terminologie multiple ayant trait à l'irlandais utilisée à la fois par les partisans de cette langue et les universitaires. On peut citer pour preuve les titres anglais et français du colloque qui multiplient les expressions censées spécifier la nature de cette langue celtique, à savoir langue « régionale », « minoritaire » et « indigène » ou « autochtone ».[1] Il apparaît donc que la langue irlandaise ait besoin d'être constamment qualifiée, en tout cas qu'elle fasse partie d'une certaine catégorie de langues (parmi lesquelles se trouvent d'ailleurs les autres langues celtiques comme le breton, le gallois ou le gaélique écossais) qui ne peuvent être glosées indépendamment de cette caractérisation. Je me propose donc d'examiner plus en avant le choix des différents qualificatifs dans la mesure où ils sont porteurs d'une certaine charge idéologique que je tenterais d'expliciter.

L'irlandais comme langue régionale

La première expression abordée est celle de « langue régionale ». Le terme « régional » renvoie chronologiquement à deux types de découpages spatiaux, parfois distincts, de nature soit purement géographique soit administrative. Ces deux éléments se rejoignent en grande partie en ce qui concerne le gaélique irlandais : le *Gaeltacht* se réfère, depuis 1956 en particulier,[2] à une entité administrative gérée par un ministère

---

[1] On fait référence ici aux titres du colloque qui a donné lieu à cet ouvrage. Le titre en français était : « Les langues régionales en Irlande », alors que le titre en anglais était : « Indigenous Minority Languages in Ireland ».

[2] Le Ministère du *Gaeltacht*, institué en 1956 par le gouvernement irlandais, a pour rôle de promouvoir la pratique de l'irlandais et de soutenir les communautés irlandophones. Avant cette date, le *Gaeltacht* avait une existence essentiellement géographique et linguistique. Aujourd'hui, le ministère qui s'en occupe s'appelle « The Department of Community, Rural and Gaeltacht affairs ».

spécifique et dont les frontières ont été clairement posées.[3] Ce processus de délimitation ne va toutefois pas sans poser problème puisqu'il cherche à mettre en place des frontières physiques ou géographiques sur des mécanismes sociolinguistiques par nature mouvants : les faits langagiers, comme tout autre phénomène social, ne sont évidemment jamais statiques. Par conséquent, les différentes commissions officielles chargées de définir avec précision le *Gaeltacht* en sont venues à affiner leur terminologie : le rapport de la première commission distingue ainsi en 1926 le *Fíor-Ghaeltacht* (zones irlandophones) du *Breac-Ghaeltacht* (zones partiellement irlandophones).[4] Le dernier rapport en date, celui de 2007, se propose de différencier trois types de districts à l'intérieur du *Gaeltacht* selon des critères à la fois officiels (découpage électoral) et linguistiques (pourcentage de locuteurs irlandophones) : le district type A dans lequel plus de 67% des locuteurs parlent irlandais, le district de type B dans lequel coexistent des réseaux irlandophones (entre 44% et 66% de la population) et anglophones et enfin, le district de type C dans lequel survivent des groupes irlandophones (moins de 44% de la population).[5] Les férus de statistiques spatiales apprécieront certainement ce découpage mais finalement, comme en témoigne d'ailleurs la carte tirée de ce dernier rapport, on aboutit à une image éclatée des locuteurs d'irlandais. Cette confusion se retrouve aussi sur place : des panneaux indiquent généralement l'entrée d'un Gaeltacht mais aucun signe n'indique au voyageur de passage qu'il en est sorti. Il n'est pas étonnant non plus que la critique la plus vive et la plus construite de la politique linguistique irlandaise, à savoir l'ouvrage de Reg Hindley paru en 1990, *The Death of the Irish Language*,[6] ne provienne non pas d'un spécialiste des langues mais d'un géographe de formation. Il dénonce notamment un fait déjà connu en Irlande depuis la fin des années 1920, à savoir le découpage parfois arbitraire des zones irlandophones pour des raisons plus politiques que linguistiques, processus qui a mené à l'inflation géographique des districts appartenant au *Gaeltacht*. Toute volonté de réduire leur dimension s'est soldée par une forte opposition à la fois des différentes organisations militantes et de certains hommes

---

[3] Le *Gaeltacht*, bien que prenant forme dès 1926, n'a pas été défini avec grande précision par la commission créée pour remplir cette office, à savoir *Coimisiún na Gaeltachta*. Le critère alors était un nombre minimum de 25% d'irlandophones mais certains districts en dessous de ce pourcentage ont aussi été inclus.

[4] Tony Crowley (2005), *Wars of Words. The Politics of Language in Ireland 1537-2004*, Oxford, University Press, p. 169.

[5] Cf. en ligne l'étude sociolinguistique menée dans le *Gaeltacht* publiée en 2007 et consultable sur le site du Ministère chargé de gérer les régions irlandophones : http://www.pobail.ie/en/AnGhaeltacht/LinguisticStudyoftheGaeltacht/ (consulté le 11/09/2008).

[6] Reg Hindley (1990), *The Death of the Irish Language*, London, Routledge.

politiques : une seule véritable modification des frontières du *Gaeltacht* a été opérée en 1956. Les dernières propositions en date, celles proposant le découpage des zones irlandophones en districts de type A, B ou C ont été, elles aussi, rejetées par le ministre en place, Éamon Ó Cuív. La raison de ce refus, si l'on met de côté la rhétorique nationaliste ou militante, tient en partie aux aides dont bénéficient les locuteurs irlandophones dans le *Gaeltacht* : retirer cet apport financier serait certainement mal vécu par les bénéficiaires et leurs représentants, dont un certain Éamon Ó Cuív, élu dans la circonscription de Galway ouest, qui seraient vraisemblablement sanctionnés dans les urnes lors d'une prochaine échéance électorale.

Le processus de délimitation de l'aire d'emploi d'une langue, qui se retrouve à bien des égards pour les autres langues celtiques (on parle aussi de *Gàidhealtachd* pour les régions où est encore parlé le gaélique écossais, de *Y Fro Gymraeg* pour la zone galloisante au Pays de Galles), implique aussi une forme de hiérarchisation sociolinguistique ou politique : il y aurait des langues régionales et une langue nationale, parlée et comprise sur l'ensemble du territoire. Or, d'après l'article 8 de la Constitution de 1937, l'irlandais est la seule langue qui remplit cette fonction : elle est la langue de la nation tandis que l'anglais, de facto la langue maternelle de la majorité des Irlandais, est « seulement » une langue officielle. Cette contradiction s'est clairement manifestée lors d'une série d'émissions télévisées, intitulée *No Béarla*, qui a été diffusée sur TG4 en 2007 sous la forme d'un reportage sur la pratique contemporaine de l'irlandais.[7] Le reporter, Manchán Magan, s'est proposé de parcourir l'Irlande durant trois semaines, pendant l'été 2006, en faisant le choix de ne parler qu'irlandais. Le résultat ne surprendra personne : à Dublin, ses tentatives de communication avec un vendeur dans un magasin ou avec un employé de l'office de tourisme se sont soldées par des mines renfrognées – et des demandes fermes exigeant qu'il parle anglais. À Galway, il s'est amusé à chanter les chants les plus paillards qu'il connaisse sans grande réaction – à part celle, amusée, de quelques personnes âgées passant à proximité. Enfin, à Killarney, il a tenté d'entraîner les clients d'une banque dans une affaire pour le moins douteuse, promettant de partager le butin s'ils l'aidaient à la dévaliser – sans plus de succès. Il en ressort donc que, d'un point de vue strictement géographique, l'irlandais est évidemment loin d'être la langue parlée sur tout le territoire national. On pourrait cependant arguer du fait qu'au niveau sociolinguistique tout au moins, elle est à la fois langue régionale et nationale : il existe un irlandais standard, enseigné dans les écoles, qui

---

[7] Pour en apprendre davantage sur cette série et visionner certains épisodes, consulter le site du producteur et animateur de la série, Manchán Magan : http://www.manchan.com/index.html (consulté le 24/09/2008).

sert de norme dans la République, voire dans toute l'île, et des variations locales qui correspondent peu ou prou aux trois provinces : les irlandais du Munster, du Connacht et d'Ulster. L'expression « Dublin Irish », également employé pour caractériser ce standard, illustre d'ailleurs une autre différence géo-linguistique, à savoir l'usage, dans la capitale et les principaux centres urbains irlandais, d'une norme qui contraste forte-ment avec la pratique des dialectes dans les campagnes de l'Ouest, à tel point que les deux types de locuteurs ont parfois du mal à se com-prendre.

L'irlandais comme langue nationale

L'expression « langue nationale » utilisée ci-dessus mérite également quelques remarques. Elle dénote évidemment un projet politique qui remonte, pour le cas de l'irlandais, au début du XXe siècle et qui per-dure, dans le discours militant, dans l'affirmation suivante : « Le but linguistique n'est pas un but en lui-même. Notre objectif est la survie du peuple irlandais en tant que nation ».[8] En clair, la langue irlandaise est un élément consubstantiel à la nation irlandaise qui s'est appuyée sur cette spécificité pour légitimer sa différence. Seulement, après un élan initial prometteur dans les années 1920, la volonté des gouvernements irlandais successifs de faire du gaélique la langue première dans les vingt-six comtés a progressivement cédé place à d'autres considérations, économiques notamment. Sur un plan sociolinguistique, la nation irlan-daise s'est construite sur un territoire où résidait une population majori-tairement anglophone. Dans le processus de définition de la nation, la langue anglaise devait logiquement être reconnue comme jouant un rôle significatif. La Constitution de l'État libre de 1922, pourtant élaborée à une époque marquée par la ferveur nationaliste, reconnaît logiquement l'anglais comme langue officielle, au même titre que l'irlandais.[9]

Depuis cette époque, qui met en place une forme de statu quo socio-linguistique, les choses n'ont guère évolué. Certes, l'amélioration de la situation politique en Irlande du Nord a mené, suite à l'Accord de Belfast, à la création en 1999 de *Foras na Gaeilge*, un organisme chargé de promouvoir la langue irlandaise sur la totalité de l'île en remplace-ment de *Bord na Gaeilge*, qui ne s'occupait que des vingt-six comtés.[10]

---

[8]   « The language aim is not an aim in itself. Our aim is the survival of the Irish people as a nation ». Seán Ó Tuama (1964), *Facts about Irish*, Baile Átha Cliath, Comhdháil Náisiunta na Gaeilge, p. 41.

[9]   « Article 4: The National Language of the Irish Free State is the Irish language, but the English language shall be equally recognised as an official language ». *Constitu-tion of the Irish Free State (Saorstát Eireann) Act*, 1922.

[10] L'Accord de Belfast a mené à la création d'instances de coopération entre la Répu-blique d'Irlande et l'Irlande du Nord, dont *An Foras Teanga*. Ce dernier est composé

La démarche de cette agence, tout comme la loi sur l'irlandais (*Official Languages Act*) promulgué en 2003 dans la République, ne dévient pas foncièrement de la double stratégie géolinguistique menée depuis plusieurs décennies : tenter de préserver la spécificité linguistique du *Gaeltacht*, et développer le bilinguisme du reste de la population. À part l'établissement d'un Commissaire de la langue chargé, suivant le modèle québécois, de veiller à ce que les dispositions légales en matière linguistique soient bien respectées dans l'administration, cette dernière loi n'apporte pas, et ne paraît pas à même d'apporter, de grands changements. Certaines mesures comme la volonté de faire disparaître la signalétique bilingue au profit de panneaux monolingues dans le *Gaeltacht* paraissent bien dérisoires quand elles ne rencontrent pas une franche hostilité de la part des autochtones (ce qui a pu être le cas pour la suppression du nom anglais de la ville de Dingle, par exemple). Le projet porté par le gouvernement irlandais, dans la mesure où il se cantonne finalement à une dimension symbolique, semble difficilement capable d'influer sensiblement sur la situation sociolinguistique existante – s'il ne se termine pas parfois en un véritable imbroglio.[11] La raison majeure derrière l'insuccès de la politique linguistique menée depuis le début du XXe siècle tient au fait que la majorité des Irlandais soutient certes l'action en faveur du gaélique mais ne se mobilise pas pour autant pour parler la langue qui sert essentiellement de marqueur identitaire. Et c'est là, à mon sens, un point crucial : les expériences réussies et récentes de renversement linguistique, comme le flamand en Belgique ou le catalan en Espagne, sont dues dans une large mesure à un mouvement nationaliste mobilisateur s'appuyant sur une base de locuteurs suffisante pour enrayer le déclin de la langue. En ce début de

---

de deux agences autonomes, *Foras na Gaeilge* et *Tha Boord o Ulstèr-Scotch*, chargées respectivement de la promotion de la langue irlandaise et de l'ulster-scots. Diarmait Mac Giolla Chríost (2003), *Language, Identity and Conflict. A Comparative Study of Language in Ethnic Conflict in Europe and Eurasia*, London, Routledge, p. 87.

[11] "Although it is 4½ years since it was removed from official status, the name Dingle is still unofficial [*sic*] painted on road signs in Co Kerry. Dingle area councillor Séamus Cosaí Fitzgerald (Fine Gael), a member of the committee to reinstate the name Dingle along with an Irish version Daingean Uí Chúis, said yesterday their requests to send a deputation to Minister for the Environment John Gormley had not been responded to. Dingle was removed from official existence in 2005 under the Placenames Order of the Official Languages Act introduced by Minister for Community Rural and Gaeltacht Affairs Éamon Ó Cuív allowed for Irish only placenames for Gaeltacht places. The new name for Dingle was to be An Daingean, it was decided, under the placenames order. However the matter was greeted with disbelief and then a wave of sustained outrage and protest by townspeople in Dingle. Whenever the name was removed from official road signs, someone would paint it back on. This continues to be the case." Anne Lucey, "Dingle committee seeks reinstatement of name", *The Irish Times*, 30/06/2009.

XXIe siècle, ces deux éléments manquent cruellement à la défense de la langue irlandaise.

Paradoxalement, la mobilisation est plus forte en Irlande du Nord où les locuteurs, appartenant pour la plupart à la communauté catholique, sont globalement beaucoup plus engagés et ont d'ailleurs contribué à la création dans les années 1960 d'un *Gaeltacht* urbain, dans Shaw's Road à Belfast. Certains pourraient penser que cette entreprise sociolinguistique s'inscrit dans un processus nationaliste plus large mais une enquête menée auprès des parents semble démontrer le contraire : les deux grandes motivations derrière l'établissement d'une école irlandophone dans la capitale nord-irlandaise ne sont pas de nature politique. Les raisons évoquées sont en effet d'ordre identitaire (l'irlandais est un marqueur identitaire fort qu'il faut préserver) et éducative (la qualité de l'éducation est évidemment meilleure dans des classes où le ratio professeur/élève y étant généralement plus bas).[12] La deuxième raison peut surprendre au vu de la situation politique spécifique à l'Irlande du Nord mais s'inscrit possiblement dans une recherche globale en Occident d'alternatives à un système figé. On retrouve des initiatives similaires en Bretagne par exemple où les écoles *Diwan* s'érigent en défenseurs de la culture et de la langue bretonne tout en niant posséder un agenda politique.

L'irlandais comme langue minoritaire

La description de l'irlandais comme langue « minoritaire » pose aussi nombre de problèmes. Commençons par la définition de cette expression empruntée ici à Bernard Poche, un sociologue français qui s'est penché sur la question. Selon ce dernier, trois grands traits généraux permettent de caractériser leur situation :

> Que peut-on donc appeler langues minoritaires ? Si l'on s'en tient à trois critères strictement *a minima* : une langue qui n'est pas la langue officielle d'un État, qui est ou a été récemment encore parlée dans la vie de tous les

---

[12] "'Irish identity' and 'quality of education' were the main advantages discussed by these respondents. Attendance at the *Bunscoil* was not seen as a way to fulfil a single aspiration. Rather, it was perceived on a wider plane. 'Irish identity' represented a broader context with which to express the attraction of the *Bunscoil*. The *Bunscoil*'s reputation for high educational standards was the factor which most respondents cited as either the first, second or third advantage which they had discussed. For many parents, the favourable pupil/teacher ratio was an important characteristic of the school". Voir : Gabrielle Maguire (1991), *Our Own Language. An Irish Initiative*, Clevedon, Multilingual Matters, p. 100.

jours par un groupe de personnes que l'on peut circonscrire approximativement dans l'espace, et qui est dotée de stabilité [...].[13]

Trois types de critères sont ici utilisés : le premier est de nature politique (c'est une langue sans statut officiel) ; le deuxième est géographique (l'usage de la langue est plus ou moins délimité dans l'espace) ; le troisième est linguistique (la langue possède une norme stabilisée même si elle n'apparaît pas toujours de manière explicite). Dans cette perspective, la distinction entre langue minoritaire et langue normée repose essentiellement sur un critère politique, c'est-à-dire sur le statut constitutionnel ou juridique qui est conféré à telle variété linguistique et qui permet ensuite un processus de normalisation. Les mouvements militants pour la défense des langues minoritaires ont d'ailleurs conscience de l'importance du politique puisqu'ils placent souvent au premier rang de leurs revendications la reconnaissance officielle de leur langue. Seulement, contrairement à d'autres langues comme celle du breton, le cas de l'irlandais est particulier dans les vingt-six comtés dans la mesure où son usage, en théorie du moins, est soutenu officiellement dans plusieurs sphères de la société telles l'école, les média, et l'administration. Le cas de la République d'Irlande est assez insolite en Europe dans la mesure où si la langue irlandaise peut difficilement être caractérisée comme langue minoritaire, le pays abrite néanmoins une minorité linguistique (les irlandophones du *Gaeltacht*) dont l'existence et la survie en tant que communauté sociolinguistique n'ont jamais été au centre des politiques linguistiques menées par les gouvernements irlandais successifs.

La situation est évidemment très différente en Irlande du Nord où l'utilisation de la langue reflétait d'autres clivages, sociaux et politiques – même si quelques rares Protestants et Catholiques y voient la possibilité d'un héritage culturel commun. Les Catholiques, longtemps cantonnés dans une position minoritaire par le pouvoir en place, pouvaient ainsi rajouter le fait linguistique à leur liste de revendications. Cependant, l'Accord de Belfast de 1998 a changé le statu quo sociolinguistique dans la mesure où deux langues minoritaires associées respectivement aux deux communautés, à savoir l'irlandais et l'ulster-scots, ont été reconnues officiellement et sont soutenues par le même organisme, *An Foras Teanga*.[14] Cette reconnaissance de l'ulster-scots tient cepen-

---

[13] Bernard Poche (2000), *Les Langues minoritaires en Europe*, Grenoble, Presses Universitaires, p. 19.

[14] Le traitement des deux langues reste toutefois sensiblement différent. Le but poursuivi par *Foras na Gaeilge* est de promouvoir la pratique de la langue irlandaise dans toute l'Irlande ("Foras na Gaeilge has the objective of promoting the Irish language on an all-island basis".) tandis que celui poursuivi par *Tha Boord o Ulstèr-Scotch* est essentiellement de faire connaître la culture de l'Ulster dont l'ulster-scots constitue

dant moins d'un véritable projet sociolinguistique que d'une manœuvre politique :

> Afin de contrecarrer les avances nationalistes dans ce domaine clé de la culture, il fallait élaborer une contre-stratégie consistant à valoriser l'« ulster-scots », variante ulstérienne du scots [...] parlé par une importante section de la population nord-irlandaise, de souche écossaise et majoritairement protestante, donc surtout unioniste.[15]

L'ulster-scots peut ainsi être considéré comme une langue mise en avant dans l'unique but de doter l'Ulster d'une identité et d'une culture propres, distinctes du reste de l'Irlande. À cette considération uniquement politique se rajoute également une forme de hiérarchisation linguistique : le scots, en Écosse comme en Irlande du Nord, est classé comme un dialecte anglais et apparaît donc moins digne d'intérêt que les gaéliques écossais ou irlandais qui comptent parmi les derniers représentants de la famille des langues celtiques sur la planète.

Cette tendance à vouloir subordonner les langues minoritaires selon leur importance sera étudiée plus en avant dans la section suivante. Pour conclure sur l'expression « langue minoritaire », qui perd finalement de sa pertinence au Sud comme au Nord, le problème majeur se pose de distinguer, d'un point de vue sociolinguistique, le groupe « minoritaire » du groupe « majoritaire » : il est difficile de mettre en avant le seul critère linguistique quand les deux groupes maîtrisent la langue anglaise et savent l'employer à bon escient, y compris dans leurs revendications. Le discours des représentants du Sinn Fein se fait ainsi entièrement en anglais même si, à l'instar de certains hommes politiques dans la République, quelques mots d'irlandais sont insérés ici ou là.

L'irlandais comme langue autochtone

L'utilisation de l'expression anglaise *indigenous language* pour qualifier l'irlandais ou les autres langues minoritaires remonte aux années 1970, et s'inspire de différents mouvements, originaires en premier lieu

---

une pierre angulaire ("The legislative remit of the Ulster-Scots Agency is « the promotion of greater awareness and the use of Ullans and of Ulster-Scots cultural issues, both within Northern Ireland and throughout the island"). Source : North /South Ministerial Council Annual Report 2001 : www.northsouthministerial council.org/nsmc_annual_report_2001-opt.pdf (consulté le 25/01/2010). De même, le budget alloué aux deux agences est loin d'être similaire : en 2002, *Foras na Gaeilge* a reçu 17 867 millions d'euros contre 2,4 millions d'euros pour *Tha Boord o Ulstèr-Scotch*. Source : Department of Community, Rural and Gaeltacht Affairs. See : www.pobail.ie/en/IrishLanguage/AnForasTeanga (consulté le 25/01/10).

[15] Wesley Hutchinson, « La Langue irlandaise en Irlande du Nord, vers une possible neutralité ? », in *Hérodote*, n° 105, 2002. See : www.cairn.info/revue-herodote (consulté le 18/09/08).

d'Amérique du Nord, réclamant des droits spécifiques pour certaines minorités. Les revendications touchant les faits langagiers ont notamment débouché deux décennies plus tard sur des textes comme la *Charte européenne des langues régionales ou minoritaires* (1992) et la proclamation de la *Déclaration universelle des droits linguistiques* (1996), documents rédigés dans le but de combler notamment le déficit législatif et juridique qui touche ces langues au niveau européen et international.[16] Le deuxième document réclame l'égalité de toutes les langues :

> La présente Déclaration part du principe que les droits de toutes les communautés linguistiques sont égaux et indépendants du statut juridique ou politique de leur langue en tant que langue officielle, régionale ou minoritaire ; les expressions « langue régionale » et « langue minoritaire » ne sont pas utilisées dans la présente Déclaration car il y est fréquemment recouru pour restreindre les droits d'une communauté linguistique, même si la reconnaissance d'une langue comme langue minoritaire ou régionale peut parfois faciliter l'exercice de certains droits.[17]

Les auteurs de cette *Déclaration* proposent la création d'un Conseil des Langues au sein des Nations Unies, organisme chargé de défendre les communautés linguistiques au vu des droits reconnus dans la *Déclaration*. Ils ont, fin 2008, fait part de leur point de vue devant le Conseil des Droits de l'Homme à Genève. Pour l'instant, leur demande n'a pas abouti tant la question est sensible : il s'agit de promouvoir l'établissement de droits linguistiques individuels ou spécifiques pour des communautés situées généralement au sein d'État-nations.

Sur le plan sociolinguistique, l'expression « langue indigène », notamment avancée par l'association militant pour le gallois, la *Welsh Language Society*,[18] permet d'éviter le piège du relativisme linguistique par ailleurs souvent développé par les défenseurs des langues minoritaires : si toutes les langues sont égales, elles doivent toutes être sauvegardées. Les langues celtiques ne seraient alors que des pratiques langagières parmi d'autres et devraient partager toute aide, financière ou

---

[16] *Déclaration universelle des droits linguistiques* (consultable en ligne à l'adresse suivante : www.linguistic-declaration.org/versions/frances.pdf (consulté le 28/09/09). Une cinquantaine d'experts de plusieurs pays, sous l'impulsion du Comité de Traductions et Droits Linguistiques du PEN Club International et du Centre International Escarré pour les Minorités Ethniques et les Nations, ont œuvré sur cette Déclaration. Celle-ci fut ratifiée par de nombreuses ONG., des collectivités territoriales et même des universités et centres de recherche.

[17] *Ibid.*, article 5.

[18] "This principle of 'indigenous language' is not unique to Wales. It is the underlying principle behind language legislation in the Basque Country and Catalunya as well as the Universal Declaration of Linguistic Rights which was submitted to UNESCO". Cymdeithas yr Iaith Gymraeg (2001), *A New Welsh Language Act for the New Century*, Aberystwyth, Cymdeithas yr Iaith Gymraeg, p. 3.

autre, accordée par l'État pour promouvoir leur usage. En Irlande, par exemple, environ 50 000 Chinois vivent à Dublin et utilisent le mandarin ou le cantonais. Un rapport réalisé par la *Gaeltacht Commission* en 2002 a montré que, bien que 90 000 personnes vivent dans le *Gaeltacht*, moins de la moitié d'entre elles parlent l'irlandais au quotidien.[19] En termes purement statistique et si l'on suivait les recommandations de la *Déclaration universelle des droits linguistiques*, priorité devrait être donnée à ces langues chinoises sur l'irlandais. Souligner le caractère autochtone de la langue, son enracinement dans un terroir particulier, permet d'échapper à ce piège. On pourrait paraphraser George Orwell et dire : « toutes les langues sont égales mais certaines langues sont plus égales que d'autres » et mériteraient donc d'être traitées en priorité.

Conclusion

Ces quelques pages ont montré que les termes utilisés pour caractériser l'irlandais véhiculent tous une vision orientée de la langue, qui soustendent une hiérarchisation de type linguistique. Une langue qualifiée de régionale ou de minoritaire se retrouve ainsi de facto dans une position inférieure par rapport à la langue officielle, généralement la langue de la nation. Pour renverser ce rapport de force, les militants invoquent l'appartenance historique de leur langue à un terroir ou un pays ou insistent sur la protection et les droits que devraient recevoir les communautés minoritaires. La situation de l'Irlande est évidemment complexe dans la mesure où tous ces termes sont également utilisés avec des implications différentes selon l'expression choisie. Qu'en est-il alors de notre interrogation première : l'irlandais peut-il seulement être une langue ? L'ensemble des qualificatifs associés à l'irlandais véhicule un substrat idéologique qui ne peut faire oublier une réalité sociologique pourtant vitale à la survie d'une langue : pour que cette dernière continue à être utilisée, il faut que son usage fasse sens au sein des groupes sociaux, en bref qu'elle soit un impératif à l'interaction sociale. En d'autres termes, il serait peut-être temps de se pencher non plus sur la langue mais sur les individus qui l'utilisent. À l'heure actuelle, seules quelques communautés plutôt vieillissantes, situés majoritairement dans l'Ouest de l'Irlande, utilisent cette langue comme moyen d'expression premier. Mais pour combien de temps encore ?

---

[19] "More people in Ireland now speak Mandarin or Cantonese than speak Irish as a first language. There are 50,000 Chinese currently living in Dublin ; a survey undertaken by the Gaeltacht Commission in 2002 found that that while 90,000 people live in Gaeltacht areas, fewer than half that number speak it on a daily basis". Mark Condren, 'Go maith : More speak Chinese than Irish', in *Sunday Tribune*, 13 February 2005.

Summary

This paper deals with a number of terms ('regional', 'national', 'minority', and 'indigenous') which are used in the worlds of academia and of language activism to qualify the Irish language – and other Celtic languages. The choice of these terms is examined in detail, as they carry a particular, often ideologically loaded, vision of the language.

What Future for the Irish Language?

Elements of Comparison with Brittany

Yann BEVANT

Université Rennes 2

As was the case more than a hundred years ago, when the movement for the preservation of the Irish language emerged, Irish appears to be in serious danger of disappearing. Yet, the figures revealed in the censuses of the present decade seem rather encouraging, as the 2002 census highlighted a marked increase in the total number of reported Irish speakers; this suggests that knowledge of Irish is spreading. Though a substantial number of Irish speakers can be found in Northern Ireland, there is no doubt that the largest section of the Irish speaking population is located in the Republic of Ireland. Therefore this article will focus on the situation in the Republic. The question of the survival of the language is not specific to Irish; other Celtic nations have experienced the same problem of preservation, though in different context. The second part of this article will provide elements of comparison with the situation of the Breton language which may cast an interesting light over language policy as well as public and private commitment in favour of the language.

In terms of the number of speakers, Irish appears initially to be in a healthy state. In the 2002 census, 1,570,894[1] persons aged three years and over were recorded as being able to speak Irish. In the 2006 census, the number of Irish speakers was estimated at 1,656,790.[2] This represents an increase of 5% compared with 2002. However, we must take a closer look at this apparent increase. First of all, when we compare the ratio of Irish speakers to the total population, we can observe that the number of Irish speakers represented 40.8% of the respondents to that question in 2006, compared with 42.8% in 2002. Moreover, the number

---

[1] Census 2002, Principal Demographic Results, Table 27, Dublin, Central Statistics Office, p. 74. Available at: http://www.cso.ie./statistics.

[2] Census 2006, Principal Demographic Results, Table 31, Dublin, Central Statistics Office, p. 79. Available at: *ibid.*

of non-Irish speakers continued to grow between 2002 and 2006 as their number rose from 2,180,101 in 2002 to 2,400,856 (that is to say an increase of approximately 10%). Immigration linked to the economic achievements of the Celtic Tiger undoubtedly played a prominent part in this increase. The demographic results of the 2006 census also indicate that the non-Irish population represented approximately 12% of the total population in the Republic of Ireland; in this respect the relative fall in the total number of Irish speakers within the population could be considered as a mere side effect of the increase in the number of non-nationals, but this trend should not hide the fact that the Irish themselves seem to be showing a renewed interest in their own language. Reasons for optimism, however, should be tempered by a more detailed analysis of the Irish speaking population.

Among those 1,656,790 Irish speakers recorded in 2006, it is necessary to draw a distinction between those who declared themselves to be daily speakers within and outside the education system and those who declared themselves Irish-speaking to some degree ("weekly," "less often," "never").[3]

In 2006, the proportion of Irish speakers who used Irish on a daily basis within the education system was much greater than the number of Irish speakers who spoke Irish on a daily basis outside the education system. For instance, of the 1.66 million people who indicated that they could speak Irish, about 485,000 people (29,3%) spoke it on a daily basis within the education system but only 53,471 speakers (3,2%) used Irish daily outside the education system. Outside the school system, those who used Irish on a daily basis represented a tiny minority (5%) compared with the Irish speakers who never used it (36%).

The statistics show also that Irish was little used as a community language. Among those who used Irish on a daily basis within the education system, only 7% of them spoke Irish on a daily basis within and outside the education system.

The growth of Irish-medium schools or *Gaelscoileanna* is undoubtedly one of the major factors which may explain the high percentage of Irish speakers within the school system. The increase in the number of children attending these Irish-medium schools outside the *Gaeltacht* is impressive. Between 1990 and 2003, the number of children attending Irish-medium primary schools rose from 13,163 to 24,619, which represents an increase of about 87% in 13 years.[4] As far as Irish-medium secondary schools are concerned, the rise was less marked. Neverthe-

---

[3] Census 2006, *ibid.*, p. 80.

[4] Diarmuid O'Neill (2005), *Rebuilding the Celtic Languages, Reversing Language Shift*, Talybont, Y Lolfa, p. 314.

less, in 2003, 5,941 students were enrolled in those schools.[5] In 2007 there were 131 Irish-medium primary schools and 38 Irish-medium post-primary schools in existence throughout the 26 counties (outside the *Gaeltacht*).[6]

Although we can observe an increase in the number of those speaking Irish on a daily basis in 2006 (339,541 in 2002[7]), it is important to bear in mind that the vast majority of the Irish speakers recorded as being able to speak Irish either never spoke it or spoke it less frequently than weekly. Thus, 1,021,418 Irish speakers – that is to say about 62% – never spoke Irish or used it less frequently than weekly.[8] It is clear that the existence of areas where Irish remains the first medium of communication remains crucial in the preservation of the language as a community language. The situation of the *Gaeltacht* therefore calls for closer study.

Irish in the *Gaeltacht*

Today the *Gaeltacht* covers parts of counties Donegal, Mayo, Galway and Kerry, all on the western seaboard, but also parts of counties Cork, Meath and Waterford. Successive governments have always claimed that the preservation of the Gaeltacht was a priority. In the 2006 census, Irish speakers represented around 70% of the population aged 3 years old and over within the *Gaeltacht*.[9] Indeed, 64,265 inhabitants out of 91,862 were reported as Irish speakers. Yet this figure represented a drop of approximately 2% compared with that of the 2002 census. The proportion of Irish speakers declined in all *Gaeltacht* areas except in the Meath and Waterford areas where the number of Irish speakers climbed from 906 to 976 and from 1,006 to 1,242 respectively between 2002 and 2006.[10]

Over the past decades, the *Gaeltacht* has faced fundamental socio-economic changes which have led to an ongoing decline in the number of Irish speakers. The decrease is primarily the consequence of both "inward and outward migration."[11] Indeed, in the 1970s, government policy for the *Gaeltacht* was to support the development of strong,

---

[5] *Idem.*

[6] http://www.gaelscoileanna.ie (accessed 30/10/2008).

[7] Census 2002, Principal Demographic Results, *op. cit.*, Table 29, p. 76.

[8] Census 2006, Principal Demographic Results, *op. cit.*, Table 32A, p. 80.

[9] *Ibid.* Table 33, p. 82.

[10] Census 2002, Table 31, *op. cit.*, p. 80 and Census 2006, Table 33, *op. cit.*, p. 82.

[11] Iarfhlaith Watson, *Broadcasting in Irish, Minority language, radio, television and identity*, Dublin, Four Courts Press, 2003, p. 12. See also: http://www.coe.int/t/dg4/linguistic/Source/IrelandCountry_report_EN.pdf (accessed 20/09/2008).

economically viable Irish speaking communities in order to stop the tide of emigration. Right from the 1970s, the policies carried out by the *Gaeltacht* Authority, *Udarás na Gaeltachta*, worked adequately since the *Gaeltacht* population rose from 70,568 in 1971 to 79,502 in 1981.[12] This tendency is still valid today as in 2002 the population was 86,517 and it rose to 91,862 in 2006. Job opportunities may account for these figures. Indeed, over the last 10 years there has been a 60% increase in the number of people working in the manufacturing industry of the *Gaeltacht*.[13]

However, it is important to bear in mind that these measures have had consequences on the number of Irish speakers. The increase of job opportunities in the secondary and tertiary sectors have caused major re-immigration of former *Gaeltacht* emigrants and their families, generally transformed into English speakers, and immigration of workers who were also native English-speakers. As a result, a great number of non-Irish speakers have been incorporated into the *Gaeltacht* community. The children of those new immigrant families have little knowledge of Irish and naturally expect education through the medium of English. These trends are precisely underlined in the study of *Gaeltacht* schools commissioned in July 2003 by the Educational Council for *Gaeltacht* Schools and published in 2004.[14] The report shows that many schools in the *Gaeltacht* find it difficult to ensure the preservation of Irish, as they are torn between the demands of parents who are monolingual in English and the wish to preserve Irish expressed by other members of the community.

The report clearly indicates that there is a close relationship between the choice of the language of instruction at school and the linguistic behaviour of the population. Among the schools located in areas in which at least 70% of the population speak Irish on a daily basis (group A), 31 schools (out of 37) use Irish for at least 71% of the teaching. In areas in which 40-60% and less than 39% of the population speak Irish on a daily basis (group B and group C), there are respectively 14 schools (out of 20) and 14 schools (out of 66) in which at least 71% of the teaching is done through the medium of Irish. So it would appear that schools located in areas in which most of the population is

---

[12]   *Ibid.*, p. 12. See also S. Mac Donacha, F. Ní Chualáin, A. Ní Shéaghdha, T. Ní Mhainín, *A Study of Gaeltacht Schools 2004*, n. p., An Chomhairle um Oideachas Gaeltachta & Gaelscolaíochta, and http://www.udaras.ie/index.php/corporate_menu/ publications/annual_reports_and_statements/1124 (accessed 20/09/2008).

[13]   http://www.udaras.ie/doicmeid/cartlann/Turascail/tur99eng.pdf   (accessed   27/09/ 2008).

[14]   S. Mac Donacha, F. Ní Chualáin, A. Ní Shéaghdha, T. Ní Mhainín, *op. cit.* See also: http:/www.rte.ie/news/2005/0610/irish.html (accessed 20/09/2008).

English-speaking (group C) are more likely to use English as a language of instruction.

Official Attitudes towards the Irish Language

It is obvious therefore that socio-economic changes have had a bearing on the linguistic situation in the *Gaeltacht*. It is interesting to observe the political response of the State to such a trend, as, since the creation of the Irish Free State in 1922, successive governments have always claimed that the revival of the Irish language was a priority. Recently the Irish government has provided funding assistance to Irish medium schools outside the *Gaeltacht*, the aforementioned *Gaelscoileanna*, and to the various Irish language voluntary organisations including notably *Udarás na Gaeltachta, Foras na Gaeilge* and other language bodies, both voluntary and state-controlled.

The present official policy is "to build a bilingual Ireland through Irish by choice and not imposition."[15] However, the Government's position becomes more ambiguous when it comes to dealing with broader and more ambitious initiatives such as the *Official Languages Act* and the establishment of new Irish speaking communities outside the *Gaeltacht* areas. In both cases, the State has shown an astonishing degree of resistance which has been denounced by associations for the promotion of Irish. This was epitomized by the recent dispute over the elimination of the funding programme for *Scéim na bhFoghlaimeoirí Gaeilge*.[16] The economic slump experienced by the country undoubtedly plays a part, but it is difficult not to question the commitment of the State on the decision to cut funds to a programme which the Department of Community, Rural and Gaeltacht Affairs considered as "one of the most successful Gaeltacht Irish language schemes" which benefitted not only the Gaeltacht, "but also some 25,000 students who seek to improve their Irish by spending time in the Gaeltacht each year."[17]

As previously mentioned, the growth of Irish-medium schools, or *Gaelscoileanna*, has undoubtedly been one of the major successes in the

---

[15] Diarmuid O'Neill, *op. cit.*, p. 293.

[16] *Scéim na bhFoghlaimeoirí Gaeilge* was a scheme dedicated to providing financial support to Gaeltacht househoulds taking in students attending Irish language Summer courses. A report from a Government agency on public expenditure (the Special Group on Public Service Numbers and Expenditure Programmes published in 2009) recommended that the scheme be discontinued.

[17] Mary Hurley, Letter to Jim Kelly, 16/06/2008, Appendix 2 "Supports for the Irish Language in the Gaeltacht," available at: http://www.commissionontaxation.ie/submissions/Government%20Depts%20-%20Political%20Parties//F07%20-%20Dept.%20Community,%20Rural%20and%20Gaeltacht%20Affairs.pdf (accessed 20/09/2008).

struggle to revive the Irish language over the past thirty years. However, a few years ago, the Irish State and more specifically the Department of Education sought to slow down this progression by introducing strict rules for recognition which have ensured that in recent years only one or two schools have opened every year.[18] Furthermore, a recent decision taken by the Minister for Education and Science has cast doubts over the real objectives of the Irish Government when it was announced that Irish-medium schools would have to teach English by the "beginning of the second term of junior infants at the latest."[19] According to the defenders of the Irish language,[20] this decision constitutes a pure contradiction and a departure from the State's own policy on language preservation. Indeed, it curbs the most effective way of promoting the language in Ireland through the medium and practice of immersion education. This ambivalent policy from the Irish State was also expressed in the much debated *Official Languages Act* which was voted in July 2003 under the pressure of *Conradh na Gaeilge* and other associations for the promotion of Irish.

The *Official Languages Act* of 2003 provides a "statutory framework for the delivery of services through the Irish language."[21] This new measure would appear to be an important step as it may help reinforce and facilitate the use of Irish in public services and thus promote equality between the Irish and English languages.

It is worth remembering that Irish ceased to be a compulsory requirement for entrants to the public service in 1974.[22] More than 30 years after the proposal of a language Act, the coalition government of *Fianna Fáil* and the Progressive Democrats published the first draft of a bill in 2002 on the improvement of the quality of services provided through Irish by State organisations to Irish citizens. After a long series of debates and amendments, the bill was finally passed in July 2003.[23] The *Official Languages Act* guarantees the right of citizens to ask and to

---

[18] Diarmuid O'Neill, *op. cit.*, p. 294.

[19] http://www.gaelscoileanna.ie (accessed 20/09/2008).

[20] See: http://www.irishtimes.com/newspaper/letters/2007/1220/1197997063089.html and http://www.gaelscoileanna.ie/index.php?page=news&lang=en (accessed 20/12/09).

[21] Muiris Ó Laoire, "The Language Planning Situation in Ireland," in *Current Issues in Language Planning*, Vol. 6, 3, 2005, p. 306.

[22] As a result, the Irish and English languages were put on an equal footing in the entrance examinations for the civil service. In the years following that decision, the ability of public bodies to provide a service of quality for those wishing to conduct business through Irish decreased. This is the reason why, towards the end of the 1970s, the Irish language movement and more specifically *Conradh na Gaeilge* launched a campaign for a Language Act.

[23] http://www.coimisineir.ie (accessed 23/09/2008).

be given oral or written information in Irish only, and it also guarantees the duty of public bodies to publish in Irish documents of public interest.

However, the *Official Languages Act* and its implementation raise certain issues which underline the reluctance of the Irish Government to push too aggressively when it comes to the use of the Irish language in the workplace.

Language activists argue that the building of a bilingual society in Ireland has to be promoted in the workplace. Today Irish is rarely used as a living language in the workplace but the implementation of the *Official Languages Act* could have constituted an important step in introducing the language into the working environment. However, the exclusion of the private sector from the terms of reference of the Act raises serious questions as to the actual commitment of the State.

It has been argued that the application of the Act to the private sector could represent a threat to the interests of the Irish economy. Indeed, the remarkable economic growth experienced by the country during the Tiger years can mainly be attributed to foreign investments from Asia, from the United Kingdom and other European countries, and especially from the United States.[24] Obviously the Irish Government feared that foreign investors would be scared off by Irish language legislation in the private sector. This lukewarm attitude actually reflects the ambivalence displayed by many Irish people towards their language, as the implementation of the Placename Order, backed up by the legislation of the *Official Languages Act* in 2005 clearly revealed.

In accordance with the 2005 Placename Order, in March 2005, only the Irish version of official place names in *Gaeltacht* areas was to be kept and began to be used in signs, official documents and maps.[25] The measure triggered controversy in the town formerly known as Dingle, located in the highly popular tourist region of south-west Ireland, and now known only by its Irish name, *An Daingean*. The inhabitants of the town have publicly expressed concern that the move from an English to an Irish name might result in a loss of business for the town. As a consequence, they requested a local referendum to determine what the locals considered to be an appropriate name for the town. The reluctance of some of *An Daingean*'s inhabitants to recognize the original Irish version of their town's name demonstrates the ambiguity that still characterizes the attitude of many towards Irish, particularly when its defence conflicts with economic interests. There is undoubtedly a paradox between the general support for the preservation of the Irish

---

[24] The present economic slump confirms Ireland's dependence on foreign capital investment.

[25] Muiris Ó Laoire, *op. cit.*, p. 302.

language and the actual reactions against the implementation of measures which go in that direction.

Ireland, however, is not the only place where a dichotomy can be observed in terms of the support brought to the protection and development of the native language. Indeed, Irish shares many problems with other minority languages in Western Europe and more specifically with other Celtic languages.

Comparisons with Breton

The Celtic languages fall into two groups: Gaelic and Brittonic (also called Goidelic and Brythonic).[26] Gaelic includes Irish Gaelic (spoken in Ireland), Scots Gaelic (in Scotland) and Manx (in the Isle of Man), while the Brittonic group comprises Welsh (spoken in Wales), Cornish (the historic language of Cornwall, no longer spoken except by a minority of enthusiasts) and Breton (in Brittany).[27] Four of these languages, Irish and Scots Gaelic, Welsh and Breton are still living community languages.[28] Just like Irish, Welsh, Scots Gaelic and Breton are today at a crossroads. Are we about to witness the last chapter in a story of a long language death? Or on the contrary, are we going to witness another stage in the struggle for survival? The future of these languages depends heavily on the support from their respective States, on the number of speakers, and on their ability to remain living community languages. The experience of the other Celtic languages may shed light on the future of Irish. Given the scope available in the article, the second part of this paper will concentrate on the situation of Breton, which is comparable to Irish in spite of major differences in terms of public funding and language status.

In 1914 over 1 million people spoke Breton west of the border between Breton and Gallo-speaking regions[29]; roughly speaking, the figure

---

[26] Darerca Ni Chartuir (2002), *The Irish Language, An Overview and Guide*, New York, Avena Press, p. 3.

[27] *Ibid.*, p. 3.

[28] Donald MacAulay (1992), *The Celtic Languages*, Cambridge, University Press.

[29] Gallo is not a Celtic language; like French, Occitan and Catalan, it derives from Latin and was spoken in some eastern parts of Brittany, more particularly in the east of the Côtes d'Armor, Ille et Vilaine and the north-east of Morbihan. Morbihan, Finistère, Côtes d'Armor, Loire Atlantique and Ille et Vilaine are the names given to administrative and political territorial units known as *départements*, created as a result of the French Revolution and of the centralised nature of the French State. However, they do not accurately reflect the traditional linguistic and cultural landscape of *pays*: it is therefore difficult to assess dialectal varieties and customs through their prism. The following website features maps illustrating the differences between present administrative structures and the geographical limits of *pays*: http://www.geobreizh.com/breizh/fra/cartes.asp (accessed 27/09/2008).

represented nearly 90% of the population of the western half of Brittany. In 1945 it was less than 75%, and today, in all of Brittany, the most optimistic estimate would be that 20% of Bretons can speak Breton. Brittany has a population of over 4 million.[30] Three-quarters of the estimated 250,000 Breton speakers using Breton as an everyday language today are over the age of 50. The decline of Breton started long before the aftermath of Second World War for a whole set of reasons, mainly related to the predominance of French in the cultural, political and economic life of the country. To put things in a nutshell, access to education and to social advancement was determined by the command of French. The trend was epitomized by the divide between poor rural Breton-speaking areas and developed industrial French-speaking urban centres, and it was reinforced by the experience of the First World War, when tens of thousands of Breton-speaking soldiers came back from the trenches as French speakers.

Fañch Elegoët, a Breton sociologist, carried out an extensive study of rural Breton speakers in north-western Brittany in the 1960s and 1970s. He found that Breton native speakers had internalized the following view of their own language:

> Breton [...] is a peasant patois, unable to guarantee communication even with the neighbouring village, even more incapable of expressing the modern world – the world of tractors, automobiles, airplanes and television. A language only good enough to talk to cows and pigs. From that you get the refusal to transmit this language to children – a language considered to be a burden, a handicap in social promotion, a source of humiliation and shame.[31]

Because Bretons came to feel that their language was vastly inferior to French in cultural terms (but also because the precondition of access to improving their social status was an excellent command of French) many parents in post Second World War Brittany made the decision to do everything possible to make sure that their children would speak French. This led to the existence of households where grandparents spoke only Breton, parents spoke Breton and some French, and children spoke only French (although they could understand some Breton even if discouraged from speaking it themselves, "for their own good"...). Thus children were being cut off linguistically from grandparents and older relatives, and a generation gap was created in linguistic terms. This

---

[30] Including the territory of *Loire-Atlantique* which the Vichy government cut off from historic Brittany in 1941 and which is today part of the *Pays de Loire* administrative region.

[31] Fañch Elegouët (1978), *Nous ne savions que le breton et il fallait parler français, mémoires d'un paysan de Léon*, Rennes, Breizh hor Bro, p. 5. My translation.

situation is confirmed by the figures: according to INSEE (National Statistics Office), out of a population of more than 4 million, there were 263,850 Breton speakers in 2007, 61% of whom were over 60.[32] The very large percentage of ageing Breton speakers clearly reveals that transmission of the language from one generation to the other has failed. Still according to an INSEE study released in 1999,[33] the rate of family transmission averaged 3%. A study released by the *Ofis ar Brezhoneg – Observatoire de la langue Bretonne* (The Breton Language Office) in 2007[34] confirmed the decline of the language from one generation to the next. The *Côtes d'Armor* has the highest proportion of native speakers aged between 18 and 30 (7.5%), but *Finistère* and *Morbihan* have experienced a serious fall in the number of native speakers. While 20% of the population over 30 still speaks Breton in *Finistère*, only 5.9% of the population aged between 18 and 30 uses the language on a daily basis. In *Morbihan*, 10% of the population over 30 is Breton speaking, while only 2.8% speak it in the 18-30 generation. All in all, one Breton speaker out of two is over 65, and three out of four are over 50. The proportion of active Breton speakers in the 18-30 generation is now under 5% in all parts of Brittany. Up to the first quarter of the 20th century the notion of a "linguistic border" between upper and lower Brittany was widely acknowledged: while French was dominant in the east,[35] Breton remained the main channel of communication in the rural areas of the west, even though cities like Brest and Lorient were French speaking. This border no longer exists, which means that, contrary to the Republic of Ireland, there is no preserved territory for the language in Brittany. Undoubtedly the absence of an equivalent to the *Gaeltacht* has had a bearing on the rapid fall in the number of young native speakers, even though there is still a strong Breton presence in *Finistère* and western *Côtes d'Armor*.

However, there has been a renewed interest in the language over the last couple of decades which has led to a substantial growth of bilingual

---

[32] INSEE (2002), *Atlas démographique départemental, Côtes d'Armor, Finistère, Ille et Vilaine, Morbihan, Loire Atlantique*, Rennes, Nantes, INSEE. Note that there is one report for each *département*.

[33] INSEE (1999), *Populations légales. Recensement de la population de 1999, Côtes d'Armor, Finistère, Ille et Vilaine, Morbihan, Loire Atlantique*, Paris, INSEE.

[34] Ofis ar Brezhoneg/Office de la langue bretonne (2007), *Ar brezhoneg e-kreizh ar roudou/La langue bretonne à la croisée des chemins, Deuxième rapport général sur l'état de la langue bretonne*, Ofis ar Brezhoneg/Office de la langue bretonne, n.p., available at: http://www.ofis-bzh.org/fr/services/observatoire/index.php (accessed 20/09/2008). The Office was created by the *Conseil régional* of Brittany in 1999.

[35] To the detriment of Gallo. A study of the erosion of the use of Gallo as a result of the influence of French would also be of great interest, but this is not the purpose of this article.

schools, and there have been clear signs that local authorities have started reconsidering their language policy so as to offer Breton greater visibility. In this regard the comparison with Ireland is quite instructive.

Breton as the Second Most Commonly Used Language in Brittany

The figures released by INSEE indicate that 6.7% of the Breton population use Breton as a daily language of communication, which represents twice as many as those using English, and more than 9 times those using Gallo, the other vernacular spoken in the eastern part of Brittany.[36] Breton speakers, however, are far from being evenly spread, both in geographical and sociological terms. Not surprisingly, the language is strongest in the west, i.e. in *Finistère*, the west of the *Côtes d'Armor* and the west of *Morbihan*, according to the 2007 report published by the *Observatoire de la langue Bretonne*.[37] In the east, most notably in *Ille et Vilaine* and *Loire Atlantique* where Breton has always been a minority language, the proportion of Breton speakers is low, and the administrative separation of *Loire Atlantique* has made things worse. Indeed, the *Conseil régional*[38] (Regional Council) of the *Pays de Loire*, to which *Loire Atlantique* currently belongs, is actively trying to build a regional identity and has little sympathy for anything that could contribute to asserting a Breton identity in *Loire Atlantique*. Another issue that must also be underlined at this stage is the fact that the report revealed that 30.6% of adult speakers were farmers, 14.4% were artisans, 13.8% industrial workers, and a mere 7.6% highly-skilled professionals and executives. Such figures clearly indicate that Breton has some difficulty in having an impact on urban areas, even though it is not exclusively confined to rural areas. Nonetheless, the overall sociological profile of Breton speakers suggests a limited number of speakers among the elite, even though some change is perceptible (see *infra*). As the table below

---

[36] According to the 1999 INSEE census, there were 33,827 Gallo-speaking persons in Brittany, but only 3,122 were between 18 and 30 years old.

[37] Ofis ar Brezhoneg/Office de la langue bretonne, *op. cit.* This study is to this day probably the most exhaustive and reliable report published on the situation of Breton.

[38] France is divided into 26 regions or *régions*. 21 are in mainland France, one is the island of Corsica, and four are overseas. The mainland regions and Corsica are further subdivided into between 2 to 8 departments, or *départements*. Each *région* and each *département* has its own capital, and the *région* and *département* levels have been given different local authority prerogatives by the State. The organisation of local authorities is currently being reviewed, in an effort to rationalise a complex system. It is clear, however, that central government is reluctant to create big regions with enlarged powers on the German or Spanish models. The following website provides maps of the French *régions* and *départements*: www.statistiques-mondiales.com/cartes/france_departments_2.htm (accessed 19/01/2010).

suggests, the situation of Breton in the western part of Brittany bears some similarity with the situation of Irish in the *Gaeltacht*, or what the situation could soon be in the *Gaeltacht*. Even here, where the largest section of the active Breton-speaking population is concentrated, Breton has become a minority language as economic activity and many of the cultural activities are carried out in French. Active public policies in favour of language development would therefore be necessary to reverse the trend.

Table 1

Number of adult Breton speakers aged 18 and over per *département*

Finistère	134,924
Morbihan	49,604
Ille et Vilaine	9,118
Loire Atlantique	7,073

Source: INSEE (1999), *op. cit.*

The Limits of Official Support

The fact is that the Breton *Conseil régional* and western *Conseils généraux* (General Councils) and local authorities in general have been supportive.[39] In terms of financial contributions, after that of the *Conseil régional*, the financial contribution of *Finistère* is by far the largest. However, it should be noted that the means of *Conseils généraux* remain limited, and to this day no *Conseil général* in Britanny has promoted bilingualism in its own services and departments as a means of giving the language any official recognition and status. In December 2004 the *Conseil régional* passed a bilingual motion entitled "une politique linguistique pour la Bretagne" (A Linguistic Policy for Brittany) which stated clear objectives for the development of the language.[40] Further, *Conseil régional* spending in favour of the language increased 42% between 2002 and 2005, as compared with a global budget increase of 13% over the same period. So there is no doubt that regional authorities are genuinely supporting Breton, but again the financial means of the Region are limited. The *Conseil régional* has refused to confine its

---

[39] See Ofis ar Brezhoneg/Office de la langue bretonne, *op. cit.* Note that whereas the *Conseil régional* has responsibility at the level of the region, the *Conseil général* has responsibility at the lower level of the department.

[40] See:http://www.ofis.bzh.org/upload/travail_paragraphe/fichier/128fichier.pdf (accessed 19/01/2010).

action to the prerogatives granted by the laws of decentralization, as its aim has been to promote a coherent, comprehensive development strategy for Brittany. It has pursued an active policy in the field of education which remains under the responsibility of the State, so as to provide financial top-ups to sectors considered as priority objectives. This has impacted on language policy as the analysis on which the Council has based its action is that economic dynamism is boosted by a strong identity, and Breton is therefore an important element in the development strategy.

Table 2 provides a comparative perspective of *Conseil régional* spending on the language in 2004.

Table 2

	Breton	Basque	Catalan	Occitan
Spending per *Conseil régional* (€)	3,930,000	840,000	600,000	2,700,000
CR spending per adult capita (€)	12.93	11.35	4.55	5.13
Number of speakers in France (INSEE)	304,000	74,000	132,000	526,000

Source: Ofis ar Brezhoneg, 2007.

In the field of education, between 2003 and 2008, the number of bilingual classes saw an increase of 39%. Yet optimism as to the future of the language should be tempered, as although there may be at present 12,333 pupils in bilingual classes, the actual percentage of children attending such classes in Brittany (*Loire Atlantique* included) in 2008 represents only 1.38% of the total Breton pupil population. Besides, contrary to Irish, Breton does not enjoy the status of national language, even though the French constitution has recently acknowledged that regional languages were part of the national heritage.[41]

Though there has been an undeniable growth over the last few decades, the pace of this growth has slowed down: the annual growth rate went down from 25% in the 1980s to 17% from 1995 to 2000, and down again to a mere 9% from 2001 to 2006. This trend implies that there will not be more than 14,000 pupils attending bilingual schools in 2010, which is far below the *Conseil régional*'s objectives.

---

[41] Article 75-1 of the French Constitution voted by Parliament, 23/07/2008. By placing this declaration under the aegis of article 75 the responsibility for the preservation of regional languages lies with regional authorities; such recognition does not contradict the fact that, for all intents and purposes, French remains the only official language of the Republic.

Two contradictory explanations are advanced. The first argument, generally put forward by those who see no point in the defence of regional languages, would be that the policy of bilingualism has run its course, and has already reached the majority of those attracted by it. The declining numbers are evidence of a growing lack of interest for bilingualism among the general public. The second explanation, favoured by language activists, is that for all its commitment, the *Conseil régional* lacks resources to reach its goals. The problem is not so much indifference as funding. However as far as Brittany is concerned the limits are set by the rules of the French State, and consequently the share of the budget allotted to the promotion of the language can not be very high. Indeed, such financial limits mean that the *Conseil régional* would have to rely on state support to carry out ambitious policies. As far as education is concerned, the Fillon law passed in April 2005 provided that education in regional cultures and languages could be dispensed within the framework of contracts between the State and local authorities of territories where such languages and cultures existed.[42] This evolution had been anticipated in the previous contract between the State and the *Conseil régional*, as an additional clause to the contract from 2000 to 2006 stipulated that the State would provide €3.2 million over the period in order to support Breton. In reality, 91% of the funding was dedicated to sustaining administrative and teaching positions, while a further 75% of the remaining money had been provided for in the contract through support to the publishing sector and communication networks. In fact the top-up amounted to €770,000 over the period, which is less than €200,000 per annum. Furthermore, job creation in education is still a State prerogative, and the *Ministère de l'Éducation Nationale*, under the aegis of the contract, agreed to the creation of 50 new jobs in primary schools in the State sector and 30 new jobs in Catholic primary schools[43] per year to meet the target of 40 new bilingual classes each year, so as to accommodate 3,000 extra pupils. The objective was reached in terms of the number of pupils accommodated, as in 2006 there were 3,081 pupils more than in 2001, but not in terms of jobs and schools. The situation was even worse in secondary education, where an extra 625 students enrolled while the target was 2,000.

---

[42]   "Un enseignement de langues et cultures régionales peut être dispensé tout au long de la scolarité selon des modalités définies par voie de convention entre l'État et les collectivités territoriales où ces langues sont en usage. Le Conseil supérieur de l'éducation est consulté, conformément aux attributions qui lui sont conférées par l'article L. 231-1, sur les moyens de favoriser l'étude des langues et cultures régionales dans les régions où ces langues sont en usage" (Article L312-10 of the Code de l'éducation).

[43]   Most Catholic schools are grant-aided and under contract with the State.

These figures reflect several difficulties. First, the situation in the primary sector seems to indicate that there is an actual public demand for bilingual schools, which the *Ministère de l'Éducation Nationale* has only been able to meet with some degree of difficulty, because not enough permanent jobs are being created. Such difficulties, which are also to be found in secondary education, act as a deterrent as fewer students than could be expected attend bilingual secondary schools.

In short, in spite of the *Conseil régional*'s willingness to sponsor and support Breton, little can be achieved without the commitment of the State, and this commitment has been lukewarm to say the least in spite of the changes brought about in the Constitution and through the Fillon Law as regards the recognition of regional cultures and languages. This ambivalent attitude is reflected in the fact that though France signed the European Charter for Regional or Minority Languages, the document was never ratified by Parliament on the grounds that article 2 of the French Constitution stipulates that: "la langue de la République est le français." (French is the language of the Republic), which entails that regional languages have no other official status than that today provided by the Fillon Law and article L312-10 enshrined in the Code of Education. As the French authorities are more concerned with the status and influence of French as an international language, it should come as no surprise that much of the money devolved to the DGLFLF (Délégation Générale à la Langue Française et aux Langues de France – High Commission on French and Regional Languages) should be dedicated to the promotion of French. In this regard, the absence of status does have an adverse effect on the development of Breton, and one can but commend the lobbying of Irish associations which led to European recognition of the language. The Breton example is good evidence that official recognition does have an important part in the fight for survival of a minority language. Irish is the official language of the Republic while Breton has virtually no status; conversely, the Irish example shows that national (and European) status is a necessary stage, even though it may not be enough.

Breton and the Private Sector

Indeed, even though official commitment is an inescapable precondition to the survival of lesser used languages such as Irish or Breton, another key factor comes into play, that is the social and economic advantages that can be expected from bilingualism. So far in Brittany 73.4% of the jobs created in relation to Breton are to be found in the teaching sector, and only 1.7% are connected to trade and industry.[44] So

---

[44] Observatoire de la langue bretonne, *op. cit.*, p. 122.

there is a clear risk that economic and social prospects remain bleak, if job creation remains limited to the educational sphere, thus conveying the impression of a dog biting its own tail. *Ofis ar Brezhoneg* has proved to be very much aware of the situation and has actively contributed to a campaign entitled *Ya d'ar Brezhoneg* (Yes to Breton) the aim of which is to encourage the use of Breton in the workplace. This campaign has met with some success as, by 2006, 579 businesses, social services and non governmental organisations had signed the charter, 258 (44.6%) of which came from the private sector. Again, the limit was financial, as *Ofis ar Brezhoneg* could not bring in more money than it did to the campaign and carry out further lobbying. The encouraging aspect is that the campaign gained momentum at a time when many small and medium-sized firms and high-profile entrepreneurs also showed an interest in the promotion of Brittany. The institute of Locarn, created in 1991 as a think tank dedicated to the elaboration of strategies (« une sorte de Davos breton, à la fois laboratoire de réflexion et centre de formation des élites entrepreneuriales locales »[45]), brings together a large number of the key actors of economic activity in Brittany such as Glon, CGPME, Legris, Coopagri, and STEF-TFE among others. In 1995, Locarn created the label *Produit en Bretagne* (Made in Brittany) which has met with considerable success and the Institute has become a staunch defender of the principle of subsidiarity, and has developed an interest in the language, as its bilingual website testifies. Indeed, the language has served the purpose of many entrepreneurs in the food processing industry; a few words of Breton on an advert are received in Paris and other places as a badge of identity synonymous with authenticity. Breton is no longer a symbol of backwardness, but a symbol of a strong, desirable identity. Yet this marketing of the language does not mean that solutions seeking to introduce Breton as a normal means of communication in the economic sphere have already been found, and little is to be expected so long as Breton does not bring added value in terms of employment. In this regard, the Bretons have gone along the lines explored by the Irish in marketing their specificity and their culture, but just like them they have stopped short of wondering what they could do for their language, and as a result what their language could do for them. As the report of *Ofis ar Brezhoneg* points out: "Why should businesses provide services in both languages if their field of activity has little to do with Breton language and culture? Bilingualism should be an indicator of the quality of products and services as is the case in Wales. Supplying goods and services in both languages may be a way of

---

[45] Olivier Millot, *Télérama*, 17/11/99: "A kind of Breton Davos Forum, which works at the same time as a think tank and as a training centre for the local business elites."

keeping customers as well as a means of attracting new ones."[46] Economic prospects would indeed facilitate transmission of the language. At this stage however, transmission has so far stumbled into another formidable sociological obstacle. While language activists have struggled for recognition of the Breton language, for visibility within French society, and for the language to be taught in schools and used in the media, in practice they have not been followed by a large section of the young generation, nor by many ageing native speakers. Members of the latter group (retired people, farmers, factory workers and artisans), are often relatively uneducated and settled in rural areas. Their practice of the Breton language is endogamous. In other words, they tend to speak Breton mainly with people who belong to the same social group (family members, friends, neighbours) and sometimes only with those who share the same vernacular practices. And if Breton is seen today by a majority in Brittany as a badge of identity, it is it not considered economically worth the effort of learning: a few distinctive words (*kenavo*, *yec'hed mat*, *Bloavezh mat*) can do the job. The ambiguity lies in fact in the notion of preservation. Is it enough to preserve traces of a linguistic heritage in the same way implements of a bygone age are preserved in museums? Or does preservation mean encouraging both popular practice of the language and its transmission through the generations? In other words, is the Breton language's present popularity merely a means for cultural distraction or marketing strategies or is it a sign of reproduction? If the first hypothesis is true, rates of transmission are likely to remain very low and the daily, active practice of Breton limited to a happy few.

Conclusion

Although we can observe political, sociological and demographic disparities between Ireland and Brittany, the use and perception of their respective Celtic languages by the populations of these countries is quite similar though not on the same scale. On the one hand, the number of Celtic language speakers has continued to decline over the past decades. Indeed, a majority of native speakers have ceased to transmit their language to the next generation. Many of them tend to consider the use of Irish and Breton as unsuited to the modern globalised world, in spite of the fact that both languages seem to be experiencing a new lease of life thanks to the promotion of the language through the education system and the public sphere. In this regard Irish has been in a much better position thanks to official recognition and the existence of the *Gaeltacht*, but the example of Brittany shows that the end of the *Gael-*

---

[46] Ofis ar Brezhoneg, *op. cit.*, p. 127. My translation.

tacht would have serious consequences for the future of the language, and that the situation could be much better had the State's commitment been more consistent. Yet in both cases the question of popular commitment cannot be ignored, and this question is obviously closely connected to the economic benefits that can be expected from language use.

If Irish is examined in this light, public support for Irish "appears to rest on two key ideological positions, the value that is placed on the language for its contribution to national distinctiveness, and the reluctance to see it disappear from public domains of Irish life and from the experience of future generations of Irish people."[47] It would therefore appear that the consensus on the notion that Irish is of particular importance for the people, society and culture of Ireland as part of the national heritage is deeply anchored in the country. However, this does not necessarily mean that people are willing to reverse the language pattern. Indeed, the dominant position of English is already a *fait accompli* and contemporary Ireland is characterized by a growing linguistic and cultural diversity which may in the end strengthen the position of English. The position of Breton with regard to French is not different and probably even worse, as Breton, contrary to Irish, enjoys no official status either at national or European level.

Yet cultural and linguistic diversity, though they certainly contribute to language change, do not necessarily constitute a threat to the survival of Irish, and there are probably lessons to be drawn from the experience of Breton and other Celtic languages. A strong English presence has not actually resulted in the destruction of Welsh in the British Isles, and up to the beginning of the 20th century Breton was still the language of the majority in the western part of Brittany. What made the difference was the perception the natives had of their own tongue and of the necessity to switch to French (or to English) in order to give their offspring a better future. In this regard, tentative steps to revitalize Breton remain incomprehensible to a large number of ageing native speakers who continue to see their language as a social and economic impediment at worst, a useless local habit at best, and see no point in language transmission. To a certain extent, this is also what is happening in the *Gaeltacht*, where many see Irish as an obstacle to trade with newcomers. One of the successes of Breton is that the marketing of the language has recently changed the way it is perceived among the younger generations: it is not – or no longer – perceived as the language of the uneducated or one that can only be used within a limited social group, but as a badge of identity people can be proud of. Yet the limit of this success is at the

---

[47] Florian Coulmas (1991), *A Language Policy for the European Community, Prospects and Quandaries*, Berlin-New York, Mouton de Gruyter, p. 262.

same time financial – lack of funding to expand the teaching of the language – and economic – the language hardly brings any added value in the workplace. There is no questioning the importance of schools and the media as vital instruments of learning and appropriation, but as the Welsh experience suggests, transmission starts with making the language not only desirable as a badge of identity to the happy few, but first and foremost economically and socially attractive and valuable to a broad cross-section of the population.

Résumé

Comme ce fut le cas à la fin du XIXe siècle au moment de la renaissance culturelle, l'avenir de la langue irlandaise semble incertain aujourd'hui. L'irlandais n'est pas la seule langue dont l'existence est actuellement menacée. Il partage les mêmes difficultés avec beaucoup d'autres langues minoritaires en Europe occidentale, surtout les autres langues celtiques, qui arrivent à un moment-clé de leur histoire. Allons-nous assister au chapitre final dans l'histoire de ces langues ou, au contraire, est-ce que nous nous dirigeons vers une nouvelle phase de la lutte pour leur survie ? La pérennité des langues celtiques dépend de plusieurs éléments-clé : le soutien de leurs États respectifs, le nombre de locuteurs, et l'utilisation de la langue comme langue vernaculaire. Peut-on mettre toutes les langues celtiques sur un pied d'égalité ? La réponse à cette question serait sans doute négative car les données varient énormément d'un pays à l'autre. Cet article se centre sur des comparaisons entre la langue irlandaise et la langue bretonne.

Les grands patrons bretons et la langue bretonne

Investissement sentimental ou engagement politique ?

Tangui PENNEC

Institut Français de Géopolitique, Université Paris 8

Pour la plupart des grands patrons bretons, leur attachement à la Bretagne et particulièrement à la langue bretonne est ouvertement revendiqué. La liste compte François Pinault, Vincent Bolloré, Michel-Édouard Leclerc, Yves Rocher, Louis Le Duff, Patrick le Lay, etc.[1] La langue constitue un des piliers des revendications identitaires qui ont connu un renouveau depuis la fin des années 1960, mais qui ont pris une tournure différente depuis les années 1990.[2] Ainsi, cette élite économique se

---

[1]   Cette liste n'est bien évidemment pas exhaustive. À noter le cas particulier de François Pinault qui ne revendique pas le breton, mais le gallo. Cependant, nous avons fait le choix d'en parler dans cette étude dans la mesure où il a montré à plusieurs reprises son attachement à la Bretagne et à l'« identité bretonne », dont la langue constitue un pilier : financement du reboisement de la forêt de Brocéliande après un incendie en 1990, financements divers lors des opérations de nettoyage de la marée noire de l'*Erika* en 1999, acquisition du Stade Rennais, participation financière dans la chaîne TV Breizh (qui, au début, propose des programmes en breton), installation du drapeau breton au fronton du Palazzo Grassi à Venise qui abrite sa collection personnelle d'art contemporain, etc.

[2]   Sur les revendications identitaires et plus précisément l'*Emsav*, voir les travaux de Michel Nicolas (1982), *Histoire du mouvement breton. Emsav*, Syros, Paris ; Michel Nicolas (2007), *Histoire de la revendication bretonne*, Coop Breizh, Spézet. L'*Emsav* est le terme par lequel on désigne le mouvement breton – du verbe *sevel*, se lever – et signifie donc le « relèvement » ou « soulèvement ». Pour Michel Nicolas, « le mouvement breton peut être défini comme un mouvement social de résistance à l'assimilation dont la Bretagne fait l'objet dans l'espace français » et dont le discours « fonde une idéologie nationale bretonne ». (Michel Nicolas (2007), *op. cit.*, p. 29). Au-delà des prémisses intellectuelles du XIXe siècle caractérisées par le celtisme (héritage des celtomanes du XVIIIe siècle), puis le bretonisme (multiplication des travaux historiques sur la Bretagne), les historiens distinguent traditionnellement trois grandes périodes dans le mouvement breton : le régionalisme conservateur, aristocratique et clérical d'avant la Première Guerre mondiale avec la création de l'Union régionaliste bretonne en 1898 ; le second *emsav* de l'entre-deux-guerres marqué par une idéologie nationaliste et dont de nombreux membres se sont ralliés à

positionne comme un nouvel acteur dans le débat régionaliste et nationaliste[3] en Bretagne. Il convient donc de s'interroger sur le rôle d'une
« bourgeoisie » entreprenante dans l'« identité » politique d'un territoire.
L'angle d'étude de la langue bretonne permet de considérer le degré
d'investissement des patrons bretons dans l'« identité » bretonne. Le
breton n'est donc pas ici analysé pour ses caractéristiques et évolutions
lexicales et grammaticales, tel que pourrait le faire un sociolinguiste,
mais pour ses dimensions géopolitiques c'est-à-dire en tant qu'enjeu de
pouvoir et de territoire.[4] La géopolitique est, en effet, une démarche qui
permet d'analyser les rapports de force et les rivalités de pouvoir sur des
territoires entre des acteurs aux représentations contradictoires.[5]

Nos propos n'ont pas pour objectif de dégager un prétendu modèle
breton patronal. Il serait en effet hasardeux et exagéré de considérer le
grand patronat breton comme un groupe social homogène. Reste que sa
situation est remarquable sur plusieurs points. Les grands patrons bre-

---

Vichy et à l'occupant nazi ; et enfin, au sortir de la guerre, un troisième *emsav* beaucoup plus multiforme : d'abord folklorique et culturel (musique et danse : Bodadeg
ar Sonerion – 1946, Kendalc'h – 1950), puis économique (Comité d'Étude et de
Liaison des Intérêts Bretons – 1950), politique (Mouvement pour l'Organisation de
la Bretagne – 1957, Union Démocratique Bretonne – 1964), activiste (Front de libé-
ration de la Bretagne/Armée républicaine bretonne – 1966) et culturel.

[3] Michel Nicolas précise que le mouvement breton n'est pas le porte-parole exclusif
des revendications identitaires. Il convient donc de clarifier les termes précisément (voir aussi la clarification apportée par Michel Nicolas dans *Histoire de la revendication bretonne*, *op. cit.*, p. 33) : nous entendons par « régionalisme » la doctrine qui vise à développer la région dans sa dimension politique et administrative et
qui doit s'affirmer par rapport à l'État qui ne garde que les seules fonctions réga-
liennes. L'autonomie régionale (politique et économique) est l'objectif recherché. Le
« nationalisme » est la doctrine qui met en avant l'existence d'une nation, en
l'occurrence bretonne, qu'il convient de promouvoir et de défendre dans un cadre
étatique comme non-étatique. L'indépendance politique, c'est-à-dire donner un État à
la nation, et donc la séparation politique, peuvent (ce n'est pas systématique) être
dans ce cadre des objectifs recherchés. D'autres auteurs proposent des dénominations
différentes pour qualifier le mouvement des revendications identitaires : Tudi Kernalegenn parle de « lutte nationalitaire » ; Béatrice Giblin préfère la notion de « nationalisme régional » ; André Lecours évoque pour sa part l'« ethnonationalisme » ;
Michael Keating utilise indifféremment les termes de « nationalisme minoritaire »,
« nationalisme périphérique », « régionalisme » ; Michel Nicolas ajoute lui le concept de « fédéralisme », etc. (Voir : Tudi Kernalegenn (2005), *Drapeaux rouges et
gwen-ha-du. L'extrême gauche et la Bretagne dans les années 1970*, Apogée,
Rennes, p. 32 ; Béatrice Giblin (1999), « Les nationalismes régionaux en Europe »,
Hérodote, n° 95, pp. 3-20 ; Michel Nicolas, (2007), *op. cit.*, p. 33).

[4] Pour une approche géopolitique des langues, voir : *Hérodote*, (2002), *Langues et
territoires*, n° 105.

[5] Sur la définition du concept de géopolitique, voir le riche préambule d'Yves Lacoste
dans le *Dictionnaire de géopolitique* (Yves Lacoste (dir.) (1995), *Dictionnaire de
géopolitique*, Flammarion, Paris) et ses nombreux éditoriaux dans la revue *Hérodote*.

tons comptent non seulement parmi les plus grands patrons français mais encore européens, voire mondiaux. Le groupe PPR (anciennement Pinault-Printemps-La Redoute) de François Pinault est le deuxième acteur mondial du luxe[6] ; Yves Rocher emploie près de 15 000 personnes dans le monde dont 4 000 en Bretagne ; le conglomérat Bolloré est un des leaders mondiaux de l'industrie papier et de la logistique et s'est récemment reconverti dans les médias ; François Régis Hutin, PDG de *Ouest-France*, est à la tête du premier quotidien francophone du monde ; le groupe Le Duff possède plus de 500 restaurants sur quatre continents ; Patrick Le Lay fut pendant près de 20 ans (de 1988 à 2007) le PDG de TF1. Ce sont surtout des patrons puissants : François Pinault et Vincent Bolloré font partie des 500 premières fortunes mondiales et la Bretagne apparaissait en 2006 comme la troisième région française pour la richesse de ses grands patrons, derrière l'Ile de France et le Nord.[7] Outre la fortune, la notoriété est un élément important de puissance : si Michel-Édouard Leclerc ne compte pas parmi les très grands patrons en matière de fortune, de chiffre d'affaire et de bénéfices économiques, il possède une renommée incontestable par ses interventions dans les débats publics en France. La participation directe ou indirecte aux questions politiques est donc un critère non négligeable. C'est bien une image de dynamisme économique que dégage cette élite bretonne. Ce sont pour la plupart des patrons pleinement intégrés à la mondialisation, accentuant ainsi leur « déterritorialisation ». Même si certains ont gardé une partie de leur siège social en Bretagne, ils possèdent tous une antenne à Paris ou dans sa région, qui est vite devenue le centre névralgique de l'entreprise. Travailler dans une « ville globale »[8] leur permet d'être reliés aux marchés mondiaux.

La situation de la langue bretonne est inverse. La pratique du breton est structurellement en déclin. Selon différentes études, le nombre de bretonnants en Bretagne et en Loire-Atlantique[9] en 2007 s'élevait à un peu moins de 210 000 personnes, alors qu'il était d'environ 270 000 en

---

[6] Le groupe contrôle entre autres les sociétés Yves Saint-Laurent, Gucci, Puma, Conforama, Fnac, La Redoute, Boucheron, etc.

[7] Calculs réalisés sur les 250 premières fortunes professionnelles de France à partir des chiffres et des informations donnés par la revue *Challenges*, le site internet des entreprises, le *Quid 2007* et l'ouvrage de Pierre-Henri de Menthon et Éric Treguier (2004), *Ces 200 familles qui possèdent la France*, Hachette, Challenges, Paris.

[8] Saskia Sassen (1996), *La ville globale*, Descartes, Paris.

[9] Notons que, si les études et les sondages sur la langue bretonne n'ont porté pendant longtemps que sur la Basse-Bretagne, les enquêtes actuelles, notamment celles dont il est ici question, prennent systématiquement en compte la région Bretagne et la Loire-Atlantique. Il n'est donc pas inutile de remarquer que c'est le territoire dit de la « Bretagne historique » qui sert désormais de référence, non sans visées géopolitiques d'ailleurs (cf. *infra*).

1999 (300 000 en comptant les locuteurs en breton dans toute la France).[10] La diminution s'explique avant tout par un vieillissement de la population bretonnante – 70% des locuteurs ont plus de 60 ans en Basse-Bretagne quand seuls 1 à 2% des moins de 18 ans pratiquent la langue en Bretagne et en Loire-Atlantique. Les grands entrepreneurs bretons, pour beaucoup originaires du territoire bretonnant (mis à part Yves Rocher et François Pinault : cf. carte 1, *infra*), ont connu le fort recul de la transmission parent-enfant : 60% des enfants recevaient le breton de leurs parents dans les années 1920 et seulement 6% dans les années 1980. De plus, la pratique de la langue est plus forte chez les agriculteurs et chez les ouvriers, que chez les cadres et les patrons. Enfin, sur un plan territorial, la langue bretonne est principalement cantonnée à sa zone traditionnelle, la Basse-Bretagne,[11] et est en repli sensible sur quelques foyers : la Cornouaille, le Trégor et le Léon (cf. carte I, *infra*). L'enseignement bilingue en Ille-et-Vilaine et la formation d'étudiants bretonnants à l'université de Rennes ne suffisent pas à

---

[10] Ces chiffres sont avant tout des ordres de grandeur, dans la mesure où ils sont le résultat de sondages et d'enquête. Pour le chiffre de 2007, nous nous appuyons sur le sondage effectué par Fañch Broudic avec TMO Régions (Fañch Broudic (2009), *Parler breton au XXIe siècle. Le nouveau sondage de TMO Régions*, Emgleo Breiz, Brest). Le nombre de locuteurs dans la zone traditionnelle de pratique du breton, c'est-à-dire en Basse-Bretagne, est évalué à 172 000. Pour le chiffre de 1999, nous reprenons les données de l'Office de la langue bretonne (Office de la langue bretonne (2007), *La langue bretonne à la croisée des chemins*, Deuxième rapport général sur l'état de la langue bretonne, Observatoire de la langue bretonne, n.p.). Elles proviennent de l'enquête « Étude de l'histoire familiale », menée par l'INSEE lors du recensement de 1999 dont on peut trouver une synthèse dans : Isabelle Le Boëtté (2003), « Langue bretonne et autres langues : pratique et transmission », *Octant*, n° 92, pp. 18-22, et ont été complétées par l'Office en partenariat avec l'INSEE Bretagne. La population scolaire bilingue et la population bretonnante d'Ille-et-Vilaine et de Loire-Atlantique ont notamment été ajoutées aux chiffres de l'Insee de 1999.

[11] Isabelle Le Boëtté (2003), *op. cit.*, p. 19 : Isabelle Le Boëtté parle d'une « langue territorialisée ». Il faut cependant souligner la présence actuelle et historique de populations bretonnantes en dehors des limites de la Basse-Bretagne, liée d'une part à la formation bilingue (école et cours du soir) en Ille-et-Vilaine, en Loire-Atlantique et à Paris, et d'autre part aux grandes vagues d'émigration commencées au XIXe siècle. L'exode connaît deux poussées importantes au lendemain des deux guerres, entre 1911 et 1931, puis entre 1946 et 1954, et est essentiellement dirigé vers Paris et sa banlieue, qui concentrent environ la moitié des émigrants. Voir Michel Phlipponneau (1970), *Debout Bretagne !*, Presse Universitaire de Bretagne, Saint-Brieuc, p. 13, et Jean Ollivro, (2005) *Bretagne. 150 ans d'évolution démographique*, PUR, Rennes, pp. 267-268. Mais, si à la fin du XIXe siècle, et probablement jusque dans les années 1960, dans certains quartiers parisiens, « l'on y entendait parler que breton » (Maurice Le Lannou (1952), *Géographie de la Bretagne*, tome 2, Plihon éditeur, Rennes, p. 395), force est de constater que la pratique du breton est de nos jours marginale en dehors de la Basse-Bretagne : en 1999, les départements où l'on comptait le plus de brittophones par rapport à la population départementale étaient l'Ille-et-Vilaine (1,3%), la Loire-Atlantique (0,7%) et les Yvelines (0,4%).

gommer la limite linguistique entre Basse et Haute-Bretagne.[12] La langue bretonne est donc dans une situation difficile et semble présenter une image à l'opposé de celle des grands patrons bretons.

Le rapprochement entre les grands patrons et la langue bretonne ne va pas forcément de soi et peut même paraître contradictoire : les dirigeants bretons symbolisent le dynamisme – économique – quand la langue bretonne donne plutôt à voir sur le long terme une image de déclin ; puis ils travaillent, pour la plupart d'entre eux, à l'échelle internationale, quand le breton est relativement bien défini dans ses limites territoriales à l'échelle locale ; enfin, ils représentent les archétypes de la sphère économique, longtemps jugée contraire au monde de la culture, qui apparaît actuellement comme le principal acteur de la promotion de la langue bretonne. Et pourtant, depuis quelques années les grands patrons bretons montrent de plus en plus d'intérêt pour la langue bretonne et s'investissent dans sa promotion. Pourquoi ? Que peut apporter la promotion de la langue bretonne aux grands chefs d'entreprise ? En retour, quelles peuvent être les conséquences pour la langue bretonne ? Les patrons participent-ils d'une revitalisation du breton, tant dans son image[13] que dans sa pratique ? Contribuent-ils à son redéploiement territorial, en dehors des limites de la Basse-Bretagne ?

L'investissement personnel des patrons bretons en faveur de la langue bretonne est clairement sentimental. Pour autant, cet investissement s'inscrit aussi dans un projet économique plus large : à l'heure de l'économie mondialisée, certains patrons proposent une nouvelle approche de la mondialisation fondée sur l'échelon régional et la culture. La langue bretonne devient ainsi un marqueur symbolique du territoire économique régional. Enfin, l'engagement d'une minorité de grands chefs d'entreprise en faveur de la langue bretonne semble correspondre davantage à l'adhésion à un projet politique régionaliste voire nationaliste.

---

[12] Fañch Broudic (2009), *Parler breton au XXIe siècle. Le nouveau sondage de TMO Régions*, *op. cit.*

[13] À ce sujet, les auteurs du *Livre Blanc de la Bretagne*, étude prospective sur la région présentant le résultat d'une réflexion de 200 décideurs bretons (économistes, chefs d'entreprises, universitaires, personnalités politiques, responsables associatifs du monde culturel, etc.) à l'initiative de l'association *Bretagne prospective* et notamment de son président, le géographe Jean Ollivro, dénoncent l'image traditionnelle accolée à la langue bretonne et le « discours pleurnichard et misérabiliste » de certains défenseurs du breton, qui « utilisent des expressions comme "sauvetage" de la langue bretonne [et] évoquent la mort "programmée" d'une langue si "dans 20 ans rien ne se passe !" ». (Bretagne Prospective (2008), *Livre Blanc de la Bretagne. Enjeux et perspectives*, Éditions du Temps, Nantes, p. 91). De manière plus générale, ce changement sémantique de la « défense du breton » à la « promotion du breton » révèle une évolution significative dans l'approche de la langue bretonne.

Les grands patrons et la langue bretonne : un attachement sentimental et identitaire

Un investissement relativement récent

La première génération de grands patrons bretons date de l'après-guerre. Les années 1960 sont celles des premiers pas d'Yves Rocher, d'Édouard Leclerc et de François Pinault. Il est frappant de remarquer le peu d'intérêt du monde économique d'alors pour la langue bretonne. Les acteurs régionaux sont effectivement davantage préoccupés par le déclin économique breton et les problèmes sociaux : pertes démographiques, sous-équipement industriel, faible productivité, déséquilibres régionaux, etc. A l'initiative du journaliste Joseph Martray, une structure relativement souple est créée en 1950, le CELIB (Comité d'Études et de Liaison des Intérêts Bretons), qui regroupe des personnalités de toutes tendances politiques (sauf les communistes), des représentants du monde économique et des syndicats. « Il ne s'agissait pas […] de réclamer un statut breton spécifique »,[14] mais d'enrayer le déclin de la Bretagne par un développement et une planification au niveau régional. Même si à terme, le CELIB contribua à réhabiliter l'idée régionale, il n'est pas question au début ni de promotion, ni de défense du breton. Fañch Broudic, spécialiste de la langue bretonne, rappelle dans sa thèse que « c'est en français que s'expriment les nouveaux jeunes agriculteurs modernistes : il est significatif qu'Alexis Gourvennec [fondateur de la Britany Ferries] et de nombreux autres leaders agricoles ne parlent pas le breton. C'est par l'intermédiaire du français que se sont faites la modernisation de l'agriculture bretonne depuis les années 1950 et son insertion dans l'économie de marché ».[15] De plus, force est de constater que les grands patrons bretons sont restés pour certains à l'écart de l'aventure du CELIB.[16] S'ils avaient en commun avec le CELIB le souci

---

[14] Et l'historienne Jacqueline Sainclivier d'ajouter que « ce ne pouvait être à l'ordre du jour moins de cinq ans après la fin d'une guerre où le régionalisme fut assimilé au séparatisme, voire à la collaboration ». Jacqueline Sainclivier (1989), *La Bretagne de 1939 à nos jours*, Ouest-France, Rennes, p. 179. Voir aussi, les écrits du géographe Michel Phlipponneau qui fut un des protagonistes du CELIB, dans : Michel Phlipponneau (1986), *Géopolitique de la Bretagne*, Ouest-France, Rennes.

[15] Fañch Broudic (1995), *La pratique du breton de l'Ancien régime à nos jours*, P.U.R., Rennes, p. 419.

[16] La puissance du réseau célibien a cependant largement contribué au développement économique régional et à l'implantation de certaines entreprises et administrations : par exemple, à la fin des années 1950, le lobbying des élus du CELIB, notamment de René Pleven, auprès du PDG de Citroën, Pierre Bercot, breton d'origine, a été à l'origine de la délocalisation de l'entreprise à Rennes. Pierre Marzin, Lannionais d'origine et polytechnicien, devenu directeur du CNET (Centre national d'études des télécommunications), et ami de René Pleven, a également joué un rôle primordial

de « sortir la Bretagne du sous-développement », ils géraient d'abord leur propre affaire économique et misaient sur le développement de l'économie locale. Yves Rocher s'est par exemple d'abord activé à enrayer le déclin de son village natal, La Gacilly. Le combat d'Édouard Leclerc se situait d'abord au niveau des blocages de la distribution en France : son objectif principal était d'instaurer le modèle du « circuit court » et de casser le monopole des notables industriels et agricoles. La première génération de patrons montre donc un faible intérêt pour la langue bretonne.

Ce n'est que depuis le début des années 1990 que le milieu patronal et économique s'est intéressé aux questions relatives à la langue bretonne.[17] Jean-Pierre Pichard, ancien président du Festival Interceltique de Lorient, constatait en 2000, qu'« il y a dix ans, les chefs d'entreprise trouvaient la bretonnité ringarde ».[18] Contrairement aux « années CE-LIB », les dirigeants économiques fréquentent désormais le monde culturel et la plupart se déclarent être attachés à la Bretagne et à la langue bretonne. Patrick Le Lay défend ardemment la langue bretonne : il est à l'origine de TV Breizh, une chaîne télévisée du groupe TF1 dont l'objectif initial était la promotion du breton. S'il ne le parle pas, il affirme arriver « à peu près à [le] lire ».[19] Vincent Bolloré se définit également comme un « défenseur de la langue bretonne », et précise que « l'imposer serait ridicule et l'empêcher serait criminel ».[20] De manière encore plus significative, l'Institut de Locarn, fondé en 1991 dans le Centre-Bretagne, regroupe de grands dirigeants économiques bretons et a pour objectif de théoriser le lien entre l'économie mondiale et la culture régionale et de former les élites entrepreneuriales bretonnes. La langue bretonne tient une place de choix dans les analyses de ce centre de réflexion et de prospective. À titre d'exemple, les conférences, les débats, les études sont traduites en breton sur le site Internet de l'institut.

---

dans l'implantation du centre à Lannion au début des années 1960. Voir, Erwan Chartier (2001), « Citroën en Bretagne », *ArMen*, n° 119, pp. 3-13 et Yvon Rochard (2001), « Lannion et la Trégor Valley », *ArMen*, n° 124, pp. 2-13.

[17] De manière plus générale, cet investissement régionaliste du patronat breton correspond chronologiquement à ce que Yann Fournis appelle dans sa thèse « l'enracinement du capitalisme en Bretagne » et le « régionalisme patronal » à partir du milieu des années 1980, après la période de fragmentation de la coalition régionaliste avec la défection des notables (1974-1986). Cette nouvelle mobilisation économique régionaliste s'inscrit dans un contexte de « désétatisation » partielle et d'intégration de plus en plus poussée des territoires dans la globalisation économique. Voir, Yann Fournis (2006), *Les régionalismes en Bretagne : la région et l'État (1950-2000)*, P.I.E. Peter Lang, Bruxelles.

[18] *Le Point*, 25 août 2000.

[19] *Bretons*, n° 2, septembre 2005, p. 14.

[20] *Le Télégramme*, 30 juillet 2003, p. 5.

Son fondateur, Joseph Le Bihan, ancien professeur d'économie à HEC, s'exprime d'ailleurs volontiers en breton. Louis Le Duff, membre de l'institut et PDG du Groupe Le Duff attache lui aussi une grande importance à la langue bretonne, qu'il maîtrise très bien. Il a publié en 2006 un livre avec le journaliste Yannick Le Bourdonnec, *Réussir... en toute franchise*,[21] qui disposerait d'une version en breton, *Doned da vad*, signée sous le nom de Loeiz an Duff.[22] Cependant, cette version n'a jamais été éditée et la maquette de la première page relève avant tout d'une opération de communication.

De nombreux chefs d'entreprise ont également signé une pétition lancée en 2004 à destination du Premier ministre, pour « la promotion de la langue bretonne », notamment pour son enseignement. Sont présents Alain Glon, président de l'Institut de Locarn et PDG du groupe Glon Sanders (aliments pour bétail), Jean-Jacques Hénaff (PDG de Hénaff), Joseph Le Bihan, Jean-Guy Le Floc'h (PDG d'Armor-Lux), etc., et, bien entendu, de nombreuses personnalités du monde culturel, universitaire, médiatique et artistique.[23] L'objectif était aussi de faire reconnaître la langue bretonne dans la Constitution française, en modifiant l'article 2, qui stipule que « la langue de la République est le français ». La teneur de la pétition n'était donc pas seulement d'ordre culturel, mais portait aussi une dimension politique forte. Cette demande a plus ou moins porté ses fruits, puisque l'amendement Le Fur, du nom du député des Côtes d'Armor, visant à permettre la reconnaissance des langues régionales dans la constitution, a été adopté le 9 juillet 2008. Cependant, ce nouvel amendement, qui précise que « les langues régionales appartiennent au patrimoine de la France » a été ajouté à l'article 75 de la constitution et non à l'article 2. Il reste que l'engagement de certains chefs d'entreprise a scellé une « union sacrée » entre le monde de la culture et celui de l'économie. Ces grands patrons ne se contentent pas d'affirmer leur soutien à la langue bretonne, ils agissent résolument pour sa promotion.

Les patrons bretons, de puissants mécènes : portées et significations

L'investissement des patrons bretons en faveur de la langue bretonne se traduit par notamment par un soutien financier. Désormais, les promoteurs du breton en appellent au mécénat des grands dirigeants bre-

---

[21] Louis Le Duff (2006), *Réussir [...] en toute franchise*, Albin Michel, Paris.
[22] *Bretons*, n° 16, décembre 2006, p. 53.
[23] *Armor Magazine*, juin 2004, p. 13 ; *Le Monde*, 14 mai 2004.

tons.[24] Cette forme de protection et d'encouragement du travail des acteurs du monde de l'enseignement, de la culture et particulièrement de la langue devient une pratique de plus en plus répandue. L'exemple de l'école bilingue français-breton Diwan à Paris est à cet égard intéressant. Fondées en 1977, les écoles Diwan sont des écoles associatives laïques où l'enseignement est dispensé en breton, utilisant la technique de l'immersion. Elles ont pour la plupart un statut d'établissement privé sous contrat ; ainsi, leur financement peut être pris en charge partiellement par l'État, pour les salaires des enseignants, et par les collectivités territoriales sous forme de subventions. L'antenne parisienne fut créée à la rentrée 2004 et a rapidement connu des difficultés financières. En effet, pour bénéficier du statut d'établissement privé sous contrat, la loi impose à l'établissement de fonctionner sans aides pendant cinq ans. Dès 2006, Diwan-Paris a été confronté à de sérieux problèmes de locaux et de trésorerie. Après un accord avec la mairie de Paris, pour la mise à disposition de locaux, la présidente de l'école, Claude Nadeau, a vivement sollicité l'aide d'entreprises, afin de contribuer au financement de l'établissement. Au titre de la loi du 1er août 2003, qui renforce le mécénat par des facilités fiscales, de nombreux grands patrons se sont portés mécènes : ainsi retrouve-t-on non seulement des entreprises de Bretagne telles CoopAgri, Glon-Sanders et le Groupe Le Duff, mais aussi des patrons bretons vivant à Paris comme les hommes de media Patrick Le Lay (TF1) et Patrick Mahé (*Paris-Match*, *Télé 7 Jours*).[25] La relation entre Louis Le Duff, PDG du Groupe Le Duff et Claude Nadeau, québécoise d'origine et présidente de Diwan-Paris, est représentative de ce nouveau partenariat entre le monde de l'économie et celui de la langue bretonne et de la culture. En 2006, lors de la réception fêtant les trente ans des magasins La Brioche Dorée (groupe Le Duff) à Saint-Malo, Louis Le Duff a tenu à s'entourer du chanteur Alan Stivell et de Claude Nadeau, qui lui ont souhaité un joyeux anniversaire en breton.

Il est possible de retenir deux éléments essentiels de cet épisode Diwan-Paris : tout d'abord, il faut noter la réflexion de plus en plus importante dans les milieux culturels bretons, en particulier ceux concernés directement ou indirectement par la langue, sur le mécénat, notamment celui des grands patrons. L'institut culturel de Bretagne, subventionné à hauteur de 75% par le conseil régional de Bretagne, reçoit des sommes

---

[24] Par exemple, les auteurs du *Livre Blanc de la Bretagne* signalent que « les entreprises bretonnes ne sont pas contre l'idée de reverser un pourcentage de leurs bénéfices à la langue bretonne. Mais il est indispensable d'aller au-delà, de diffuser l'idée d'un mécénat d'un type nouveau, à la bretonne » (Bretagne Prospective, *op. cit.*, p. 113).

[25] Site Internet de Diwan Paris : http://diwanparis.free.fr/20entreprises.html (consulté le 10/09/09).

importantes de dirigeants et d'entreprises bretons comme le patron de media, Patrick Le Lay, l'industriel Jean-Jacques Hénaff, le quotidien *Ouest-France*, la banque Crédit Mutuel de Bretagne, etc.[26] De plus, la présence importante de patrons bretons à Paris est un vecteur de diffusion territoriale non négligeable de la langue bretonne en dehors de son foyer originel, à savoir dans la capitale. Ainsi, la création d'une école Diwan à Paris est présentée comme « le projet de toute la diaspora bretonne ».[27] Cette représentation qu'il existerait une « diaspora bretonne » dans le monde, dont un des facteurs de cohésion résiderait dans la langue, est récente[28] et de plus en plus courante dans certains milieux culturels et économiques, dont le monde patronal. L'Institut de Locarn est par exemple un des piliers du projet « Diaspora Économique Bretonne », créé au début des années 2000, dont le but affiché est le développement économique de la Bretagne dans la mondialisation à travers la promotion de son image et la croissance des exportations.[29] De son côté, l'école Diwan-Paris donne de fait à voir l'existence d'une « diaspora bretonne » construite autour de la langue dans la capitale.[30] Outre les objectifs économiques, le terme de diaspora relève aussi d'une dimension politique et sociale : il suggère en définitive, premièrement, qu'il existe un peuple, en l'occurrence breton, ce qui relève idéologiquement des courants de pensée régionaliste et nationaliste,[31] et deuxièmement, que les Bretons installés en dehors de Bretagne conservent des

---

[26] Entretien avec Yvonig Gicquel, ancien président de l'institut culturel de Bretagne, le 10 avril 2007 à Lorient.

[27] Site internet de Diwan-Paris : www.diwanparis.free.fr (consulté le 10/09/2009).

[28] Jusque dans les années 1970/1980, il était question d'« émigration bretonne » (cf. Elie Gautier (1953), *L'émigration bretonne. Où vont les Bretons émigrants ? Leurs conditions de vie*, Bulletin de l'entraide bretonne de la région parisienne, Paris) et non de « diaspora bretonne ». D'ailleurs, le terme de diaspora fut d'abord uniquement utilisé pour décrire la dispersion de la communauté juive, puis fut généralisé à d'autres communautés à partir des années 1980. L'OBE (Organisation des Bretons Émigrés) fut créée en 1970, mais a été relancée surtout dans les années 1990. En 2005, l'organisation a changé de nom et est désormais appelé *Bretons du Monde*. Sur le concept de diaspora, voir les écrits du géographe Michel Bruneau, notamment : Michel Bruneau (2004), *Diasporas et espaces transnationaux*, Economica, Paris.

[29] Site de l'Institut de Locarn : www.institut-locarn.com. Voir aussi : *Ouest-France*, 6 juin 2006.

[30] L'office de la langue bretonne propose de développer ce projet « dans les plus grandes villes de France pour que les nombreux Bretons qui y travaillent puissent scolariser leurs enfants dans les deux langues ». in : Office de la langue bretonne (2007), *La langue bretonne à la croisée des chemins*, Deuxième rapport général sur l'état de la langue bretonne, Observatoire de la langue bretonne, p. 52).

[31] *Le peuple breton* est par exemple l'organe de presse de l'Union démocratique bretonne (UDB), parti autonomiste de gauche ; et, à l'autre extrémité, Adsav, parti indépendantiste et nationaliste, se nomme « parti du peuple breton ».

liens importants avec le territoire d'origine, développent une conscience identitaire plus ou moins forte et aient une certaine cohésion.[32]

En retour, qu'apporte cet engagement à ces nouveaux mécènes ? Certains y voient une manne financière. Pour Jean-Bernard Solliec, directeur général de la coopérative CoopAgri, son investissement auprès de Diwan permet « de conforter notre notoriété auprès de la diaspora bretonne, très forte à Paris, et d'inciter les gens à consommer nos produits de retour en Bretagne ».[33] Ce soutien financier à la langue bretonne donne aux patrons bretons une image de patrons attachés à la Bretagne. Claude Nadeau, la présidente de Diwan-Paris, avait bien compris cette logique puisqu'en 2006, elle reprenait la notion d'« entreprise citoyenne », pour qualifier l'investissement des patrons en faveur de la langue bretonne. Elle appelait ainsi les « gens d'affaires de Bretagne [à] montrer leur dynamisme et leur implication pour leur région ».[34] C'est pourquoi, ce mécénat ne concerne pas le seul domaine de la langue, mais recouvre une dimension plus généralement identitaire.

Effectivement, cet engagement pour le breton s'apparente pour certains dirigeants à une véritable quête d'identité. Pour Louis Le Duff, Diwan « réunit à la fois [s]es racines et [s]es convictions, parce qu'avant de savoir où l'on va, il faut savoir d'où l'on vient ».[35] Comment comprendre cette récente quête identitaire ? Est-ce une volonté de trouver des repères dans un contexte de mondialisation économique exacerbée et souvent présentée comme débridée ? Le temps du protectionnisme national étant révolu, l'échelon régional ne fonctionnerait-il pas comme une enveloppe rassurante capable de protéger les patrons contre les coups durs et les incertitudes imposées par la mondialisation ? Ne répondrait-elle pas aussi à une recherche d'ordre plus spirituel ? Patrick Le Lay explique que « chaque Breton doit faire quelque chose pour son

---

[32] Relevons simplement qu'il est difficile d'évaluer le degré de cohésion des Bretons installés dans la région parisienne, malgré la présence de nombreuses amicales et associations de Bretons, d'une Maison de la Bretagne dans le XVème arrondissement, de « dîners celtiques », etc. À ce titre, Maurice Le Lannou souligne au sujet des premiers émigrés bretons à Paris à la fin du XIXe siècle/début XXe siècle, en s'appuyant notamment sur les ouvrages de l'abbé Elie Gautier, leur manque de cohésion, « l'assimilation rapide au milieu local dans les domaines linguistique, politique et religieux » et la « singulière aptitude à la débretonnisation » (Maurice Le Lannou, *op. cit.*, pp. 394-402). Voir aussi sur cette question de la cohésion des Bretons de Paris : Annick Madec (2006), « Les Bretons de Paris : un groupe-témoin » pp. 199-222, in Elsa Carrillo-Blouin (coord.) (2006), *Le monde en Bretagne, la Bretagne dans le monde*, Brest, CRBC/UBO.

[33] *Les Échos*, 29 juillet 2004, p. 3.

[34] www.diwanparis.free.fr (consulté le 09/09/2009).

[35] Blog de Louis Le Duff : www.entoutefranchise.typepad.com (consulté le 09/09/2009).

pays dans son domaine de compétence »[36] et relève que « [l]es conceptions [des entrepreneurs bretons] sont celles du patronat chrétien, la
Bretagne ayant été très influencée par le Sillon de Marc Sangnier ».[37] Ce
catholicisme d'inspiration sociale, créée à la fin du XIXe siècle dans la
ligne de conduite tracée par Léon XIII dans l'encyclique *Rerum Nova-
rum* (1891), a pour but originel de concilier le libéralisme économique
et le message de solidarité de l'Évangile en œuvrant pour l'assistance et
l'entraide et préconise le ralliement à la République. Il a eu un rôle très
important dans la création de syndicats et de coopératives en Bretagne.[38]
C'est également cette sensibilité à la doctrine sociale de l'Église qui est
à l'origine de la fondation du quotidien *L'Ouest-Éclair* devenu en 1944
Ouest France, premier quotidien à l'échelle nationale en nombre de
tirage depuis 1975. Les valeurs portées par la démocratie chrétienne
(humanisme, famille, soutien à l'Europe, à l'école confessionnelle)
continuent encore à inspirer la ligne éditoriale garantie par le PDG
François-Régis Hutin.[39] Mais, dans le contexte actuel, cette approche
sociale du catholicisme semble s'être désormais focalisée sur la défense
de la communauté bretonne et notamment de sa langue. Rappelons que
la plupart des grands patrons bretons ont reçu une éducation catholique
relativement poussée et continuent d'être imprégnés par ses valeurs.[40] À
ce titre, certains d'entre eux, notamment l'institut de Locarn, ont soutenu la venue du pape Jean-Paul II en Bretagne en 1996[41] et contribué à
l'édition d'une plaquette bilingue français/breton sur « l'histoire de la
Bretagne à l'époque de Clovis, et les principaux textes de Jean-Paul II et
de l'Église sur les minorités et les cultures minoritaires ».[42] Leur enga-

[36]   *Bretons*, n° 2, sept. 2005, p. 15.
[37]   Cité par Christophe Deloire, *Le Point*, 25 août 2000.
[38]   Sur le catholicisme social et plus généralement la question religieuse en Bretagne,
       voir : Christian Brunel (2003), « L'évolution religieuse de la Bretagne », pp. 539-553
       in : *Toute l'histoire de Bretagne*, Morlaix, Skol Vreizh, et Michel Lagrée (1992),
       Religion et cultures en Bretagne (1850-1950), Paris, Fayard.
[39]   Michel Lagrée, Patrick Harismendy, Michel Denis (2000), *L'Ouest Éclair, Nais-
       sance et essor d'un grand quotidien régional*, Rennes, PUR ; Guy Delorme (2004),
       Ouest-France, histoire du premier quotidien français, Rennes, Apogée.
[40]   François Pinault issu d'une famille pratiquante et de culture républicaine, fut
       scolarisé au collège eudiste Saint-Martin à Rennes ; Édouard Leclerc est passé par le
       petit puis le grand séminaire et son fils Michel-Édouard Leclerc fut également élève
       d'un petit séminaire à Viry-Châtillon en région parisienne.
[41]   Joseph Le Bihan fondateur de l'institut de Locarn et Auguste Génovèse, directeur des
       usines Citroën de Rennes de 1985 à 1996 et président de l'institut de Locarn de 1995
       à 1999, siégeaient avec d'autres personnalités du monde économique, culturel et po-
       litique au sein du « Comité pour une visite du pape en Bretagne » (COVIP). *Le Télé-
       gramme*, 20 mai 1996 et 11 juin 1996.
[42]   *Le Télégramme*, 11 juin 1996. Quelques mois avant l'arrivée du pape, le COVIP
       s'est opposé aux évêques de France pour protester contre ce qu'il a appelé « le "dé-

gement pour la langue bretonne et plus généralement pour la Bretagne peut alors apparaître comme une quête teintée d'une certaine religiosité, entendue dans le sens de dévouement : les chefs d'entreprise bretons seraient, en quelque sorte, redevables de leur appartenance à la Bretagne et de leur communauté de naissance. Faire du catholicisme social avec l'« identité bretonne » et le breton revient à une sorte de « catholicisme identitaire ».[43]

Les media bretons jouent également un rôle important dans la construction d'une image « bretonne » des patrons. Ils diffusent des représentations de patrons actifs, dynamiques, attachés à la cause bretonne et particulièrement à la langue bretonne. Le journaliste, Yannick Le Bourdonnec, fin connaisseur du milieu des dirigeants bretons, insiste sur le rôle de la presse qui selon lui « a renvoyé un regard bienveillant et flatteur des grands patrons bretons ».[44] Il a réalisé de nombreuses interviews de grands patrons dans le quotidien régional *Le Télégramme* pendant l'été 2003 : son but, dit-il, était de « faire adopter un discours régionaliste aux grands patrons afin que les Bretons, qui sont assez légitimistes, puissent suivre ».[45] À ce titre, Thibaut Courcelle a montré le rôle de la presse quotidienne régionale dans la création d'une « identité » bretonne.[46] Les magazines et autres revues à connotation bretonne, comme *Armor Magazine* et *Bretons*, s'inscrivent dans le même discours. Tous deux multiplient ainsi les unes mettant en scène des patrons bretons : *Armor Magazine* a décerné sept fois la

---

tournement" de la visite du pape [...] pour en faire un rassemblement des "Églises du grand Ouest" » et a dénoncé le « battage médiatique autour du baptême de Clovis, évènement qui ne concerne nullement la Bretagne qui était indépendante et christianisée bien longtemps avant ». Cité par *Le Télégramme*, 11 juin 1996. L'édition de la plaquette bilingue résulte de cette protestation.

[43] À ce titre, une frange de l'Église s'est affirmée comme un nouvel acteur dans le débat identitaire en Bretagne en revendiquant son attachement à la langue et à la culture bretonnes à travers notamment la Lettre pastorale (rédigée en français et en breton) de Mgr Gourvès, alors Évêque de Vannes en 2003. Il souligne qu'« un lien très fort a [...] longtemps existé entre le fait d'être Breton et de s'affirmer Catholique » et que « la langue jouait un rôle important dans le couple ainsi formé ». Il appelle désormais les services de l'Église de Vannes à « donner à la langue et à la culture bretonnes la place qui leur revient lors des cérémonies religieuses » et « favoriser la diffusion de certains programmes en langue bretonne » (François-Mathurin Gourvès (2003), *Le renouveau de la culture bretonne : un défi pour l'Église*, Lettre pastorale, Évêché de Vannes). Notons que c'est également Mgr Gourvès qui fut à l'origine de la venue du pape Jean-Paul II en Bretagne en 1996.

[44] Entretien avec Yannick Le Bourdonnec, le 15 mars 2007 à Paris.

[45] *Id.*

[46] Thibault Courcelle (2003), « Le rôle de la presse quotidienne régionale bretonne dans la création d'une "identité bretonne" : étude comparative de *Ouest-France* et du *Télégramme* », *Hérodote*, n° 110, pp. 129-148.

décoration de « Breton de l'année » à un dirigeant breton ; c'est donc environ une décoration sur trois depuis 1977 qui fut attribuée à un chef d'entreprise.

Au-delà de l'investissement purement sentimental et identitaire, la langue bretonne est également un moyen pour de nombreux patrons de s'insérer différemment dans la mondialisation de l'économie.

La langue bretonne, un nouvel enjeu économique dans la mondialisation de la Bretagne ?

Une langue abordée comme fondement culturel et symbole identitaire qui doit servir la mondialisation économique de la Bretagne

Afin d'appréhender l'attachement des grands patrons bretons à la langue bretonne, il convient de comprendre la représentation récente que se font beaucoup d'acteurs en Bretagne de la mondialisation économique. Claude Nadeau défendait en 2006 son appel aux entreprises bretonnes pour le sauvetage de Diwan-Paris en argumentant qu'« une Bretagne forte culturellement, c'est une Bretagne forte économiquement ».[47] Pendant très longtemps, le monde de la culture et celui de l'économie étaient jugés imperméables, et paraissent encore pour certains antinomiques. Cependant, comme le soulignait le journaliste Yvon Rochard, lors du lancement en 2000 de la télévision en breton, TV Breizh, « les industriels bretons […], depuis quelques années [ont] découvert les délices de l'union libre entre économie et culture ».[48] Comment expliquer la percée fulgurante de cette nouvelle approche du couple économie/culture dans la pensée contemporaine ? Le journaliste et militant breton Jean Bothorel apporte un élément de réponse : il affirme que Patrick Le Lay « a compris que la quête identitaire, loin de s'opposer à la mondialisation, en est, au contraire, l'enfant légitime, le compagnon naturel ».[49] À son tour, Claude Nadeau, affirme qu'« à l'heure de la mondialisation des échanges, la Bretagne représente l'accord parfait entre le profond ancrage dans ses racines et l'ouverture vers le monde et vers l'avenir » et que la langue bretonne représente dans ce contexte « une plus-value importante ».[50] La culture et le mar-

---

[47] www.diwanparis.free.fr (consulté le 09/09/2009).

[48] Yvon Rochard (2000), « TV Breizh. Première chaîne privée régionale et bilingue d'Europe », *ArMen*, n° 116, p. 6.

[49] Jean Bothorel (2001), *Un terroriste breton*, Calmann-Lévy, Paris, p. 10. Jean Bothorel est l'auteur d'une biographie sur François Pinault et d'une autre sur Vincent Bolloré.

[50] www.diwanparis.free.fr (consulté le 10/09/2009).

queur linguistique seraient donc dans la mondialisation un facteur déterminant dans l'attractivité économique du territoire breton.[51] Posséder un « logiciel culturel »[52] serait en quelque sorte indispensable dans la compétition économique mondiale et permettrait l'ouverture à de nouveaux marchés. L'Institut de Locarn est sans aucun doute le plus grand théoricien de cette nouvelle approche du monde. Son fondateur, Joseph Le Bihan parle de « glocalisme » pour traduire le partenariat entre la culture et l'économie dans la mondialisation : la culture serait au local ce que l'économie serait au global. L'Institut de Locarn est à ce sujet particulièrement représentatif : ainsi, à « stratégies internationales », l'institut a accolé le mot « cultures ». « Le but de l'association est d'appuyer cet élargissement du champ d'actions des acteurs du développement économique de la Bretagne sur un approfondissement de l'identité culturelle de la région ; […] et ce notamment par […] l'enracinement de l'internationalisme de la Bretagne sur son histoire, sa culture, son identité […] ».[53] En 2007, un séminaire traitait explicitement du « scénario glocal »,[54] également appelé par les membres de l'institut de « scénario glocarn », tant l'Institut de Locarn en est l'exemple type. Michel Houdebine, PDG d'une entreprise d'agroalimentaire et membre de l'institut, voit dans la mondialisation, « une chance pour le redéploiement du local ».[55] Sa conclusion est claire : « Économie et culture, même combat ».[56] La « glocalisation » est donc une nouvelle approche de la mondialisation économique au sein de laquelle la langue régionale apparaîtrait comme un pilier de la culture locale.

Ainsi, la langue bretonne est reléguée par certains acteurs économiques et culturels au rang de symbole « identitaire » et devient un élément incontournable de ce qu'ils appellent le « logiciel culturel »[57] breton. Dans cette optique de « glocalisation », de nombreux patrons bretons contribuent indéniablement à enfermer la langue bretonne dans ce que l'ethnologue suédois Orvar Löfgren a appelé un « kit » identi-

---

[51] Voir le chapitre « Changer les idées reçues. Les dynamiques réelles entre langue, culture et économie » dans : Bretagne Prospective, *op. cit.*, pp. 73-117.

[52] Yannick Le Bourdonnec (1996), *Le miracle breton*, Calmann-Lévy, Paris, p. 225.

[53] Statuts de l'association « Institut de Locarn, cultures et stratégies internationales », 5 avril 1991.

[54] www.institut-locarn.com.

[55] Michel Houdebine (2000), *Vive les maquis économiques*, Ad Lib, Rennes, p. 34.

[56] *Ibid.*, p. 48.

[57] Yannick Le Bourdonnec (1996), *op. cit.* Dans le *Livre Blanc de la Bretagne*, les auteurs signalent aussi que « la langue en tant que moyen de communication […] est une base fondamentale de la culture bretonne » et se demandent plus loin s'il ne faudrait pas « étendre la notion de culture à la notion d'identité ». (Bretagne Prospective, *op. cit.*, p. 89 et p. 109).

taire, repris par Anne-Marie Thiesse dans son ouvrage intitulé *La Créa-tion des identités nationales*.[58] Il n'est pas inutile d'en rappeler les fondements tant la notion d'« identité » est abordée de manière essentia-liste et comprise comme une donnée « naturelle » dans les milieux nationalistes et régionalistes et non comme une construction historique précise et datée.[59] Ce kit comprend plusieurs éléments symboliques comme un paysage typique, un folklore, des héros nationaux, des lieux de mémoire, une langue, des représentations officielles (drapeau, hymne), des traditions culinaires, etc. Depuis le début des années 1990, les entreprises ont compris qu'exploiter le « label breton » pouvait être particulièrement lucratif. Thibault Courcelle parle de « régionalisme business ».[60] Chaque élément du « kit » est d'une manière ou d'une autre potentiellement commercialisable. Ce « business culturel » est non seulement bénéfique à l'économie, mais il est aussi présenté comme un moyen de survie pour la culture et la langue. Jakez Bernard, alors Vice-président de l'association « Produit en Bretagne » chargé du volet culturel, expliquait que « pour que la culture perdure, il faut qu'elle soit marchande ».[61] La langue bretonne, en tant que pilier du « kit identi-taire », n'échappe bien évidemment pas à la règle de la commercialisa-tion.

---

[58] Orvar Löfgren (1989), « The Nationalization of Culture », *Ethnologia Europea*, Volume XIX, pp. 5-24, cité dans : Anne-Marie Thiesse (1999), *La Création des identités nationales. Europe XVIII-XXe siècles*, Seuil, Paris. Concernant plus spécifi-quement l'histoire de France, la publication des *Lieux de mémoire* dirigés par Pierre Nora à partir de 1984, puis les travaux de Suzanne Citron en 1987 sur *Le Mythe na-tional. L'histoire de France en questions*, ont joué un rôle pionnier pour mettre en évidence les fondements du « roman national » (P. Nora), ce récit patriotique édifié par les historiens du XIXe siècle (E. Lavisse) à la gloire de la nation française. Ce n'est que dans les années 1990 que s'est ancrée l'idée que les nations étaient des constructions et non des essences.

[59] À ce titre, Catherine Bertho a étudié les différentes étapes de la construction de l'image de la Bretagne au XIXe siècle. Elle a montré qu'elle évoluait en trois temps, selon des objectifs politiques et idéologiques bien précis : sous la Restauration, c'est l'image d'une Bretagne sauvage qui ressort ; puis à partir de 1850, la Bretagne est perçue comme une province conservatrice, paysanne et réactionnaire ; enfin, au tour-nant du siècle, c'est l'image de Bécassine qui donne à voir la Bretagne. Catherine Bertho (1980), « L'invention de la Bretagne. Genèse sociale d'un stéréotype », *Actes de la recherche en sciences sociales*, n° 35, pp. 45-62.

[60] Thibault Courcelle (2003), « Le rôle de la presse quotidienne régionale bretonne dans la création d'une "identité bretonne" : étude comparative de *Ouest-France* et du *Té-légramme* », *Hérodote*, n° 110, p. 148.

[61] Propos tenus lors du colloque « Du CELIB à Produit en Bretagne », organisé par l'Institut culturel de Bretagne, à Ploemeur, le 30 septembre 2006. Voir aussi : *Ouest-France*, 27 septembre 2006, cahier spécial du colloque de l'Institut culturel de Bre-tagne.

L'opération « Produit en Bretagne » est, à ce sujet, particulièrement intéressante. « Produit en Bretagne » est une association d'entreprises créée en 1995 « pour promouvoir l'achat citoyen breton ». Elle a été lancée à l'initiative de quatre chefs d'entreprise du Nord Finistère et plus particulièrement du Léon. Sous l'impulsion de Jean Bannier du Crédit Mutuel de Bretagne et de Jean-Yves Chalm du *Télégramme*, le réseau s'est mis en place avec l'aide de Jean-Claude Simon de la coopérative Even et de Claude Pujol du distributeur É. Leclerc. Aujourd'hui, « Produit en Bretagne » dispose d'une véritable force de frappe car l'association regroupe 200 entreprises, qui représentent 100 000 emplois et 15 milliards d'euros. La langue bretonne est devenue un élément central de sa communication, notamment lors des campagnes publicitaires menées en mai 2007 et mai 2008 dans les transports franciliens.[62] Aussi, depuis 2007, l'association a passé un partenariat avec l'Office de la langue bretonne, afin de créer une interface en breton sur son site Internet.

Comment expliquer cette campagne de publicité en breton dans l'agglomération parisienne, c'est-à-dire dans un espace où il est susceptible d'être le moins compris ? Conformément à l'idée de « glocalisme », la langue bretonne n'est pas considérée comme un moyen de communication mais bien comme un produit commercial, qui met en avant un aspect du « kit identitaire ». La ville, qui plus est celle de Paris, est avant tout un grand marché économique. De plus, c'est un moyen pour diffuser la langue bretonne, en dehors de son territoire originel de la Basse-Bretagne. Une vaste campagne de publicité a également été mise en place à Nantes et à Rennes, dès 2006.[63] Encore une fois, ce sont de potentiels marchés de consommation. Mais surtout, en choisissant d'être présent dans ces deux villes, « Produit en Bretagne » cherche à diffuser la langue bretonne dans le territoire de l'ancien duché de Bretagne. L'objectif est donc de faire coïncider le territoire de l'usage de la

---

[62] Après un premier essai en 2006, 350 panneaux « Produit en Bretagne » avec le message en breton « Plijadur penn da benn » (« du plaisir du début à la fin ») ont été affichés du 22 au 31 mai 2007 dans le métro parisien, mais aussi dans 120 magasins et grandes surfaces de la capitale et de sa région. L'opération a été renouvelée en 2008. Notons pour mai 2009, le nouveau logo « Breizh da dan va » (« la Bretagne à savourer »), destiné aux campagnes publicitaires dans les Pays de la Loire et en Ile-de-France. Site internet de l'association, www.produitenbretagne.com. Voir aussi : www.blog.breizh.bz/?207-produit-en-bretagne-fait-le-printemps (consulté le 09/09/2009).

[63] Campagne de publicité réalisée au second trimestre 2006 dans les transports et dans les grandes surfaces de Rennes et de Nantes, mettant en avant le drapeau breton et la langue bretonne (logo « Plijadur penn da benn ») et dont le message portait sur l'achat militant en faveur du développement de l'emploi régional. Site internet de l'association, www.produitenbretagne.com (consulté le 09/09/2009).

langue bretonne avec celui de la Bretagne dite « historique ».[64] L'économie milite indéniablement pour le rattachement de la Loire-Atlantique à la Bretagne en se servant du breton dans ses campagnes publicitaires : bien qu'en anglais, le slogan « I love Nantes... depuis toujours » affiché sur les bus et tramways nantais en 2006 en est révélateur. L'association appuie également la politique de « bretonnisation » de l'espace urbain menée par la ville de Rennes, dont le but est de (ren)forcer sa légitimité de métropole-capitale de toute la Bretagne. Il n'en demeure pas moins que le territoire historique de la langue, à savoir la Basse-Bretagne, ne correspond pas et n'a jamais correspondu au territoire de la Bretagne : même s'il a pu y être parlé pour diverses raisons, notamment économiques, le breton n'a jamais été la langue quotidienne, ni à Nantes, ni à Rennes.[65] Au-delà du simple marketing « identitaire », « Produit en Bretagne » reprend les principes d'un nationalisme régional fondé sur une idée d'unité de la Bretagne. Yvonig Gicquel, ancien Président de l'institut culturel de Bretagne, résumait bien cette tendance : « si il n'y avait pas l'esprit régionaliste chez les patrons bretons, l'association "Produit en Bretagne" n'aurait jamais vu le jour, Locarn n'aurait jamais vu le jour ».[66] Il est à noter que « Produit en Bretagne » a pour siège social l'Institut de Locarn, ce qui traduit un lien entre les deux organismes. En se servant de la langue bretonne, l'économie participe au développement du régionalisme, mais peut-être pas toujours de manière aussi intentionnelle que ne l'affirmait Yvonig Gicquel. Pour une frange de patrons, l'idéal régionaliste et politique est premier, car il doit servir la mise en place d'une nouvelle économie mondiale fondée sur la glocalisation. Pour le reste des dirigeants économiques, l'approche n'est pas autant idéologique, mais en utilisant la langue bretonne comme argument de vente, ils contribuent à l'enfermer dans le « kit identitaire » et fixent par là même les bases du régionalisme.

Un intérêt paradoxal et contesté

Cependant la promotion de la langue bretonne peut parfois se heurter aux logiques économiques bien établies et devenir une mauvaise affaire commerciale. Au début de l'association « Produit en Bretagne », les

---

[64] Barbara Loyer (2005), « Bretagne », *Nouvelle géopolitique des régions françaises*, Fayard, Paris, p. 308. À ce titre, les auteurs du *Livre Blanc de la Bretagne* donnent l'exemple de l'opération de communication en breton menée par l'« enseigne U » à Verne-sur-Seiche, en Ille-et-Vilaine, et concluent qu'« utiliser la langue bretonne marque symboliquement l'entrée en Bretagne ». (Bretagne Prospective, *op. cit.*, p. 83).

[65] D'ailleurs, François Pinault, originaire de Trévérien en Ille-et-Vilaine, n'oublie pas de rappeler qu'il parle gallo.

[66] Entretien avec Yvonig Gicquel, le 10 avril 2007 à Lorient.

chefs d'entreprise ont refusé que la langue bretonne soit utilisée dans les slogans.[67] De même, le journaliste Yannick le Bourdonnec, qui a réalisé les entretiens avec les grands patrons bretons au *Télégramme*, signale que « Louis Le Duff avait refusé de faire paraître le titre de son article en breton, bien qu'il soit bretonnant ».[68] Dans certaines circonstances, l'étiquette « Bretagne » et donc la langue bretonne ne semblent plus autant vendeuses, notamment lorsque les marchés s'éloignent du simple business culturel. Louis Le Duff a décidé de vendre ses produits aux États-Unis « dans une décoration inspirée d'une chaumière normande avec un feu de cheminée » car c'est la vision de la Normandie du débarquement qu'auraient les Américains de « l'art de vivre à la française ».[69] Pareillement, de nombreux grands patrons bretons n'ont pas adhéré à l'association « Produit en Bretagne », et leurs produits ne sont donc pas estampillés du logo. Louis Le Duff n'est pas membre, ni Yves Rocher, ni Vincent Bolloré et encore moins François Pinault. On comprend aisément que sur les marchés étrangers, la qualité « produit en Bretagne » des croissants ou des cosmétiques « produits en Bretagne » n'élargit pas automatiquement la clientèle. Les chefs d'entreprise sont avant tout des acteurs économiques. Vincent Bolloré résume cette position : « l'affectif compte mais il s'arrête là où commence la déraison. […] L'affectif mal utilisé peut coûter très cher et, dans certaines décisions, se retourner contre les intérêts de l'entreprise ».[70] L'attitude des chefs d'entreprise bretons est semblable à celle du reste de la population bretonne. Suite à un sondage réalisé fin 2001, Fañch Broudic a montré les distorsions entre d'un côté l'unanimité des Bretons pour conserver la langue et d'un autre côté, leur réserve quand à son utilité dans la société.[71] Quand la langue bretonne s'avère être lucrative, n'est-ce pas finalement qu'un simple appoint économique pour les patrons bretons ? Jean Bannier, un des quatre fondateurs de « Produit en Bretagne » déplore les dérives de l'association qui mettent le marketing breton avant l'économie régionale : ce serait devenu aujourd'hui plus une « organisation de nature commerciale et de marketing qu'un regroupement de chefs d'entreprise axé sur l'achat citoyen breton et donc la défense d'emplois ».[72] Il y a incontestablement un certain opportu-

---

[67] Bretagne Prospective, *op. cit.*, p. 92.

[68] Entretien avec Yannick Le Bourdonnec, le 9 avril 2007 à Carhaix. Il s'agissait de l'article au sujet de Louis Le Duff réalisé par Yannick Le Bourdonnec, paru dans *Le Télégramme* pour la série estivale « Grands patrons et Bretons » : *Le Télégramme*, 14 août 2003.

[69] Louis Le Duff, *in* Ronan Le Flécher, Didier Le Gorrec (2006), *La Bretagne : tout le monde en parle*, Éditions des Dessins et des Mots, Bannalec, p. 92.

[70] *Le Télégramme*, 30 juillet 2003, p. 5.

[71] Fañch Broudic (2007), *Le breton, une langue en questions*, Emgleo Breiz, Brest.

[72] Entretien avec Jean Bannier, le 5 avril 2007 au Relecq-Kerhuon.

nisme économique de la part de nombreux chefs d'entreprise, qui ont compris que le label « Bretagne » et l'utilisation de la langue bretonne pouvaient ouvrir des marchés et être particulièrement lucratifs.

C'est cette approche de la langue et plus généralement de la culture, qui est dénoncée par certains écrivains. Françoise Morvan, dont l'essai autobiographique sur le nationalisme et la dérive identitaire en Bretagne[73] suscita beaucoup de débats, s'insurge contre ce « régionalisme business » : elle dit constater que

> la mainmise de l'économique et du politique sur la culture est, de toute façon, désastreuse. [...] La censure s'exerce de manière détournée : on ne vous publie pas, on ne vous donne pas de subventions, on vous ignore et on promeut la Fest Yves (c'était l'une des grandes actions du Centre régional du livre : offrez des livres bretons pour la saint Yves), le folklore frelaté, la poésie bardique et le n'importe quoi en breton unifié.[74]

En 2001, un musicien, Jean-Michel Veillon, a refusé le prix « Produit en Bretagne » et s'en est expliqué dans un texte dénonçant notamment « la logique de "Produit en Bretagne" » selon laquelle « la culture bretonne doit s'adapter à l'économie en cours, car sa valeur ne dépend que de son aptitude à être commercialisée ».[75] À l'initiative du poète François Rannou, un collectif de plus d'une centaine d'écrivains appelé « Gardons les yeux ouverts »,[76] a été créé en 2000, afin de résister à cette intrusion de l'économie dans la culture. Il dénonce lui aussi la sélection de la culture au profit de la seule culture « identitaire » et relève que « les critères retenus pour évaluer une œuvre ne sont ni esthétiques ni littéraires »,[77] mais que seule l'utilisation du breton ou la référence à la Bretagne sont désormais valorisées.

Enfin, il convient de noter que certains patrons bretons ont une approche différente de la langue bretonne et se montrent plutôt réticents quant à sa promotion. Michel-Édouard Leclerc précise que son « attachement à la région et à sa culture ne passe par la langue. Je ne parle pas le breton. [...] je ne suis pas sensible aux sonorités très gutturales du breton ». Il place également la question de la langue bretonne sur le terrain politique : « Je ne me reconnais pas toujours, loin de là, dans les divagations idéologiques et le fatras politique qu'on veut lier à cette

---

[73] Françoise Morvan (2002), *Le Monde comme si. Nationalisme et dérive identitaire en Bretagne*, Actes Sud, Arles.

[74] Entretien avec Françoise Morvan, le 20 janvier 2007 à Rennes.

[75] Cité par Françoise Morvan : entretien avec Françoise Morvan, le 20 janvier 2007 à Rennes.

[76] www.lmda.net/direct/petition001019.html.

[77] François Rannou (2005), *Une littérature de refondation*, www.europe-revue.info/2005/bretagneintro.htm.

cause ».[78] L'approche de la langue bretonne par les dirigeants économiques bretons est donc multiple. Si certains d'entre eux montrent une
certaine distance vis-à-vis du breton, d'autres l'utilisent comme res-
source économique. Un troisième groupe de patrons a enfin une approche plus idéologique et politique de la langue et les intérêts économiques semblent alors passer au second plan.

Carte 1

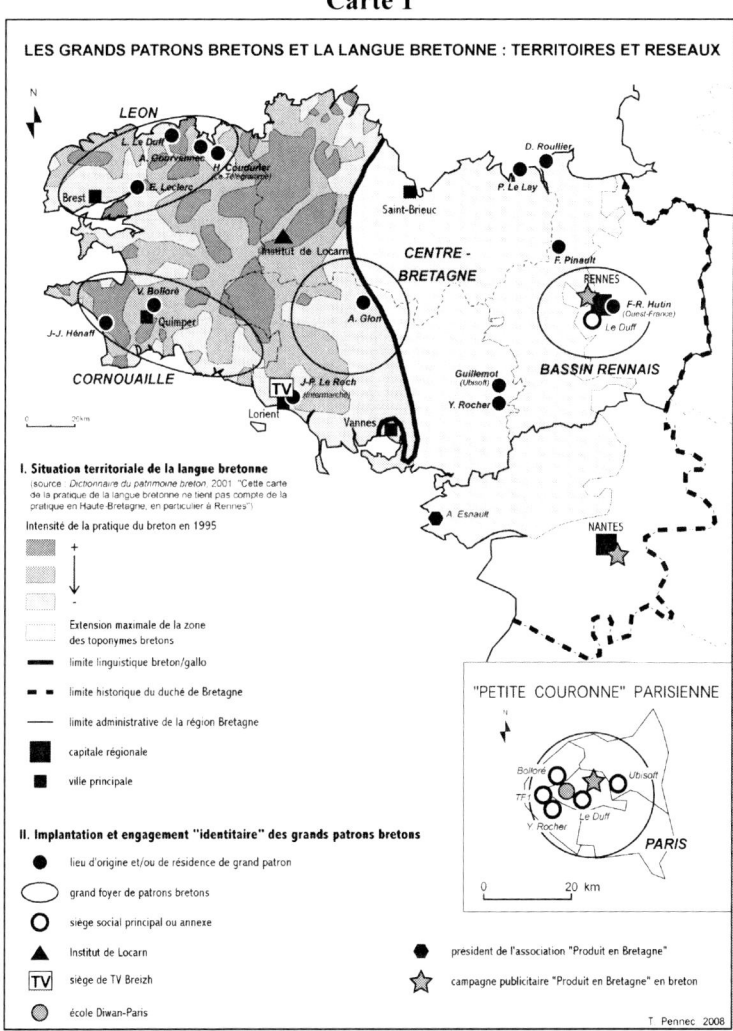

---

[78] Michel Édouard Leclerc (2004), *Du bruit dans le Landerneau*, Albin Michel, Paris,
pp. 66-67.

Summary

Captains of industry of Breton origin – people like François Pinault, Vincent Bolloré, Michel-Édouard Leclerc, Yves Rocher, Louis Le Duff, Patrick le Lay, etc. – are among the most important not only in France but also in Europe, not to say the world. Most of them would openly state their attachment to Brittany and more particularly to the Breton language. The objective of this article is not to look into their involvement in the social or economic sphere, but rather to look at things from a geopolitical perspective. Indeed, in their defence of the Breton language, the power of these employers takes on a political dimension. This economic elite has thus become a new player in the regionalist debate in Brittany. What role does a business bourgeoisie play in the political identity of a territory?

Les territoires de la langue basque

Conflits et représentations

Barbara LOYER

Université Paris 8

Le cas de la langue basque présente un grand intérêt méthodologique car une même langue minoritaire est parlée dans trois territoires aux caractéristiques juridiques et politiques différentes : deux en Espagne, la communauté autonome d'Euskadi et la communauté autonome de Navarre, et un en France, la partie occidentale du département des Pyrénées Atlantiques reconnue comme « pays »[1] en janvier 1997 par arrêté préfectoral.

L'euskara : une très ancienne langue de paysans convertie en langue nationale

La communauté autonome d'Euskadi, est constituée de trois provinces, Biscaye, Guipuscoa, Alava. Les premières élections du Parlement autonome eurent lieu en 1980. Elles portèrent au pouvoir le parti nationaliste basque (PNV : *Partido Nacionalista Vasco*) qui a gouverné ce territoire sans discontinuité jusqu'en 2009. Pour la première fois, en mai 2009, un président non nationaliste basque (Patxi López, Parti socialiste) a été élu à la tête du gouvernement autonome. Ce contexte est évidemment très important à prendre en compte en ce qui concerne la politique linguistique depuis trente ans. En effet, la société est massivement hispanophone, notamment dans les villes, mais la langue basque est au cœur du projet des nationalistes basques. Depuis trente ans, ils ont œuvré pour lui donner toutes les fonctions d'une langue d'État : on la

---

[1]   Territoire de projet caractérisé par une cohésion géographique, économique, culturelle ou sociale, pour le développement de contrats de pays au sens de la loi du 4 février 1995, dite loi Pasqua ou LOADT (Loi d'Orientation pour l'Aménagement et le Développement du Territoire). Elle est complétée par l'article 25 de la loi du 25 juin 1999, *Loi d'Orientation de l'Aménagement Durable du Territoire* dite loi Voynet (Décret d'application n° 2000-909 du 19 septembre 2000, paru au *Journal Officiel* le 20 septembre 2000).

parle au Parlement, dans les administrations, à l'école, à l'université. La langue basque doit être la langue de l'enseignement national, et les grandes œuvres littéraires enseignées à l'école sont traduites en euskara (langue basque). Le président de la communauté autonome basque de 1999 à 2009, Juan José Ibarretxe, ne la connaissait pas et l'a apprise durant ses mandats. En 2002, 94 018 672 euros ont été consacrés par l'ensemble des institutions gouvernementales à la promotion de la langue basque.[2]

Pour atteindre ce résultat, une loi de « normalisation » de l'usage de la langue basque fut votée en 1982.[3] Cette loi établit la co-officialité de l'euskara et de l'espagnol sur tout le territoire de la communauté, le bilinguisme de l'administration, le format des traductions des documents officiels. Elle prévoit les modalités d'apprentissage de l'euskara par les écoliers et le personnel administratif (article 14). Cela représente une véritable révolution dans l'histoire de la langue basque. Sans revenir sur le très long passé de cet idiome, dont on ne connaît pas les racines tant il est ancien, on rappellera néanmoins qu'il a toujours été une langue du peuple, surtout rurale. Il n'y a pas eu d'État basque qui aurait dans le passé créé des archives dans cette langue. Les aristocrates puis les bourgeois ont adopté la langue espagnole. Le basque, comme le breton en France, a été la langue des gens de la campagne ou de ceux qui venaient servir les grandes familles de la ville, et c'est une des raisons supplémentaires qui ont amené les couches sociales supérieures à la délaisser. L'Église, en revanche, a utilisé l'euskara, pour être au plus près de ses ouailles. L'enjeu du contrôle ecclésial était particulier dans cette région car elle est le berceau de la compagnie de Jésus (Azpeitia, ville natale de Saint Ignace de Loyola, se trouve dans l'actuelle communauté autonome. Saint François-Xavier était un noble de Navarre, province limitrophe de la communauté autonome basque).

À la date où fut votée la loi de normalisation, le nombre de bascophones était en recul, surtout dans la jeunesse, et les personnes qui parlaient le basque ne savaient souvent ni le lire ni l'écrire car il n'y avait pratiquement aucun texte dans cette langue à part les missels. Le mouvement en faveur d'un renouveau linguistique a démarré dans les années 1960. La période antérieure était en effet très défavorable. Le fondateur du nationalisme basque au début du XXe n'a pas tout de suite accordé d'importance à l'euskara, et la guerre civile espagnole est arrivée très vite après la fondation du parti nationaliste basque (1898). De la victoire du général Franco (1939) à sa mort (1975) la langue

---

[2] Viceconsejería de Política Lingüística, Departamento de Cultura, http://www1. euskadi.net/euskara_adierazleak/Dialog/Saveshow.apl (consulté le 25/04/09). Ce site du gouvernement donne des chiffres pour 2000 et 2002.

[3] Ley 10/1982 de Normalización del Uso del Euskera.

basque est minorée par le pouvoir[4] La loi de 1982 marque donc un tournant d'une portée exceptionnelle. Elle accorde le droit de s'adresser en basque et en castillan à l'oral ou par écrit avec l'administration, et celui de recevoir l'enseignement dans les deux langues officielles.

La construction d'une langue d'État

Cette révolution est à la fois linguistique et politique. Linguistiquement, elle mène à imposer une version unifiée du basque car ses usages s'étaient différenciés d'un extrême à l'autre de la zone bascophone au point de poser des problèmes d'intercompréhension. L'avènement d'une langue urbaine relègue alors la langue rurale et traditionnelle des différentes provinces et aboutit à l'imposition d'une norme nationale. Il a fallu inventer des nouveaux mots pour faire entrer dans l'euskara les concepts modernes. La société basque dans son ensemble a accepté cet effort. Il y a eu également très peu de résistance à la mise en place d'un système d'enseignement axé sur la croissance de l'enseignement bilingue. Le nationalisme espagnol du régime franquiste a servi de socle, après la mort du dictateur, pour bâtir un consensus en faveur d'une politique linguistique favorable aux langues régionales, que la société percevait comme une juste réparation. D'après les statistiques de la communauté autonome, en 2006, 37,3% des habitants étaient recensés comme bascophones (774 894) au lieu de 30% en 1996 (636 816 personnes). En 2006 40% étaient complètement ignorants de cette langue contre 49% en 1996.[5] La progression du nombre de personnes se déclarant soit bilingue soit « presque bilingue » est due en grande partie à la mise en place d'un système éducatif organisé en trois branches. Le modèle D, où tous les cours sont en basque, le modèle B, où certains cours sont en basque et d'autres en espagnol, le modèle A, où tous les cours sont en espagnol mais où l'on reçoit un enseignement du basque (NB il n'y a pas de lettre C en basque). La nécessité de parler l'euskara pour accéder à un nombre important d'emplois est un des éléments-clés expliquant la croissance, sur le long terme, des inscriptions dans les modèles B et D. En 2008, 55 % des élèves sont inscrits dans le modèle D (tout en basque), 23% en bilingue, et 20% dans le modèle A (espa-

---

[4]   La représentation commune est celle d'une féroce répression franquiste contre l'usage du basque. Mais elle est relative. Les gens continuent à la parler, l'académie de la langue basque, *euskaltzaindia*, n'a jamais cessé ses travaux, et un mouvement culturel en basque (*Ez dok amahiru*) s'est développé dès les années 1960. En revanche, rien n'est fait pour que son usage se développe, au contraire.

[5]   Eustat, *Evolución de la población de 2 y más años por nivel global de euskera, territorio histórico y año. 1996-2006*, disponible à : www.eustat.es/elementos/ele0000400/tbl0000487_c.html (consulté le 20/04/09).

gnol).[6] Ces pourcentages devraient aller en augmentant puisque la proportion d'élèves suivant tous les enseignements en langue basque est plus élevée en maternelle (68,9%).

La mise en œuvre concrète de ce qui fut perçu comme un beau symbole de fraternité pose cependant quelques problèmes. Concernant les fonctionnaires, par exemple, selon le degré de responsabilité du poste administratif, un niveau correspondant de maîtrise de l'euskara est exigé. La loi prévoit que la part de la connaissance linguistique dans les concours administratifs sera établie par le gouvernement autonome basque. Les fonctionnaires peuvent être libérés d'une partie de leur service pour assister à des cours afin de se mettre au niveau requis. Certains y parviennent, d'autres non. Il faut savoir en effet que la langue basque est difficile à maîtriser.[7] L'euskara a une grammaire et un vocabulaire absolument différents de ceux des langues romanes, il se construit sur la base de déclinaisons multiples fort complexes. Les analyses concernant les relations entre les citoyens des régions officiellement bilingues doivent tenir compte des difficultés ou facilités d'apprentissage de chaque langue. Rendre le catalan obligatoire dans une partie de l'Espagne ne change pas autant la vie des gens car tout Espagnol comprend plus ou moins le catalan. C'est la même chose pour le galicien, langue romane très proche de l'espagnol. En revanche, la diffusion du basque pose des problèmes spécifiques liés aux difficultés de la langue. Certaines personnes n'ont pas atteint le niveau requis pour leur poste. Elles ont alors été employées à des tâches subalternes, ce qui a parfois suscité des protestations. Pour les embauches nouvelles, il faut avoir le niveau.

Les polémiques sur le poids de l'euskara dans les critères de sélection sont récurrentes. Ainsi, par exemple, lors de la publication en novembre 2008 par le service basque de la Santé du barème des compétences exigées pour être infirmière ou technicien spécialiste en anatomie pathologique. Dans les deux cas, l'expérience professionnelle compte au maximum pour 55 points, la formation, les enseignements, et la recherche au maximum 15 points. Mais la langue basque compte 17 points si vous avez un diplôme de niveau 2, et 8,5 points si vous avez le niveau 1.[8] Pour une personne convaincue que l'euskara est la langue nationale

---

[6] Gobierno vasco, Departamento de educación, *Estadísticas sobre el Sistema Educativo 2007-2008*, disponible à : http://www.hezkuntza.ejgv.euskadi.net/r43-573/es/contenidos/informacion/dia4/es_2025/adjuntos/07_08/FOLLETO_c.pdf (consulté le 15/03/09).

[7] L'auteur a étudié l'euskara durant 18 mois dans le cours municipal de la ville d'Hernani au Guipuscoa.

[8] Osakidetza, Servicio vasco de Salud, Directora general, resolución 4240/2008, et 42/35/2008, de 28 de noviembre.

basque, ce barème n'a rien de scandaleux. Pour quelqu'un qui n'est pas nationaliste mais qui connaît bien la langue basque, il peut être apprécié comme un atout précieux ou dénoncé comme un barrage pour certains bons praticiens. Pour une autre personne, non nationaliste basque et qui ne maîtrise pas la langue basque, il est discriminatoire. Enfin, pour un Espagnol qui pense que l'unité du marché du travail est un des piliers de l'unité de l'Espagne, ce genre de barème accordant une place importante à la langue régionale est politiquement dangereux car il contribue à affaiblir l'ensemble national espagnol.

Le bilinguisme : une représentation géopolitique

Depuis mai 2009, pour la première fois depuis bientôt 30 ans, le président de la communauté autonome basque n'est pas nationaliste basque. Il a fallu que le parti socialiste (25 sièges) et le parti populaire (droite espagnole : 13 sièges) signent un accord pour l'investiture du candidat socialiste à la présidence face à celle du candidat nationaliste basque (les partis nationalistes basques disposent au total de 36 sièges). Cet accord fait une place notable à la question linguistique. Il prévoit par exemple l'« adoption d'un critère adéquat d'évaluation de la connaissance du basque comme compétence (*mérito*) dans les différentes offres publiques d'emploi pour le recrutement de personnel du gouvernement basque, qui cherche un équilibre avec la ponctuation des compétences professionnelles » [c'est à dire que la connaissance de la langue donne moins de points]. Les paragraphes sur la liberté de l'enseignement en basque ou en espagnol sont également nombreux. L'état d'esprit général du pacte est traduit par la phrase : « éviter activement la volonté (*pretención*) de fractionner la société basque en communautés linguistiques différenciées, c'est-à-dire promouvoir la connaissance et l'usage de l'euskara dans le respect de la liberté (*desde la libertad*). Empêcher et éviter les actions sectaires, l'imposition de sanction et l'utilisation partisane de la langue ».[9]

On retrouve ces subtilités de langage à grande portée politique au sujet d'un décret du gouvernement nationaliste basque (2008) qui stipulait que l'objectif de l'enseignement était de « s'identifier comme citoyen basque dans un environnement multiculturel en considérant (*valorando*),

---

[9] « Adopción de una valoración adecuada del conocimiento del euskera como mérito en las diferentes OPEs en la contratación del personal dependiente del Gobierno Vasco que busque el equilibrio con la puntuación correspondiente a los méritos profesionales. – Evitar de forma activa la pretensión de fraccionar la sociedad vasca en comunidades lingüísticas diferenciadas, para lo que se fomentará el conocimiento y el uso del euskera desde la libertad. Impedir y evitar las actuaciones sectarias, la imposición de sanciones y la utilización partidista del idioma ». *Bases para el cambio democratico al servicio de la sociedad vasca*, preacuerdo PP/PSOE, *Diario Vasco*, 31 mars 2009.

de manière positive, la langue et la culture basques comme la langue d'appartenance et de référence ».[10] Les socialistes demandaient que cette phrase devienne : « s'identifier comme citoyen conscient et critique dans un environnement multiculturel, en considérant de façon positive tant l'euskara que le castillan ».[11] Dans son discours à la candidature, le futur président a dit[12] : « Notre diversité est aussi linguistique. En Euskadi, deux langues coexistent, l'euskara et le castillan, et l'objectif de mon gouvernement sera de renforcer cette coexistence (*convivencia*) en évitant la formation de ghettos ou de communautés séparées par les langues ». Le journal des nationalistes basque, *Deia*, notait le lendemain qu'il n'avait parlé que dix minutes en basque et que son niveau de langue n'était pas très bon.[13] Ce qui est en jeu ici est la dimension bilingue de la culture basque au sein de l'État espagnol. Les adversaires nationalistes et non nationalistes se disent chacun défenseurs du bilinguisme, les uns pour justifier les efforts en faveur du basque, les autres pour justifier une politique de rééquilibrage des représentations géopolitiques sur les deux langues.

Cependant, si le lien entre langue et nationalisme est fort, il n'est pas systématique, ou plutôt, il n'est pas étroitement lié à la connaissance effective de la langue basque par l'électeur. Ce qui est à étudier pour l'observation du bilinguisme d'un point de vue géopolitique c'est la représentation du bilinguisme autant que la pratique du bilinguisme. Bon nombre d'électeurs nationalistes basques ne connaissent pas la langue basque. De même, l'augmentation du nombre de bascophones dans la communauté autonome basque n'a pas empêché que les nationalistes basques perdent le pouvoir. En 1980, ils avaient rassemblé 54% des suffrages (avec 40% d'abstention). En 2009, ils obtiennent 48,2% des votes (51,7% en incluant les voix de la Gauche Unie qui les soutient au Parlement), avec une abstention plus faible (35%), et un nombre insuffisant de députés pour faire élire le président. L'arrivée d'une génération nouvelle de citoyens où l'on trouverait, en nombre plus

---

[10] « Identificarse como ciudadano y ciudadana vasca en un entorno multicultural, valorando de forma positiva tanto la lengua y cultura vasca como las lenguas y culturas de pertenencia y referencia, para que a partir de las identidades múltiples construya cada uno su propia identidad de forma inclusiva, así como para construir un marco de referencia común compatible en el respeto a las diferencias y que facilite la convivencia ». :   www.euskadi.net/cgi-bin_k54/bopv_20?c&f=20081125&a=20080 6543 (consulté le 24/04/09).

[11] Sur le site du Parti socialiste de Euskadi, daté du 25/10/2007 : http://www. socialistasvascos.com/varios/Currculum-de-la-Educacin-Bsica-para-la-CAPV-V131.php?sbc=167&sec=239 (consulté le 23/04/09).

[12] Le 5/05/2009.

[13] *Deia*, 6/05/2009, Humberto Unzueta, *El adiós de Ibarretxe eclipsa a Patxi López*, intertitre : « Suspenso en euskera para López ».

important encore qu'aujourd'hui, des électeurs à la fois bascophones et non nationalistes basques pourraient durablement découpler la question nationale basque et la question linguistique.

L'avenir dira comment évolue la relation entre langue et nation dans cette communauté autonome, et si l'alternance entre des gouvernements nationaliste et non nationaliste basque dans un territoire qui devient progressivement bilingue s'imposera comme une banalité ou non. Il n'est pas sûr cependant que le premier gouvernement non nationaliste basque parvienne à installer durablement dans la communauté autonome la pratique de l'alternance politique, car il va prendre les rennes du pouvoir dans un contexte de grave crise économique après trente ans de développement rapide suite à l'entrée dans l'UE.

Pour analyser des politiques linguistiques il faut donc distinguer la réflexion sur la langue comme patrimoine linguistique et celle qui porte sur la langue comme objet politique. Le cas de la communauté autonome basque montre que la langue est le support de représentations géopolitiques en même temps qu'elle est un outil pour consolider des projets géopolitiques. Mais cet outil n'est pas une arme infaillible dans un système démocratique où l'électeur choisit finalement à qui il confie la direction de la cité. L'argument linguistique n'est qu'un élément de son choix.

Le basque en Navarre : un autre rapport de force

La langue basque se parle, on l'a dit, au sein de divers territoires dans lesquels son statut est différent. En Navarre, elle est co-officielle seulement dans une partie de la communauté autonome. Une enquête sociolinguistique du gouvernement de la communauté autonome basque en Navarre (2006) estime à 81% le nombre de non bascophones (413 900 sur 600 000 habitants).[14]

On rappellera que la Navarre est une région aux milieux naturels très divers : elle s'étend des Pyrénées pluvieuses et boisées, au nord, au plateau de Castille chaud et sec, au sud. Paysages, architecture, langues parlées, tout diffère entre les deux Navarre, sachant que le centre de la région est une série de dégradés de ces deux extrêmes, et que les liens entre eux ont toujours été très étroits car la Navarre est traversée par les plus importantes routes de Compostelle. Du point de vue de son patrimoine naturel et architectural, c'est une région exceptionnelle.

---

[14] *IV Encuesta Sociolingüística*. 2006. Gobierno Vasco Departamento de cultura, Vitoria-Gasteiz, 2008. http://www.euskara.euskadi.net/r59-738/es/contenidos/libro/iv_inkesta_soziol/es_ink/iv_inkesta_soziolinguistikoa.html (consulté le 25/04/09).

La langue basque en Navarre est parlée dans la montagne, zone dont les villages, les maisons, le folklore, sont très similaires à ceux de la majeure partie de la communauté autonome basque voisine. Il y a unité culturelle évidente entre la Navarre du Nord, les territoires limitrophes de la communauté autonome basque et ceux de France.

Les nationalistes basques pensent que la Navarre doit absolument faire partie de la nation qu'ils cherchent à bâtir : l'idée de nation est antérieure au contrôle du territoire, elle se décline comme une évidence aussi « naturelle » que les paysages. Mais, en Navarre, il leur faut batailler avec des citoyens qui pensent tout à fait différemment et accordent de l'importance à d'autres faits historiques.

La Navarre en effet fut un des plus anciens royaumes d'Espagne, et celui qui s'est le plus tardivement incorporé à la couronne de Castille (pour les nationalistes basques ce fut un royaume basque, et il a été incorporé de force). Je n'ai pas l'espace ici pour raconter l'histoire intéressante d'un royaume aux limites changeantes, mais il faut retenir que le régionalisme navarrais est un sentiment puissant à tous les niveaux de la société. Ce n'est pas un nationalisme navarrais. Le but des partis majoritaires est de faire respecter une tradition de compromis (on dit *pactismo*) aboutissant au respect de certaines libertés anciennes maintes fois reconnues par les régimes successifs d'Espagne, y compris celui du général Franco qui respecta l'autonomie fiscale de la Navarre. Néanmoins, cette autonomie n'a de sens pour eux qu'au sein de l'Espagne. Toutes proportions gardées, la Navarre ressemble un peu à la Bavière allemande (600 000 habitants dans la première, 12 millions dans la seconde). Pour ces partis majoritaires, le nationalisme basque n'est rien moins qu'un insupportable impérialisme.

La langue basque en Navarre est très largement associée par la majorité des Navarrais au nationalisme basque.[15] Cependant, au nom de la démocratie et de la protection d'un patrimoine linguistique, une loi a également été votée en Navarre, dite « ley del vascuence », pour respecter les droits des bascophones. Le terme « vascuence » est le nom donné à la langue basque en Navarre ; par ce biais elle est distinguée de l'« euskara », terme employé dans la communauté autonome basque. Grammaticalement ce sont tout de même les normes du basque unifié qui sont utilisées en Navarre. La loi navarraise de 1986[16] représente la même révolution que dans la Communauté autonome basque, à la

---

[15]   Il y a bien sûr des Navarrais bascophones non nationalistes basques, notamment dans la vallée du Baztan au nord est de la province, zone très faiblement peuplée, mais aussi ailleurs, par lassitude ou hostilité envers le militantisme nationaliste basque et l'ETA.

[16]   Ley Foral 18/86, de 15 de diciembre de 1986, del Vascuence. Regulación de su uso normal y oficial.

différence près qu'elle crée des zones où son statut diffère. Une zone bascophone, une zone mixte, et une zone non bascophone. La liste des communes de chacune des zones est citée dans la loi.

Carte 1 : les zones linguistiques
de la communauté autonome de Navarre

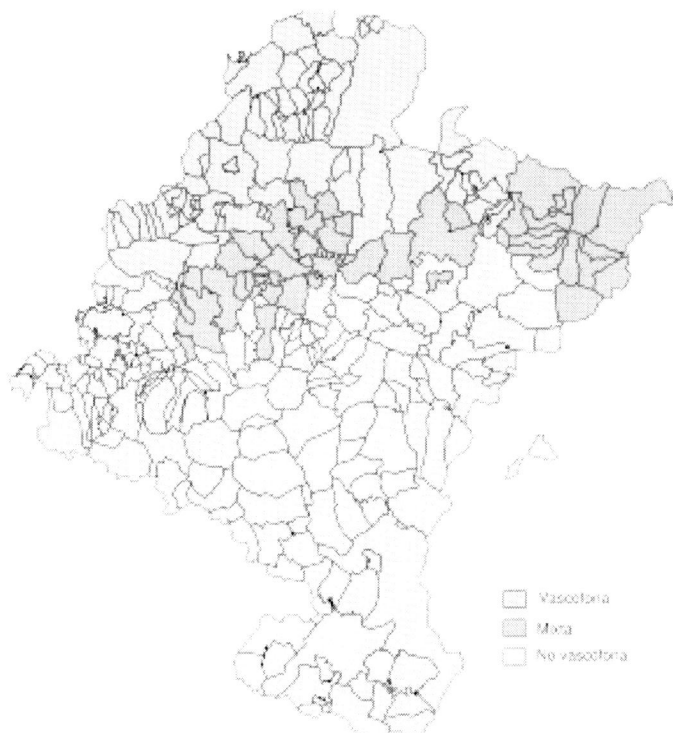

Source : http://fr.wikipedia.org/wiki/Fichier:Navarra_Zonificacion_linguistica.svg.

L'article 2 de la loi établit que le castillan et le « vascuence » sont les langues de Navarre ; tous les citoyens ont le droit de les connaître et de les utiliser. Le bulletin officiel du Parlement de Navarrre est publié dans les deux langues. Les toponymes historiques, en basque au nord, en castillan au sud, et parfois dans les deux langues selon l'usage local, sont respectés comme tels. Dans la zone bascophone le citoyen peut employer indistinctement les deux langues officielles avec l'administration. Dans la zone mixte, l'administration doit former le personnel nécessaire pour rendre possible l'exercice des droits linguistiques des citoyens s'ils le demandent. Les services centraux de l'administration régionale font de même.[17] Dans la zone bascophone tous les modèles d'enseignement comprennent l'apprentissage du basque, que ce soit dans des cours de langue basque (modèle A) ou des cours en langue basque (modèles B et D). Dans la zone mixte sont proposés les modèles A, B, D mais aussi le modèle G ou l'élève ne reçoit aucun enseignement de la langue basque. Dans la zone non bascophone la loi prévoit que seront proposés les modèles A (cours de basque), ou G, mais il y a aussi des classes d'immersion en basque dans les écoles associatives. En 2007-2008, sont inscrits dans le modèle D (tous les cours en basque), 77% des élèves de la zone bascophones, 24% de ceux de la zone mixte, 4% de ceux de la zone non bascophone. Dans le sud de la Navarre, hors zone mixte et bascophone, 73% des élèves ne suivent aucun cours de langue basque (modèle G).

Les désaccords portent sur l'existence de ces zones. Pour les nationalistes basques, il y a en Navarre deux communautés de citoyens : une bilingue (euskara/espagnol), une dite monolingue en espagnol ; ils voudraient que l'ensemble de la population devienne bilingue et que la même loi s'applique partout. Mais la plupart des Navarrais pensent qu'ils ne sont pas Basques et ne voient pas pourquoi ils devraient s'astreindre à cet effort.

Les bascophones de Navarre diront qu'ils ont l'esprit ouvert puisqu'ils sont bilingues et que les hispanophones qui ne veulent pas apprendre le basque sont au contraire fermés au dialogue. Les hispanophones ne souhaitant pas apprendre la langue basque diront quant à eux qu'ils préfèrent le dialogue avec d'autres cultures, dans d'autres langues ; ou que le bilinguisme basque/espagnol n'est pas une démarche d'ouverture au même titre que l'apprentissage du chinois ou de l'anglais. Le débat sur le bilinguisme est empreint de jugements de valeur au sujet du sectarisme des uns et des autres. D'un point de vue géopolitique, l'analyse met l'accent sur les représentations liées aux territoires et à la nation, et s'attache à faire apparaître les acteurs porteurs de ces représentations géopolitiques. Plus l'analyse porte sur un territoire de dimension restreinte plus elle s'intéresse à l'influence de personnes concrètes, de groupes au sein des partis, de personnalités.

Pour les nationalistes basques, le bilinguisme doit être développé chez tous les individus vivant en Navarre. Par ce biais, c'est le territoire qui doit devenir bilingue afin que la langue ait une existence sociale et

---

[17] Decreto Foral 29/2003, de 10 de febrero, por el que se regula el uso del vascuence en las Administraciones Públicas de Navarra. BON nº 19 de 12 de febrero de 2003 : http://www.navarra.es/home_es/Actualidad/BON/Boletines/2003/19/Anuncio-4/ (consulté le 24/04/09). Texte en français sur : http://www.tlfq.ulaval.ca/axl/europe/ navarre-decret-2003.htm (consulté le 24/04/09).

politique consolidée. Ils réclament donc un changement de la loi afin d'abolir la différence entre les trois espaces linguistiques en Navarre, c'est-à-dire que les droits dont ils jouissent dans le Nord soient appliqués partout. D'une part, une telle extension permettrait de créer une image cartographique (icône nationale) englobant toute la Navarre à partir de la situation institutionnelle. Pour l'instant la loi contraint, si l'on veut être rigoureux, à faire une carte limitant la partie bilingue au tiers de la Navarre. D'autre part, la partie en zone basque est la moins peuplée (50 000 habitants, contre 274 300 en zone mixte, essentiellement regroupés dans la capitale, Pampelune, et 184 600 en zone non bascophone). Les leviers qu'offre la loi dans un vaste espace géographique ne donnent d'influence que sur une faible partie de la population. Enfin, cette revendication est également une façon de combattre l'idée que la langue basque est une langue « étrangère » à la partie méridionale de la Navarre (puisqu'elle vaut autant dans les concours que le chinois ou l'anglais).

La nation et ses langues étrangères

L'idée qu'une langue est autochtone ou étrangère est centrale pour comprendre la portée des disputes : l'adjectif autochtone renvoie à un droit lié à l'ancienneté de l'enracinement. La présence du basque au sud de la Navarre fait l'objet de polémiques. Une partie affirme que le basque n'a jamais été parlé dans le Sud de la Navarre, l'autre qu'elle a disparu de cette zone sous la pression des langues romanes. Les linguistes nationalistes basques (Luis Mitxelena, par exemple) prennent beaucoup de précautions pour suggérer qu'on y parlait peut-être basque[18] ; d'autres avancent des arguments toponymiques pour affirmer au contraire qu'elle est d'évidence une langue autochtone.[19] D'un point de vue politique, il n'y a pas de représentation intermédiaire entre la langue autochtone et la langue étrangère. Ceux qui refusent que les Navarrais aient tous à apprendre l'euskara pensent que cette langue est « étrangère » au sud. Les nationalistes basques pensent quant à eux que

---

[18] « On pourrait éradiquer l'idée [...] que les limites de la langue basque [...] coïncidèrent avec celles de la Vasconie historique, dont la définition n'est d'ailleurs pas la même pour tous. En réalité, tout indique que ses frontières furent très découpées et qu'elles délimitaient un territoire discontinu ». Luis Mitxelena, *Sobre historia de la lengua vasca*, Saint Sébastien, 1988, p. 26. Voir aussi : Euskaltzaindia, Real Academia de la lengua vasca, *El libro blanco del Euskara*, Bilbao, sans date, p. 346 selon lequel, la Ribera (vallée de l'Ebre) « es la región de mayor peso demográfico y también la que plantea mayor problemas cuando se trata de su caracterización lingüística en razón de los avances de la Reconquista ».

[19] Par exemple : Page personelle de Jabier Sainz Pezonaga sur la toponymie historique de Tierra Estella et lexique en basque populaire de la Ribera de Navarre, disponible à : http://www.euskalnet.net/jabiersainz/ern/lexico.htm.

l'espagnol est une langue étrangère dans la montagne[20] et que seule la réalité des rapports de force historiques l'a rendu indispensable *a posteriori*. Dans l'histoire, l'étranger, et la menace venue de l'étranger, est un élément fondamental pour la cristallisation des nations que nous connaissons aujourd'hui. La représentation de l'espagnol comme une langue étrangère est ici aussi très importante pour consolider le sentiment national basque, et la menace qui pèse sur l'avenir de la langue joue son rôle aussi dans ce processus. De même, la représentation du basque comme langue autochtone au sud de la Navarre est fondamentale pour légitimer la carte du projet national.

Une revendication sur un petit espace, quelques communes, n'est pas interprétée de la même manière, elle n'a pas le même contenu politique, si elle apparaît comme la partie tactique d'une stratégie nationale à long terme. L'existence d'un projet national amène l'observateur à voir la question linguistique comme un élément d'une action plus complexe. En effet, le nationalisme est une idée étroitement liée au fait linguistique et le bilinguisme est apparemment difficile à associer à la nation : on le voit au Canada où, pour défendre la langue française, les Québécois ont centré leur stratégie sur le territoire de la nation, reléguant le combat pour un million de ceux qu'on appelle Canadiens français, francophones résidant hors du Québec.[21] En Navarre, du fait de l'existence d'un mouvement nationaliste basque qui se confond presque avec l'ensemble des bascophones, l'enjeu des rivalités ne peut guère s'analyser seulement d'un point de vue linguistique. Il est géopolitique car, dans l'esprit des nationalistes, les progrès du projet national sont intimement liés à la croissance de l'usage de la langue nationale, ici le basque. Toute subordination politique de l'euskara, sous forme de langue régionale navarraise, leur apparaîtrait comme une faiblesse insurmontable du projet linguistique visant à faire de l'euskara « la » langue des citoyens de la nation basque.

Leurs opposants pensent que cette revendication est donc une première étape sur le chemin du bilinguisme et d'un processus lent, mais constant, de rapprochement entre la Navarre et Euskadi (communauté autonome basque) pour fonder un ensemble unitaire regroupant les deux territoires. Cette utopie paraît lointaine, compte tenu des réalités ac-

---

[20] Les débats en Catalogne sont du même tonneau : les Catalans seulement hispano-phones sont accusés de ne pas parler la langue du pays, comme si l'espagnol n'était pas une langue locale. À partir du XVe siècle, l'espagnol devient la langue de cour du royaume d'Aragon à la place du catalan et se diffuse dans les villes. Les Catalans illustres deviennent bilingues ou, plus rarement, monolingues espagnol.

[21] Joseph Yvon Thériault (ed.) (2008), *L'espace francophone en milieu minoritaire au Canada*, Montréal, Fides. Ce livre fait apparaître des thèses contradictoires sur le fait de savoir si les Québécois ont « abandonné » les Canadiens français.

tuelles, mais c'est pourtant bien contre ce projet à long terme que s'organise la politique linguistique des non nationalistes basques (certains d'entre eux peuvent être qualifiés de nationalistes espagnols, d'autres se définissent prioritairement comme Navarrais). Majoritaires, ils ne se méfient pas moins des stratégies géopolitiques nationalistes basques et sont convaincus que les revendications linguistiques sont leur cheval de Troie. Ils ne croient pas à un sentiment régional navarrais porté par les militants bascophones : ceux-ci en effet plaident également que les zones linguistiques sont une atteinte à la cohésion sociale de la province car elles différencient les Navarrais entre eux selon le territoire où ils habitent.

Les rivalités sont fortes et les électeurs les font rebondir régulièrement en changeant les équilibres politiques au Parlement. Ainsi, en avril 2008, un débat parlementaire a porté sur l'extension de la zone mixte à quelques communes de Pampelune dont la population avait augmenté ces dernières années. Pour l'instant, le Parlement l'a rejetée. Mais ce vote aurait été différent si un élu nationaliste ne s'était pas absenté le jour du scrutin (la modification des limites des zones linguistiques requiert la majorité absolue des voix). En effet, depuis que les indépendantistes de gauche de Navarrre ont coupé les ponts avec l'ETA (avec la création du parti Aralar en 2002), les nationalistes basques ont retrouvé l'influence qu'ils avaient perdue depuis les années 1990. Ils représentent en 2007, 23% des suffrages et 12 députés sur 50. Le parti socialiste, qui a aussi 12 députés, et la Gauche Unie, 2 députés, peuvent voter sur certains points, notamment la question linguistique, avec les nationalistes basques. Dans le cas présent, le parti a voté un jour pour l'élargissement de la zone mixte, mais la fois suivante contre. Ses positions varient en fonction de rapports de force internes ou des alliances parlementaires à Madrid. La rivalité linguistique et politique entre nationalistes basques et navarrais est donc plus que jamais d'actualité.

En France : quelle relation entre la langue régionale et la langue nationale ?

La comparaison avec la France amène à s'interroger à nouveau sur la relation entre les locuteurs bilingues dans ce qu'on appellera ici les deux langues « locales », euskara et français, et les locuteurs ne connaissant que l'une des deux, le français. Ce concept de « langue locale » est utilisé pour signifier que le français et le basque sont les deux langues parlées localement depuis des siècles. Sans nier l'inégalité des fonctions des deux langues, il les met de ce point de vue sur le même plan, ce qui permet d'éviter l'association implicite entre langue basque et culture basque. Ce que fut la culture rurale basque, berceau de la langue, disparaît en effet avec l'urbanisation. Bien qu'il s'agisse du même idiome au sens linguistique, la langue rurale des siècles passés n'est pas assimilable à la langue devenue urbaine depuis qu'on l'enseigne à l'école, même en zone rurale, car la culture qui y est associée est différente. Le lien entre langue et culture basque existe évidemment, mais il est à préciser et n'est pas exclusif du lien entre langue française et culture basque.

L'enquête sociolinguistique du gouvernement autonome basque d'Espagne (2006) estime que 22 % (51 800) de la population du Pays basque français de plus de 16 ans est bilingue et 68% (158 600 personnes) ne connaît pas du tout l'euskara. Dans cette partie de l'espace linguistique basque le sentiment régional est prégnant, mais l'euskara n'est que partiellement associé à un mouvement nationaliste. En novembre 1933, parut – avec une édition en français et une autre en euskara – une brochure de 45 pages, œuvre de l'abbé Pierre Lafitte (1901-1985), intitulée : *Eskual-Herriaren alde (Pour le Pays Basque). Court commentaire du programme eskualerriste à l'usage des militants* qui reprenait la devise du Parti Nationaliste Basque, *Jainkoa eta Lege Zaharra* (Dieu et la Vieille Loi). Il demandait la reconnaissance de la langue basque et son officialisation ainsi que la défense et la promotion des coutumes et des traditions basques. Mais on trouve aussi dans les années 1920 un nationaliste français d'extrême droite défendant les traditions basques, Jean Ybarnegaray (1883-1956), ancien combattant de la guerre 1914-1918, et qui s'était déclaré favorable aux « Basques de Franco » par anticommunisme (en Espagne le PNV s'était allié au Front Populaire). Dans les deux cas, la langue basque était perçue comme un patrimoine précieux dans une conception traditionaliste de la société et la référence aux voisins basques du sud est importante. Mais la distance avec l'Espagne a été ensuite accentuée par les 37 années de dictature franquiste, durant lesquelles la frontière fut quasiment fermée et la société espagnole prit un grand retard économique par rapport à la France des années 1960. Aujourd'hui, malgré le développement de relations transfrontalières et l'installation de nombreux Espagnols dans les villes côtières proches de la frontière, on est surpris de constater une assez grande ignorance de la situation politique et linguistique de Navarre et de la Communauté autonome basque. La référence au côté espagnol, même quand on est de langue maternelle basque, est loin d'être automatique.

Il est impossible en si peu de pages de faire une présentation de l'histoire du Pays basque au sein de la nation française. Disons pour simplifier que deux types de représentations s'opposent aujourd'hui au sujet de la langue basque, bien que les individus adoptent des versions souvent nuancées de l'un ou l'autre des extrêmes. La première est celle d'un rouleau compresseur français écrasant les langues et cultures régionales. La deuxième est celle des processus parallèles et cumulatifs de diffusion autoritaire de la langue française dans l'enseignement public et d'abandon de la langue régionale par des populations rurales ou fraîchement urbanisées, désireuses d'atteindre la modernité que leur offrait la langue française. Depuis les années 1980, les évolutions législatives[22] ont permis un développement réel de l'enseignement en deux langues dans l'éducation nationale et privée sous contrat. J'ai rapporté dans un numéro d'*Hérodote* intitulé *Langues et territoires*,[23] comment s'est déroulé le développement de l'enseignement du basque dans les écoles publiques au côté de deux autres filières privées, l'une catholique, l'autre associative proche de l'idéologie nationale basque. Depuis, la situation a évolué avec la création, en 2004, de l'Office Public de la langue basque qui est chargé de mettre en place et de suivre la politique concernant l'enseignement de l'euskara.[24] L'Office est une sorte de médiateur entre les services de l'État et les mouvements associatifs pour le développement de la connaissance de la langue basque. Des mesures de promotion ou d'organisation de la demande des familles donnent des

---

[22] Circulaire 82-261 du 21 juin 1982, dite « Circulaire Savary ». *BOEN*, n° 26, 1er juillet 1982. « L'enseignement des langues régionales dans le service public d'éducation nationale ». Cette circulaire organise les enseignements de langues et cultures régionales de la maternelle à l'université et autorise les expérimentations, telles les ouvertures de classes bilingues. L'enseignement des langues et cultures régionales peut être considéré comme une matière spécifique.

Circulaire 95-086, dite « Circulaire Bayrou » du 7 avril 1995. *BOEN*, n° 16, 20 avril 1995. Cette circulaire permet la mise en œuvre de plans pluriannuels concertés entre rectorats et collectivités territoriales en vue des « enseignements de langues et cultures régionales ».

Circulaire 2001-166, dite « Circulaire Lang » du 5 septembre 2001. *BOEN*, n° 33, 13 septembre 2001. Elle précise le « Développement de l'enseignement des langues régionales à l'école, au collège et au lycée ». Décret du 3 janvier 2002. *JO* du 5 janvier 2002. Création d'un « Concours spécial de Recrutement de Professeurs des Écoles, en langues régionales ».

Loi d'orientation et de programme pour l'avenir de l'école, n° 2005-380, 23 avril 2005, article L312-10. JO du 24 avril 2005. *BOEN*, n° 18, 5 mai 2005. Cette loi stipule qu'« un enseignement de langues et cultures régionales peut être dispensé tout au long de la scolarité selon des modalités définies par voie de convention entre l'État et les collectivités territoriales où ces langues sont en usage ».

[23] *Hérodote*, n° 105, 2002.

[24] Office Public de la langue basque, Groupement d'Intérêt Public associant l'État, la région Aquitaine, le département des Pyrénées Atlantiques, le syndicat intercommunal de soutien à la culture basque, et le Conseil des Élus du Pays basque. Cf. : OPLB, *Projet de politique linguistique* (brochure), décembre 2006. La communauté autonome basque peut aussi, par le biais de l'Office, investir dans la langue basque en France. En 2009, « Dans la continuité du dispositif initié en 2007, le partenariat avec la Communauté Autonome d'Euskadi sera renouvelé et permettra la mise en place d'un fonds de 1 380 000 € géré par l'Office Public de la Langue Basque. Le fonds sera alimenté à hauteur de 920 000 € par l'OPLBasque et 460 000 € par la Communauté autonome d'Euskadi ». Site de l'OPLB : http://www.mintzaira.fr/fileadmin/documents/presentation/2_2009KO_AITZINKONTUA.pdf (consulté le 24/04/09).

résultats notables sur le plan quantitatif et territorial. Il y a une planification de l'enseignement du basque sur le territoire du pays « Pays basque », depuis l'école primaire jusqu'au lycée.

En 2008-2009, 86 écoles primaires de l'éducation nationale (48% des établissements) offrent un enseignement bilingue à 4 160 élèves (24% des élèves). Dans 30 écoles primaires privées catholiques (56% des établissements), 1 780 élèves sont scolarisés en bilingue (29% des élèves). Enfin, 22 écoles primaires associatives conventionnées offrent un enseignement tout en basque à 1 639 élèves. Dans les trois filières confondues, 7 579 élèves suivent donc un enseignement en basque, soit environ un tiers des élèves dans 54 % des établissements. Au niveau du collège, l'objectif de la parité horaire entre cours en français et cours en basque dans les filières bilingues est rarement atteint,[25] car la formation des enseignants spécialisés (non polyvalents à l'inverse de ceux du primaire) est une difficulté supplémentaire. Pour l'instant, dans les collèges bilingues de l'enseignement public, 3 heures 30 d'histoire et géographie sont délivrées en basque (en plus des 3 heures d'études de l'euskara) et l'objectif est d'étendre l'offre de cours en basque aux mathématiques, aux SVT, à la Physique-Chimie, jusqu'à la parité horaire.[26] Le nombre d'enfants scolarisés dans le système bilingue diminue avec l'entrée au lycée. Il existe deux filières distinctes avec des classes composées seulement d'élèves bilingues et des classes composées d'élèves non bilingues. Il serait intéressant de voir à quel point se constituent des groupes à forte cohésion d'élèves bilingues ayant étudié ensemble tout au long de leur scolarité, où si le nombre croissant d'élèves inscrits en cursus bilingue a comme résultat un brassage des élèves dans des classes et des milieux diversifiés. Le volet enseignement de la politique linguistique en langue régionale est donc bien engagé, la proportion des enfants suivant un enseignement bilingue étant supérieure au niveau de la maternelle (39%) que dans les autres niveaux.

Les développements futurs de cette politique sont envisagés sans que leur traduction géopolitique, leur relation aux deux nations en présence, française et basque, ne soit posée. Le projet de politique linguistique adopté par l'Office Public de la langue basque en 2006 aborde pourtant la question de l'avenir professionnel des nouveaux bilingues. Il y a en effet une grande différence entre la génération des plus de 50 ans qui ont appris le basque à la maison et accédé à l'emploi par le biais de la langue française ; pour eux le bilinguisme dissociait la langue de la

---

[25] Parité horaire reconnue légale par le Conseil Constitutionnel, décision du 12 mai 2003.

[26] Entretiens avril 2009 : Jean Sarraillet, inspecteur pédagogique pour la langue basque, Académie de Bordeaux, Estebe Eyherabide, directeur de l'OPLB, Pascal Sarpoulet, chargé de mission langue occitane, Académie de Bordeaux.

maison, du village, éventuellement des débats au conseil municipal, c'est-à-dire la langue d'un entre soi, du français parlé hors de cette sphère. Ce bilinguisme inégal, les spécialistes l'appellent diglossie,[27] n'était pas vécu comme un problème pour les locuteurs, mais a provoqué la décadence de la transmission familiale de l'euskara perçu comme un outil linguistique inutile pour construire une vie professionnelle satisfaisante. C'est pourquoi, les militants plaident aujourd'hui pour un usage social accru de l'euskara. Ainsi peut-on lire dans le chapitre « vivre la langue » du document d'orientation de l'Office Public :

> L'absence de place dans la vie sociale et le manque de prestige qui est alors associé à la langue peuvent [...] compromettre les acquis de l'apprentissage à l'école, du fait de la frustration des locuteurs qui, après avoir appris le basque, ne perçoivent pas que la connaissance et l'usage de la langue soient utiles et gratifiants, mettant ainsi en évidence que les efforts réalisés pour rapprendre le basque ne sont pas compensés par l'utilité qu'il en a (*sic*) ou la satisfaction qu'il en tire (*sic*). Le risque est que le basque soit alors considéré comme une simple matière d'étude, et que la motivation pour l'utiliser et la transmettre se perde. Dans ce cas, les avancées obtenues notamment dans l'enseignement pourraient s'avérer stériles. Pour qu'une langue se développe, elle doit aussi acquérir statut et prestige social, en ayant toute sa place dans la société sans quoi les efforts faits en faveur de la transmission sont vains. Quand une langue en difficulté ne garde qu'une fonction vernaculaire, culturelle et emblématique, qu'elle est peu présente dans la vie publique, dans le monde du travail ou les médias, elle est vite perçue comme inutile et tend à décliner [...] La langue basque doit donc aussi trouver sa place dans la vie sociale.[28]

En France, pour l'instant, la distinction entre le bilinguisme chez l'individu et le bilinguisme politique n'est pas pensée. Les débats sont très fortement orientés par les sociolinguistes qui dissertent au sujet du statut ou du développement de l'usage de la langue dite minoritaire et sur les conditions nécessaires à ce développement. La démarche géopolitique aborde la question sous un angle différent : elle pose la question de la relation entre des langues nationales et des langues régionales, ou entre des langues nationales coexistant sur un même territoire. Elle inscrit la problématique des langues dans le cadre des États nations, des nations sans État mais non démunies de pouvoirs (le cas de la communauté autonome basque), et de l'Union Européenne. Très souvent, lors des entretiens, les personnes interrogées insistent sur l'idée que la

---

[27] Marie-Louise Moreau (ed.), *Sociolinguistique, concepts de base*, Sprimont, Mardaga, 1997.

[28] Projet de politique linguistique, « Un objectif central : des locuteurs complets. Un cœur de cible : les jeunes générations ». Bayonne, Office Public de la Langue basque, décembre 2006, p. 39.

question linguistique ne doit pas être « politisée » au Pays basque français. La « politique » apparaît comme un spectre qu'il faut écarter, une crainte, sans doute fondée sur l'intuition du risque de zizanie contenu dans le développement du bilinguisme social, au-delà de l'école.

Sur quoi se fonderait la discorde ? Sur le fait que, dans le cas présent, deux nations revendiquent le territoire et l'identité des citoyens qui s'y trouvent. La nation basque de façon exclusive, car elle est en construction, mais avec une réussite relative dans les territoires français et navarrais.[29] La nation française de manière plus complexe parce qu'elle existe en tant qu'État et puissance européenne depuis des siècles.[30] La crainte de voir croître des rivalités internes entre des sentiments qui peuvent devenir exclusifs (basque ou français) alors qu'ils étaient inclusifs (basque et français) est donc liée à la dimension nationale de la question linguistique qui entraîne l'entrée des deux langues dans le domaine du pouvoir judiciaire. La loi de 1982 en Euskadi prévoyait par exemple non seulement que l'on puisse travailler dans les deux langues, mais aussi que l'on ait le droit de « s'exprimer en basque dans n'importe quelle réunion ». Cela laisse entrevoir le potentiel conflictuel de l'usage de l'une et l'autre langue qu'il faut réguler légalement.

Il est délicat de prévoir les effets politiques de l'évolution linguistique. En effet, si l'évocation de la nation basque divise en France, celui des « réparations historiques » apparaît comme unificateur. On entend très souvent dire, chez des bascophones ou non, qu'il faut racheter d'une manière ou d'une autre tout le mal qui a été fait contre la petite langue lors de la construction de la grande nation. La décadence des langues régionales serait une faute dans l'histoire de la nation française. Le sentiment d'être « responsable de sa langue » est important. Toute forme de questionnement des objectifs à moyen terme de la diffusion de la langue basque est ainsi aisément assimilée à de l'hostilité. Du coup, on parle beaucoup de la langue basque, au chevet de laquelle on se fait voir, mais assez peu de l'avenir d'une société bilingue au sein de la nation. La Nation Française s'est construite par la diffusion de sa langue et des idées que celle-ci a permis de véhiculer. Peut-on imaginer que son modèle linguistique évolue au XXIᵉ siècle non pas sur la base d'une

---

[29] L'ancien président du PNV, Jon Josu Imaz, avait proposé une co-souveraineté entre la France et Euskadi sur le Pays basque nord, mais il a été désavoué au sein de son parti par ceux qui soulevaient une contradiction majeure de la proposition : pour être co-souverain il faut d'abord être souverain.

[30] « La formulation bipolaire de la conscience individuelle – Basque et Français – est devenue au cours du XIXᵉ siècle, moment historique le plus intense pour la fabrication de l'imaginaire national, une réalité et une évidence culturelles ». Dans Pierre Bidart (2003/3), « Héritage, dynamique et tension au Pays basque français », *Éthnologie française*, Paris, PUF, vol. 33, pp. 443-450.

rédemption du passé, mais d'une capacité de cohésion et d'innovation avec les nouvelles donnes de la modernité ?

L'absence de réflexion sur ce que pourraient être les implications du développement du bilinguisme régional est, à mon sens, bien illustrée par le fait que sur le site de l'académie de Bordeaux la carte de « l'aire de développement de la langue basque » correspond à la représentation de la « nation » basque et ne prend pas en compte les zones linguistiques navarraises. Cela signifie que la dimension politique du bilinguisme n'est pas envisagée dans le volet enseignement, ce qui semble paradoxal dans un pays où la diffusion de la langue française par le biais de l'école a été une des clés de la consolidation d'une identité nationale.

**Carte 2 : Représentation du « Pays basque »
sur le site de l'Académie de Bordeaux**

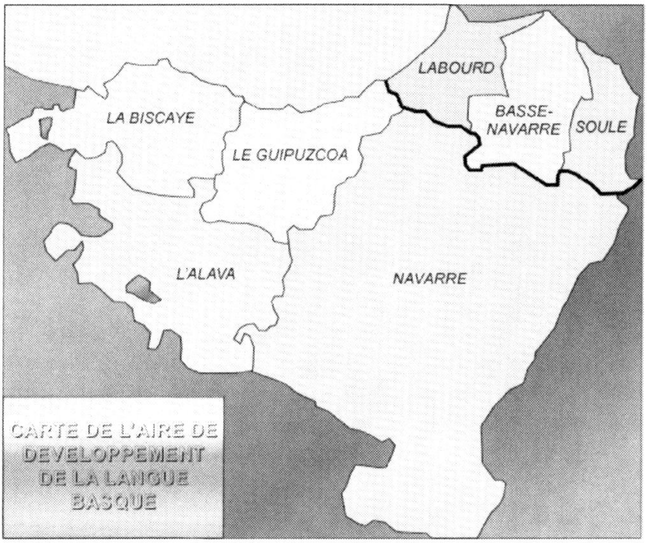

Source : Inspection Académique des Pyrénées-Atlantiques[31]

Une carte plus précise est pourtant possible, comme celle qui est publiée par une association navarraise de défense de la langue basque (*Euskara kultur elkargoa*).[32] Elle montre le pourcentage d'élèves inscrits dans l'enseignement en basque (on ne sait pas comment est faite la somme entre les divers systèmes et les années cumulées) ainsi que, en cartouche, les statuts de la langue. C'est aussi une carte de la nation basque. Elle permet de visualiser le chemin à parcourir, du point de vue

---

[31] http://crdp.ac-bordeaux.fr/langues/basque/cartbasq4.htm.
[32] Disponible à : http://www.euskarakultur.org/eke/images/index/eh_mapa.pdf.

nationaliste, pour que tout soit de la même couleur correspondant aux trois quarts des élèves scolarisés en euskara, au XXIIe siècle peut-être.

Les deux cartes montrent le Pays basque français sans le reste du département des Pyrénées Atlantiques. C'est pourtant un aspect essentiel de la question du côté français[33] car la revendication d'un département séparé de la partie béarnaise des Pyrénées Atlantiques peut être interprétée comme une étape d'un long processus d'unification des sept territoires, une marche vers l'utopie.

La situation relativement consensuelle au Pays basque français repose aujourd'hui à la fois sur le rôle joué par les classes bilingues de l'éducation nationale, qui rendent compatibles les deux sentiments d'appartenance, français et basque, et sur la faible audience électorale des nationalistes basques jusqu'à aujourd'hui. Le développement linguistique se déroule dans un contexte électoral où les électeurs du Pays « Pays basque » votent majoritairement pour des partis non nationalistes basques, UMP, Modem, Parti Socialiste. La croissance du nationalisme basque est ralenti par l'existence de l'ETA, car le terrorisme fait l'objet d'un rejet assez puissant pour avoir été contenu côté français, bien que les éléments d'une croissance de la violence existent.[34] Mais l'ETA déposera les armes, souhaitons-le, ce qui ouvrira des perspectives nouvelles.

Parmi ces perspectives se trouvent aussi celle qu'ouvrent des citoyens français de Basse Navarre, partie centrale du pays « Pays basque », amants de l'histoire locale, ou soucieux de ne pas laisser s'imposer sur cet espace la seule représentation de la nation basque. Ils tentent en effet à leur tour de réactiver une autre figure géo-historique, le royaume de Navarre, qui s'étendait outre Pyrénées et englobait la Basse Navarre aujourd'hui française. L'actuel gouvernement de la Communauté autonome de Navarre en Espagne subventionne des livres retraçant l'histoire de cet espace transpyrénéen, qui sont publiés en français, en espagnol et en basque, les trois langues aujourd'hui officielles dans les limites de l'ancien royaume. En 2012 des célébrations rappelleront l'incorporation du royaume de Navarre au royaume de Castille (1512) et la séparation d'avec la partie nord. Pour les nationalistes basques c'est la fin du « royaume basque », la perte de leur indépendance. Pour les *navarristas*, c'est le début de l'alliance avec l'Espagne.

Plusieurs ensembles spatiaux se superposent ainsi sur l'espace linguistique basque de France (voir Carte 3) : un territoire administratif, le

---

[33] Barbara Loyer (2003), « Identités et pouvoir local : le cas de la revendication d'un département Pays basque », *Hérodote*, n° 110, pp. 103-128.

[34] Barbara Loyer, Christian Aguerre (2008), « Terrorisme et Démocratie », *Hérodote* n° 130, pp. 112-145.

département français des Pyrénées Atlantiques (qui fait lui-même partie de la région Aquitaine), partagé en deux sous-ensembles, le pays « Pays basque » et le Béarn. Un territoire historique, la basse Navarre, partie du royaume de Navarre. Et enfin un territoire utopique, la nation basque, appelée aussi Euskadi ou Euskal Herria.

Conclusion

Dans le contexte de la construction européenne, la projection dans l'avenir des nations française, espagnole, et basque dépendra des évolutions politiques internes à ces trois territoires. Le côté français fait l'objet de représentations plus ou moins concurrentes entre elles, et le rapport entre langue et culture, entre langues et histoire, y est complexe. En Navarre, la question linguistique ne peut être dissociée des rivalités nationales de l'Espagne et l'évolution de l'euskara sur le plan territorial dépend aussi des résultats électoraux des nationalistes basques. En Euskadi, le changement de pouvoir introduira peut-être pour la première fois au niveau des instances dirigeantes l'idée que la culture locale, même au cœur de la nation basque, est un mélange.

La philosophie de la démarche vers une autre culture à partir de l'apprentissage linguistique ne peut se décliner de la même façon si l'on parle d'un individu et d'une société. Dans une société, l'usage d'un idiome ou son absence d'usage détermine des rapports de pouvoirs plus ou moins déséquilibrés et les rivalités inhérentes à la démocratie s'engouffrent dans la merveilleuse réalité des langues. Ces rivalités sont l'objet de l'approche géopolitique.

Summary

The space where the Basque language, or Euskara, is spoken is more limited than the surrounding political territories. There are three distinct areas where the language is spoken: the Autonomous Basque Community or Euskadi, Navarra in Spain and the department of the Pyrénées Atlantiques in France. In the Autonomous Basque community, Euskara is the official language in the three provinces which make up the region even though the use of the language is quantitively very different in each of the three. In Navarra, the Autonomous Community is made up of only one province and Euskara is an official language on part of the territory, in the mountainous region of the Pyrenees. The department of the Pyrénées Atlantiques is made up of two distinct areas: the Béarn and a "Pays Basque." Basque has no official status in these areas but the various structures set up within this framework are working to increase the penetration of the language and the French Department of Education has set up bilingual institutions where some children study subjects in Basque and others in French. In each of the territories the language question poses different problems. This article will examine recent developments in Navarra, the region in which the linguistic balance is more tenuous than in Euskadi, and where the battle for the status of Euskara is a subject of constant political confrontation.

Carte 3 : La langue basque : un ensemble spatial complexe

La langue basque : un ensemble spatial complexe

Océan Atlantique

Bayonne — FRANCE

□ Pau

Bilbao   San Sebastian   Pyrénées Atlantiques

EUSKADI

Vitoria   Pamplona   NAVARRA

ESPAGNE

© C Trépier mai 2009

0   157 km

I) Différents types de limites politiques

   A) Limites administratives en vigueur

Communauté autonome basque : Euskadi   Pays "Pays basque" (loi française de 1997)

Communauté autonome de Navarre   Frontière franco-espagnole

Département des Pyrénées-Atlantiques

   B) Limite historique

Ancien royaume de Navarre

   C) Limite utopique   *Source :*

La nation basque   *Barbara Loyer*

II) Le statut de la langue basque

Coofficiel

Enseigné

□ Ville importante

Pyrénées Atlantiques Département français

NAVARRA Communauté autonome

FRANCE Pays

Autres départements français

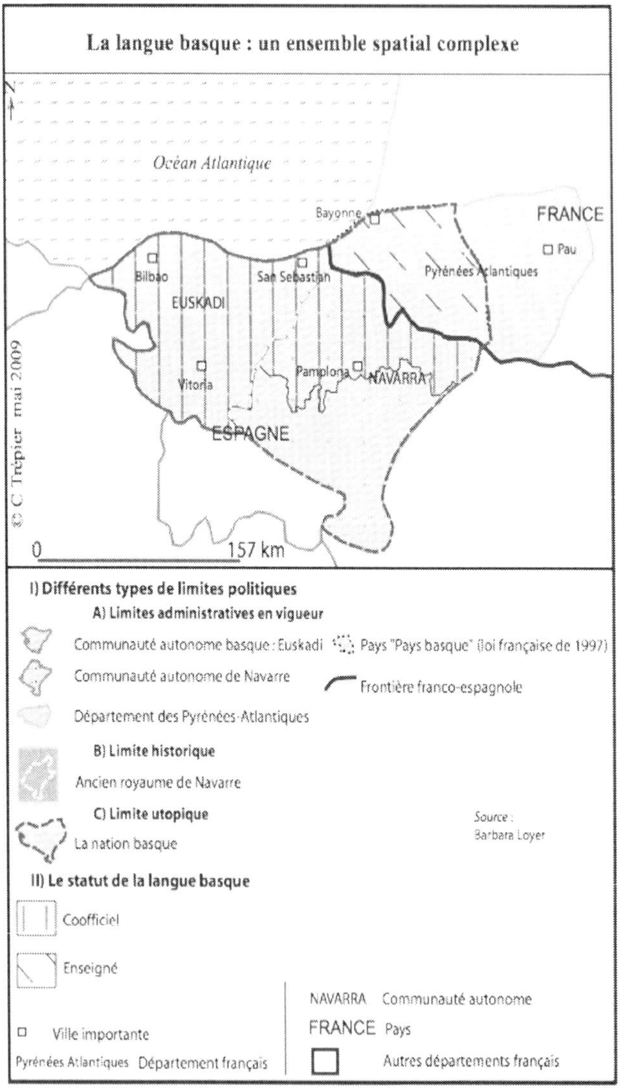

Les patrons catalans et la langue
Attitudes diverses

Cyril Trépier

*Institut Français de Géopolitique, Université Paris 8 et
Facultat Economia i Empresa, Universitat de Barcelona*

Éléments contextuels

Les entrepreneurs de Catalogne : une cible stratégique pour les discours nationalistes sur la langue catalane comme sur l'indépendance

Seul grand parti de Catalogne ayant l'objectif de l'indépendance dans ses statuts, le parti Esquerra est depuis fin 2003 membre d'un gouvernement tripartite dirigé par les socialistes catalans. Ce parti indépendantiste vise entre autres à séduire le patronat. En cela, Esquerra suit le modèle récent du Scottish National Party (SNP) en Écosse, qui au cours de sa campagne pour les élections du 3 mai 2007 au parlement écossais, a reçu le soutien de dirigeants économiques majeurs.[1] De même, Esquerra vise l'héritage de la coalition nationaliste modérée CiU, créée par Jordi Pujol. Depuis fin 2006, Esquerra détient entre autres la vice-présidence du gouvernement autonome, et les rênes de la politique linguistique. Sur l'usage du catalan comme sur l'indépendance, Esquerra envoie au patronat catalan des messages assez parallèles. Dans les deux cas, le parti indépendantiste joue sur le pragmatisme des patrons en revendiquant la défense de leurs intérêts. Dans les deux cas également, il s'adresse aux patrons pour qu'ils entraînent l'ensemble de la société. Cela ne signifie nullement que les patrons catalans qui utilisent le catalan le fassent nécessairement pour des motifs nationalistes. Il peut s'agir d'une simple stratégie de marché. Toutefois, les patrons catalans effectuent leurs choix linguistiques dans un contexte politique où Es-

---

[1] Xavier Solano i Bello (2007), *El Mirall escocès*, Barcelona, Dèria editors-La Magrana.

querra lance depuis la *Generalitat* des politiques destinées à les rapprocher de l'indépendantisme.

Bien entendu, ces choix linguistiques répondent aussi à la prise en compte d'une mondialisation que les patrons catalans voient comme une compétition de tous contre tous que tous les territoires, dont la Catalogne, ont les mêmes chances de gagner.

En ce sens, généraliser le catalan dans le fonctionnement des entreprises peut représenter un autre enjeu pour les indépendantistes : faire valoir l'idée que le marché espagnol est destiné à perdre de l'importance pour l'économie catalane au profit du reste de l'Union européenne, de l'Europe de l'Est ou encore de la Chine. Pour les patrons catalans, il s'agit plus simplement d'ajouter ou non le catalan à une liste de langues qui peut être longue pour les entreprises les plus internationalisées.

Le contexte sociologique actuel de la politique linguistique catalane

La carte suivante (Fig. 1) montre la répartition des entreprises et celle de la population catalanes.

Figure 1

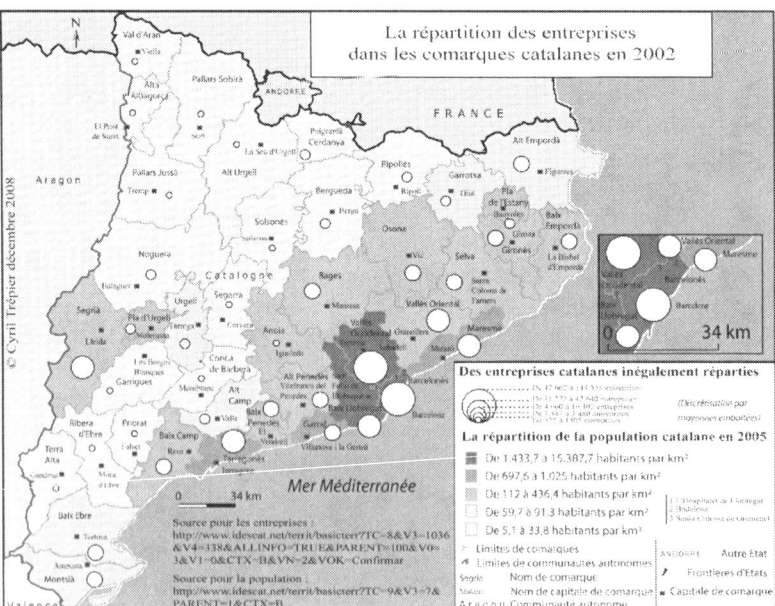

Le tableau ci-dessous (Fig. 2) donne les résultats d'une enquête de l'Institut catalan de la statistique sur la compétence linguistique dans la population. En termes d'expression en langue catalane, la tranche d'âge des 15-29 ans, seule à avoir connu la normalisation linguistique dans l'éducation, se place presque toujours en tête. C'est très net pour la compétence écrite. Une enquête réalisée en 2001 auprès de 389 entreprises adhérentes à l'association patronale Cecot[2] confirmait cette hypothèse en montrant que les entreprises qui avaient accru l'usage du catalan l'expliquaient très majoritairement par l'augmentation du niveau linguistique chez leurs employés.

Figure 2. La connaissance du catalan par l'ensemble de la population et les 15-29 ans en 2007

	Comprennent le catalan	Savent parler le catalan	Savent lire le catalan	Savent écrire le catalan
Les 15-29 ans	91,80%	88,12%	81,30%	76,50%
Population totale	93,80%	75,60%	73,00%	56,30%

Source : Institut catalan de la statistique : http://www.idescat.cat/dequavi/ Dequavi?TC=444&V0=15&V1=1 Consultation le 17/11/2009.

En outre, les pratiques linguistiques des entreprises interviennent dans un contexte marqué par le phénomène récent et massif de l'immigration extracommunautaire. Elle concernait en 2006, 10,9% de la population de Catalogne et 7,2% de celle de l'ensemble de l'Espagne.[3] La même année, la Catalogne était la deuxième communauté autonome après Madrid en nombre d'obtention de la nationalité espagnole par résidence.[4] Entre 1998 et 2007, cette immigration a été plus forte en variation annuelle en Catalogne que dans l'ensemble de l'Espagne, avec 26% dans cette communauté autonome contre 24,3% dans l'ensemble du pays.[5]

Selon le sociologue Amado Alarcón,[6] spécialiste des usages linguistiques des entreprises catalanes, la plupart des nouveaux emplois créés en Catalogne sont occupés par des travailleurs issus de l'immigration

---

[2] Amado Alarcon (2004), *Economía, política e idiomas, intercambio lingüístico y sus efectos sobre la eficiencia y la distribución*, Madrid, CES, p. 120.

[3] Cecot (2008), *Informe sobre la inmigració a Espanya i a Catalunya. Reflexions de cara al futur*, Barcelona, Cecot, p. 9.

[4] Anuario de la inmigración en España, 2006, Madrid, Ministerio de Trabajo e Inmigración, voir : www.mtas.es

[5] Cecot (2008), *op. cit.*, p. 7.

[6] Entretien avec l'auteur, 24/11/2008 par téléphone.

récente. Selon Bernat Joan,[7] secrétaire Esquerra à la Politique linguistique, 47% des employés d'hôtellerie restauration sont issus de l'immigration récente. Pour eux, l'espagnol est indispensable pour obtenir un premier travail. Mais comme les travailleurs venus du reste de l'Espagne dans les années 1940 à 1960, ils perçoivent le catalan comme un indispensable outil de promotion sociale, et une clé pour obtenir un meilleur emploi. Certains d'entre eux apprennent par conséquent les deux langues et non pas seulement l'espagnol comme ils en sont parfois accusés. Nous le verrons par la suite, ce phénomène a conduit l'administration catalane et des patrons à organiser des cours de catalan pendant les heures de travail souvent dans les locaux des entreprises.

Un tissu économique catalan marqué par les entreprises familiales

Le graphique ci-dessous (Fig. 3) montre la répartition par secteur d'activité des entreprises ayant leur siège social en Catalogne en 2008,[8] avec une très nette prédominance du secteur des services.

Figure 3

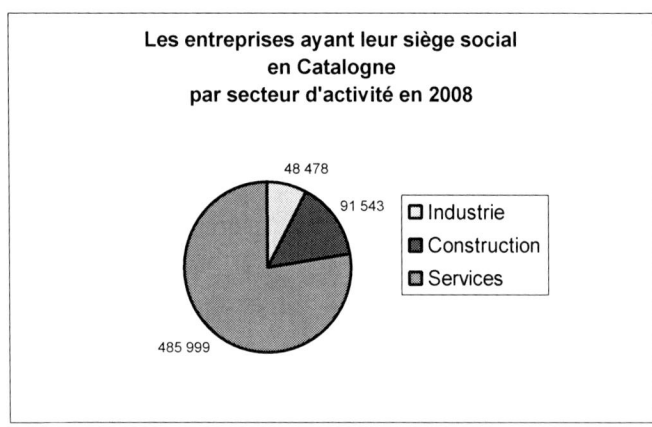

© C. Trépier

Parmi les entreprises catalanes, les petites et moyennes entreprises familiales dominent largement. Sur 635 445 entreprises répertoriées en Catalogne en 2008, 327 047 étaient des personnes physiques contre 28.

---

[7] Entretien avec l'auteur, 20/ 11/ 2008 à Barcelone.

[8] Institut catalan de la statistique, « Empreses amb seu a Catalunya. 2008. Per sector d'activitat i nombre d'assalariats de l'empresa » : http://www.idescat.cat/pub/?id =eee&n=2.1.1 (consulté le 17/11/2009).

690 sociétés anonymes et 216 283 sociétés limitées. De même, les entreprises comptant entre 0 et 9 salariés sont très majoritaires dans le tissu économique catalan, dont elles représentent 93%, une proportion presque identique à celle observable à l'échelle de l'Espagne.[9]

Figure 4

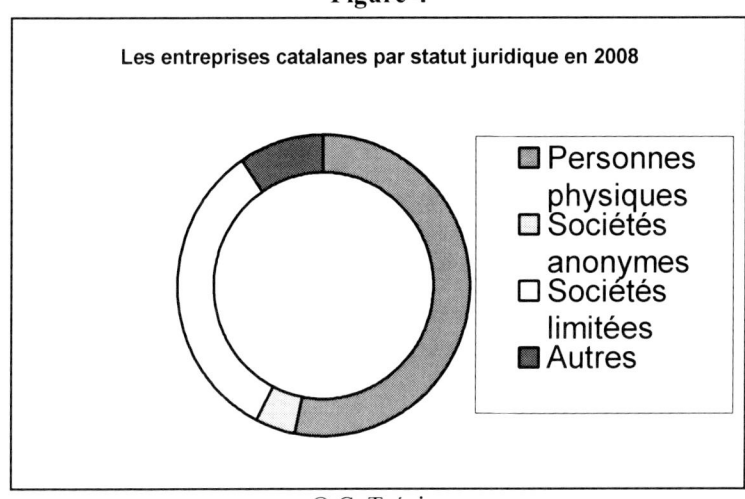

© C. Trépier

Figure 5

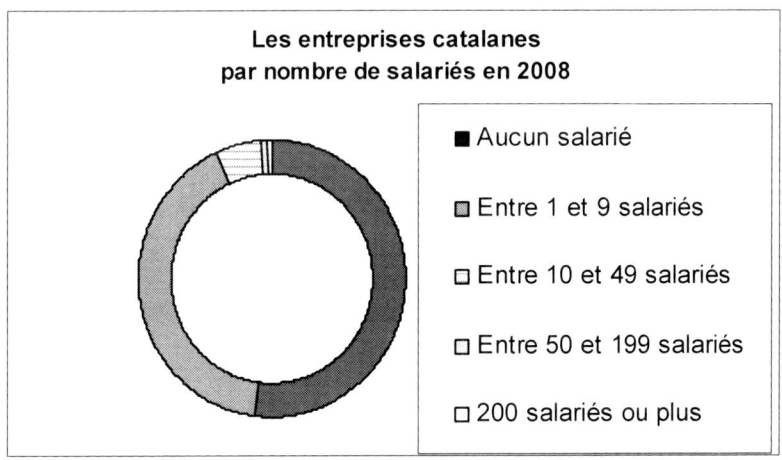

© C. Trépier

[9] Institut catalan de la statistique : http://www.idescat.cat/economia/inec?tc=3&id=6004 (consulté le 17/11/2009).

Même les grandes entreprises sont le plus souvent familiales et très anciennes en Catalogne. Toutefois, bien qu'il n'existe pas de statistiques précises sur ce point, le tissu économique catalan se compose aussi d'entreprises créées par des Espagnols issus de l'immigration intérieure.

Le cadre juridique actuel des pratiques linguistiques des entreprises en Catalogne

Les usages linguistiques des entreprises catalanes s'inscrivent dans le contexte juridique espagnol selon lequel tous les produits doivent être étiquetés au moins en espagnol.

Seuls les produits bénéficiant d'une Dénomination d'Origine contrôlée (DOC) et les produits artisanaux sont obligatoirement étiquetés en catalan, et dispensés de l'étiquetage obligatoire en espagnol.

Le Statut d'autonomie de 1979 définit le catalan comme l'unique langue propre (*llengua propia*) de Catalogne. Cette disposition a servi de base à de nombreuses législations ultérieures en faveur du catalan dans la Communauté Autonome, et alimente encore beaucoup de discours dans ce sens.

La législation espagnole dessine le cadre d'usage obligatoire du castillan dans l'ensemble du territoire espagnol. En revanche, la législation linguistique de Catalogne ne prévoit que l'usage du catalan sur le territoire autonome. C'est le sens de la formule « au moins en catalan », très fréquente dans la législation de Catalogne et les dépliants qui la résument. Cette formule n'exclut en rien l'usage d'autres langues comme l'espagnol. Mais le législateur catalan sait en l'employant, que, pour certains usages linguistiques comme la raison sociale, beaucoup de dirigeants d'entreprise emploieront le plus souvent une langue et une seule.

Les documents de proposition de services tels que les catalogues ou brochures commerciales ainsi que les menus des restaurants et l'affichage des tarifs de l'hôtellerie, doivent être rédigés au moins en catalan, tout comme l'affichage fixe des magasins. Les entreprises de service public, ce qui inclut évidemment des entreprises privées dans les domaines de l'eau, de l'électricité, des communications et des transports notamment, doivent donner en catalan les informations diffusées par haut-parleur, dans les factures, et les notifications écrites aux clients.

Les informations données sur l'ensemble des produits vendus en Catalogne, commerciaux ou industriels, particulièrement concernant l'alimentation, la santé et la sécurité, doivent être libellées au moins en catalan.

Pour Amado Alarcón,[10] la législation linguistique est plus strictement appliquée depuis l'arrivée au pouvoir en coalition des indépendantistes d'Esquerra, fin 2003. Situés dans les capitales des quatre provinces de Catalogne et à Tortosa, cinq « Bureaux de garantie linguistique » sont habilités depuis 2005 à recevoir les plaintes de consommateurs pour défaut de catalan dans les entreprises en relation avec le public. En dernier recours, ces plaintes peuvent valoir à l'entreprise visée des sanctions financières dont le montant sert à financer le développement du catalan. Pour le secrétaire à la Politique linguistique, Bernat Joan, le nombre de ces plaintes de consommateurs baisse nettement depuis plusieurs années.[11]

Le Statut d'autonomie catalan de 2006, approuvé par référendum en Catalogne en juin 2006 et visé par plusieurs recours devant le Tribunal Constitutionnel espagnol, crée surtout le devoir, non de parler catalan, mais de comprendre les clients qui s'adressent aux entreprises en catalan. C'est le devoir de « disponibilité linguistique » introduit par l'article 34, Chapitre III du Statut. Il stipule que « les entités, entreprises et établissements ouverts au public en Catalogne sont assujetties au devoir de disponibilité linguistique dans les termes qu'établissent les lois ».[12] Cela n'interdit pas aux employés de répondre en espagnol.

Plus généralement, l'innovation principale du nouveau Statut d'autonomie en matière linguistique a consisté à placer le catalan et le castillan au même niveau. En effet, selon la Constitution espagnole de 1978 et le Statut d'autonomie catalan de 1979, connaître l'espagnol était un devoir, connaître le catalan, un droit. Avec le Statut d'autonomie catalan de 2006, la connaissance du catalan également devient un devoir. À l'évidence, le droit des consommateurs à employer le catalan crée un devoir des employés à le comprendre.

Ces dispositions réglementaires s'appuient sur un éventail d'incitations, financières mais aussi techniques de la *Generalitat* comme des lexiques spécialisés en catalan ou les cours de catalan pour adultes sur lesquels nous reviendrons. Ajoutons que, sur un territoire comme celui de la Catalogne, un nombre significatif d'entreprises a besoin d'être en relation commerciale avec la *Generalitat*. La concurrence locale qui en résulte constitue un autre moyen, informel mais efficace, pour l'admi-

---

[10] Entretien avec l'auteur, 24/11/2008 par téléphone.

[11] Entretien avec l'auteur, 20/11/2008 à Barcelone.

[12] « Les entitats, les empreses i els establiments oberts al públic a Catalunya estan subjectes al deure de disponibilitat lingüística en els termes que estableixen les lleis ». Generalitat de Catalunya (2006), *Estatut d'Autonomia de Catalunya*, Barcelona, Generalitat de Catalunya, p. 25 (consulté 27/11/2009). Disponible à : http://www.parlament.cat/porteso/estatut/eac_ca_20061116.pdf.

nistration catalane, de s'assurer du respect par ces entreprises de la législation linguistique en vigueur.

Une approche généralement pragmatique des langues par les entreprises

Un facteur-clé : la personnalité du chef d'entreprise

Selon Bernat Gasull, un sociologue qui dirige les études de l'association catalaniste, Plateforme pour la Langue (Plataforma per la Llengua) : « La question, c'est qui commande, et quel est son point de vue ».[13] Le degré de sensibilisation du chef d'entreprise à l'égard du catalan déterminera souvent si le développement de cette langue doit primer sur le coût initial qu'exige son introduction. C'est d'autant plus vrai que quand une entreprise industrielle catalane maîtrise sa distribution, le choix des langues employées relève presque toujours de sa direction générale et non du marketing ou d'un service particulier. Même lorsque la loi catalane s'applique, la personnalité de l'entrepreneur reste un moteur fondamental de ses pratiques linguistiques. Soulignons, avec le sociologue Amado Alarcón, que les syndicats d'employés peuvent aussi plaider pour le catalan, par exemple pour obtenir les contrats et les bulletins de salaire dans cette langue.[14]

Le facteur générationnel : des jeunes entrepreneurs souvent plus sensibles au catalan

Acteurs et observateurs de la politique et de l'économie catalanes s'accordent pour dire que la nouvelle génération de patrons est plus revendicative sur le plan du nationalisme que la précédente qui a davantage connu la dictature franquiste. Cela se reflète souvent par un plus fort usage du catalan, que, contrairement à la génération précédente, ils ont pu apprendre à l'école où il est obligatoire. Les organisations catalanistes proposent au patronat catalan des études de marchés sur l'impact potentiel du catalan dans le reste de l'Espagne. Pour Bernat Gasull, les jeunes patrons accordent une plus grande importance dans leurs décisions à ces études de marchés qu'à la crainte d'éventuelles réactions négatives de consommateurs du reste de l'Espagne.[15]

Selon Xavier Cambra,[16] secrétaire général de l'association patronale Femcat, « pour les entrepreneurs, la langue est instrumentale ». Créée en

---

[13] Entretien avec l'auteur, 18/11/2008 à Barcelone.

[14] Amado Alarcon (2004), *Economía, política e idiomas*, *op. cit.*, p. 204.

[15] Entretien avec l'auteur, 18/11/2008 à Barcelone.

[16] Entretien avec l'auteur, 15/11/2008 à Barcelone.

2005, cette association patronale catalane met en avant la jeunesse de ses membres, et revendique une participation de 10% au PIB catalan. Les nationalistes présentent souvent Femcat en exemple de la nouvelle génération d'entrepreneurs plus ouverts à leurs arguments, ce qui ne fait qu'ajouter à l'intérêt du propos de son secrétaire général. Le site Internet de l'association – http://www.femcat.cat/ – est proposé en catalan et en anglais.

Xavier Cambra dirige aussi les éditions Dèria. Se pencher sur le secteur de l'édition en Catalogne est intéressant à plusieurs titres dans une étude des pratiques linguistiques des entreprises catalanes. En effet, comme ce fut longtemps le cas pour l'industrie textile, les plus grandes entreprises éditoriales espagnoles demeurent largement concentrées en Catalogne. Sans être le plus important secteur de l'économie catalane, l'édition reste donc une activité emblématique. En outre, la production de livres est une des activités économiques où les choix linguistiques sont déterminants.

On comptait en 2006, 245 éditeurs en Catalogne, dont 91 publiant en catalan.[17] La même année, sur toute la production éditoriale catalane, 70,3% des livres étaient édités en espagnol, 28,5% en catalan, et 1,2% en d'autres langues.

Dèria editors, est né en 1995. Il a publié d'abord en catalan puis a traduit en espagnol une partie de son catalogue, et notamment des titres de sa collection de livres d'entretien « Què pensa », consacrée à des dirigeants politiques, mais aussi à des artistes et des journalistes. Le livre d'entretiens de l'ancien président du parti indépendantiste Esquerra, Josep-Lluís Carod-Rovira, est par exemple disponible en catalan et en espagnol chez cet éditeur. Le site Internet – http://www.geocities.com/deriaeditors/ – propose le catalan, l'espagnol et l'anglais. On peut comparer Dèria à un autre jeune éditeur catalan basé à Barcelone, Mina.

Né en 2005 et publiant uniquement en catalan, Mina est un autre éditeur centré sur les livres d'actualité, connu notamment pour sa collection d'essais politiques, L'Arquer, où sont parus entre autres certains des derniers ouvrages publiés par les dirigeants actuels du parti Esquerra, Joan Puigcercós et Joan Ridao, mais aussi, plus récemment encore, la traduction en catalan du livre de Barack Obama, *L'audace de l'espérance*. Le site de Mina – http://www.mina.cat/www/mina/ca – est uniquement en catalan. Il est intéressant de noter que des éditeurs récents choisissent le catalan dès leur apparition.

---

[17] http//www.20.gencat.cat/docs/CulturaDepartament/Cultura/Documents/Arxiu/Arxius%20GT/ECC_2007_juliol2008.pdf (consulté 03/11/2008).

S'adapter à la clientèle dans une économie mondialisée : catalan, espagnol, mais aussi anglais

La lecture de la mondialisation comme une lutte de tous contre tous revient régulièrement dans le discours des entrepreneurs sur leurs usages linguistiques. Aux yeux de David Garrofé, secrétaire général de l'association patronale CECOT, située à Terrassa, au nord de Barcelone : « Le marché est absolument global. Il faut soigner le marché espagnol comme tous les autres. On ne met plus de frontière entre la Catalogne, l'Espagne et l'Europe ».[18] Josep Tragant, patron d'une entreprise de construction employant une centaine de personnes dans la comarque de Bages, résume un point de vue très répandu sur l'usage économique des langues : « L'idéal est de s'exprimer dans la langue où l'on travaille le plus. Si cette langue est l'anglais, qu'on l'utilise quand il le faut. Si c'est l'espagnol, qu'on l'utilise. Il faut avoir un large éventail de capacités linguistiques pour s'exprimer dans la langue la plus efficace selon le moment ».[19] De nombreux patrons catalans veulent voir améliorer l'enseignement de l'anglais, et voient le multilinguisme comme une opportunité.

En Catalogne, l'étiquetage en catalan peut difficilement provoquer à lui seul un achat en dehors des produits culturels. Mais il peut être vu comme un gage d'authenticité. De même, l'usage du catalan par un vendeur peut favoriser la confiance d'un client, surtout envers une entreprise étrangère.

Autre facteur important : l'environnement sociolinguistique des entreprises

Le sociologue Amado Alarcón désigne l'environnement sociolinguistique des entreprises comme un facteur essentiel de leurs pratiques linguistiques.[20] Or, le degré de pratique et de connaissance du catalan peut varier sensiblement entre les classes sociales, et entre les territoires de Catalogne. Ce phénomène s'est trouvé accentué par les mouvements d'immigration successifs.

Cela joue logiquement sur les entreprises qui pourront être influencées à utiliser plutôt le castillan ou le catalan selon la langue majoritairement parlée par leur clientèle proche. S'il n'y a pas d'incompatibilité entre l'usage du catalan et l'implantation dans un espace très urbanisé comme l'aire métropolitaine de Barcelone, la tendance générale consiste à y fonctionner davantage en castillan qu'en ayant son siège à Vic ou à

---

[18] Entretien avec l'auteur le 08/04/2008 à Terrassa.
[19] Entretien avec l'auteur le 04/04/2008 à Manresa.
[20] Amado Alarcon (2004), *Economía, política e idiomas, op. cit.*, p. 119.

Gérone par exemple. Le contraste est notable lorsque l'on compare la proportion d'enseignes en catalan à Barcelone et Gérone. Une enquête sur les grandes entreprises en 2002 montrait que le catalan était la principale langue de travail de 40,4% des entreprises de l'aire métropolitaine de Barcelone et de 84,4% des provinces de Lleida, Gérone et Tarragone.[21] Pour Joan Rovira, patron d'une petite entreprise industrielle dans la comarque d'Osona, dans la troisième ceinture industrielle, « personne ne concevait que quelqu'un exerçant une fonction d'encadrement dans la comarque ne parle pas catalan ».[22]

Toutefois, la langue majoritaire peut également varier à l'intérieur d'une ville, comme celle de Sabadell. Comme d'autres villes industrielles catalanes, Sabadell a en effet vu dans les années 1950 et 1960, des périphéries ouvrières et majoritairement hispanophones, se construire autour d'un centre historique de classe moyenne et majoritairement catalanophone. Cette géographie de la langue s'est en grande partie maintenue jusqu'à ce jour, les déménagements d'un district de Sabadell à l'autre étant assez faibles en dehors des populations jeunes.

Degré de qualification et exigence de connaissance du catalan au sein de l'entreprise

Souvent, les employeurs mentionnent davantage l'exigence de l'anglais dans les offres d'emploi que celle du catalan. Ils présupposent que la maîtrise de cette langue est acquise. Mais l'exigence explicite du catalan semble apparaître de plus en plus fréquemment. Selon une enquête de 2007,[23] 44,4 % des entreprises commerciales, d'hôtellerie et de transports demandaient le catalan. Si l'on exige davantage le catalan, cela indique que tous les candidats ne le parlent pas. Il redevient ainsi un critère de sélection. Selon les secteurs d'activité, le catalan sera demandé ou non, et les entreprises qui le demanderont, exigeront un niveau de compétence dans cette langue adapté à la fois au secteur d'activité et aux compétences du poste à pourvoir. Ce niveau sera plus haut pour un poste de direction ou au contact du public. Ces mêmes facteurs détermineront l'exigence ou non d'un diplôme linguistique par l'entreprise qui peut également choisir de l'évaluer au cours de l'entretien. Quatre niveaux de connaissance du catalan existent officiellement, du niveau élémentaire, A, au niveau supérieur, D. À chacun de ces quatre niveaux

---

[21] Joan-Maria Romaní (2004), « Usos lingüístics a les grans empreses amb vocació internacional presents a Catalunya l'any 2002 », Barcelona, Generalitat de Catalunya, Departament de Vicepresidència, p. 33.

[22] Entretien avec l'auteur le 26/09/2008 à Manlleu.

[23] Secretaría de política lingüística (2008), « Els usos lingüístics a petites i mitjanes empreses de Catalunya ».

correspond un certificat spécifique.[24] Quand elle existe, l'exigence du catalan exclut dans les faits une partie des candidats aux postes concernés et les zones géographiques dont ils sont issus.

Deux facteurs n'influent pas toujours dans le même sens : la taille de l'entreprise et l'origine géographique du chef d'entreprise. Une grande entreprise peut, par sa taille, réduire le coût lié à l'ajout d'une langue à son étiquetage. C'est l'une des raisons pour lesquelles l'usage du catalan n'est pas incompatible avec les grandes entreprises.

Par ailleurs, il est tout à fait possible de voir des entrepreneurs originaires du reste de l'Espagne utiliser le catalan dans la communication externe de l'entreprise, tout comme des entrepreneurs nés en Catalogne et catalanophones peuvent communiquer en interne en catalan et en externe en espagnol. Ajoutons que les entrepreneurs de Catalogne ne diffèrent pas fondamentalement de l'ensemble de la société catalane. Ne pas être natif de Catalogne n'empêche en rien de s'y sentir attaché. Dirigeant d'une PME de fabrication textile dans la comarque intérieure d'Osona, Joan Rovira, natif de Catalogne, souligne cette réalité : « De nombreux entrepreneurs viennent de l'immigration espagnole ou d'ailleurs. Récemment, poursuit-il, je dînais avec l'un des grands entrepreneurs de la construction dans la comarque, né en Galice. Il m'a dit : "Je ne suis pas Galicien. Je suis Catalan. Je suis né en Galice, mais je suis Catalan, car je suis arrivé ici à vingt ans pour gagner ma vie, parce que c'est ici que j'ai travaillé, fondé une famille et gagné ma vie".[25]

Plus généralement, les usages linguistiques des entreprises de Catalogne présentent de nombreuses facettes. Une entreprise peut utiliser le catalan ni en interne, ni en externe, mais financer des études sur l'usage de cette langue. Symétriquement, l'utilisation du catalan en interne n'implique pas forcément son utilisation dans les relations avec le public.

---

[24] Secretaria de política lingüística,: http://www20.gencat.cat/portal/site/Llengcat/menuitem.1ab5a94fef60a1e7a129d410b0c0e1a0/?vgnextoid=5f19f9465ff61110Vgn VCM1000000b0c1e0aRCRD&vgnextchannel=5f19f9465ff61110VgnVCM1000000 b0c1e0aRCRD&vgnextfmt=default (consulté le 17/11/2009).

[25] Entretien avec l'auteur, le 26/09/2008 à Manlleu.

Usage économique des langues, persuasion et confrontations

Des multinationales étrangères aux PME catalanes : toutes sollicitées pour le catalan

Les multinationales étrangères présentes en Catalogne sont elles aussi sollicitées pour utiliser le catalan, tant par l'administration catalane que par un tissu associatif catalaniste très actif. L'une de ces associations, la Plateforme pour la Langue, est allée voir avec succès les dirigeants mondiaux de la multinationale Ikea au début des années 2000.[26] L'argument utilisé auprès des multinationales pour utiliser le catalan est souvent celui-ci : elles emploient dans d'autres pays des langues nationales ayant moins de locuteurs que le catalan, mais n'utilisent pas le catalan en Catalogne.[27]

Que l'interlocuteur soit une entreprise catalane, une société espagnole implantée en Catalogne, ou une multinationale étrangère, le discours est à la fois incitatif et moral. Les partisans de la langue catalane insistent sur l'intérêt commercial de son introduction tout en soulignant que les consommateurs catalans ont le droit d'être servis dans la langue propre de la Catalogne. Si les multinationales étrangères et les sociétés du reste de l'Espagne utilisent généralement peu le catalan, il existe tout de même quelques exceptions. On peut voir entre autres dans les rues de Catalogne des publicités en catalan de multinationales de la téléphonie mobile comme le britannique Vodafone, premier opérateur mobile d'Europe, ou le français Orange, troisième opérateur mobile d'Espagne, ou de sociétés ayant leur siège dans d'autres communautés autonomes, comme la caisse d'épargne asturienne, Cajastur.

Surtout, il est très intéressant d'observer que le catalan n'est pas le monopole des entreprises catalanes. En effet, la société qui édite le plus de livres en catalan pour les concours publics en Catalogne, est andalouse et non catalane. L'entreprise Mad a son siège à Alcalá de Guadaíra, près de Séville et se spécialise dans les livres de préparation des concours publics dans toute l'Espagne. L'introduction du catalan en 2002 lui a permis de doubler ses ventes en Catalogne qui représente actuellement 8% de son activité annuelle. Le site Internet de Mad – www.mad.es – l'indique, la société possède un réseau de librairies partenaires couvrant les dix-sept communautés autonomes d'Espagne ainsi que les villes de Ceuta y Melilla. On peut donc commander des manuels en catalan partout en Espagne. Une partie de l'activité de Mad

---

[26] Entretien de l'auteur avec Bernat Gasull, le 18/11/2008 à Barcelone.
[27] *Id.*

peut donc nous renseigner sur les Espagnols du reste de l'Espagne qui souhaitent aller vivre et travailler en Catalogne et apprendre le catalan avant leur départ.

Les huit plus grandes entreprises catalanes de boissons sont toutes des entreprises familiales

Elles ont leur siège en Catalogne et enregistrent chacune un chiffre d'affaires annuel d'au moins un million d'euros. En 2000, le catalan était absent ou pratiquement absent de leur étiquetage.[28] La carte suivante (Fig. 6) indique l'emplacement de leur siège social et leurs choix linguistiques actuels.

Figure 6

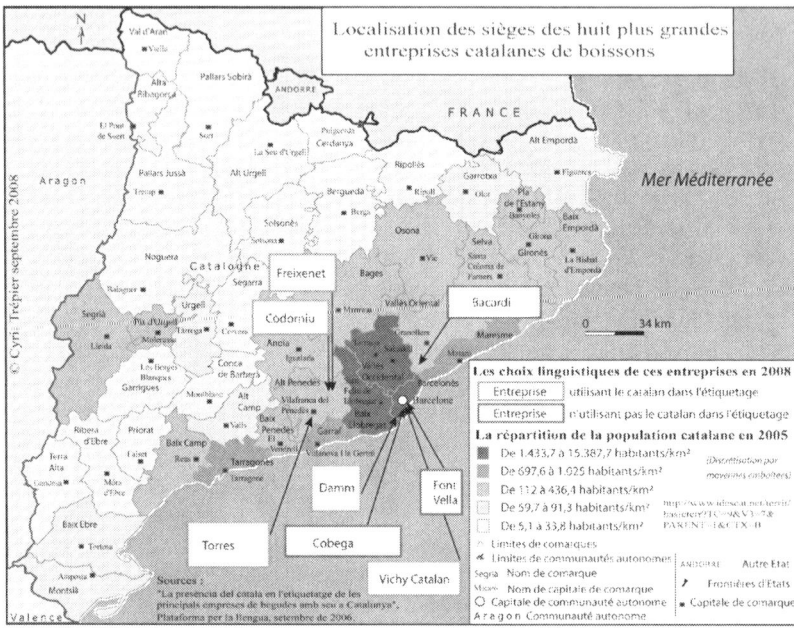

Toutes ont fait l'objet de campagnes d'associations catalanistes pour introduire le catalan. Cinq l'ont fait, souvent parce qu'un concurrent l'avait fait avant sans rencontrer de difficultés. Un précédent favorable semble donc pouvoir peser davantage qu'une étude de marché.

---

[28] Plataforma per la Llengua (2009), *El català en el món socioeconòmic*, Barcelona, Plataforma per la Llengua, p. 42. http://www.plataforma-llengua.cat/media/as sets/1320/ catala_mon_socioeconomic_2009.pdf (consulté le 30/11/2009).

Damm produit principalement de la bière. Elle introduisit cette bois-son en Catalogne à la fin du XIXe siècle. Le site Internet de Damm – www.damm.es – propose l'espagnol, le catalan et l'anglais. D'après Bernat Gasull de la Plateforme pour la Langue, c'est le précédent du brassier Cervezas Möritz qui a convaincu Damm d'introduire le cata-lan.[29] Dans son étude de 2009 intitulée *El català en el món socioe-conòmic*, (Le catalan dans le monde socio-économique), la Plateforme pour la Langue notait la généralisation de l'usage du catalan parmi les nouveaux brassiers, industriels ou artisans.[30]

Les trois entreprises Torres, Codorniu et Freixenet bénéficient de dé-nominations d'origine contrôlée (DOC). Cela les oblige à étiqueter en catalan les produits concernés, mais elles ne l'ont pas toujours fait.[31]

Toujours selon Bernat Gasull, le fabricant de vins et de cavas Torres ne s'est pas laissé convaincre tout de suite par la Plateforme pour la Langue, même quand celle-ci a conduit une étude de marché indiquant une absence de risque dans l'hypothèse d'une introduction du catalan. L'association catalaniste a dû redoubler de force de persuasion pour persuader Torres.[32]

Dans un entretien publié dans un supplément du mensuel valencien *El Temps* en octobre 2007, le président de la société Bodegas Torres, Miguel A. Torres, semblait confirmer l'affirmation de Bernat Gasull. Voici un extrait de cet entretien :

Question – Concernant l'étiquetage en catalan, quelle est votre position ?

– Nous avons déjà presque tous nos produits étiquetés en catalan et en espa-gnol, et heureusement, nous n'avons eu aucune plainte dans le reste de l'État. Nous sommes une grande entreprise et nous ne pouvons pas faire deux lignes de produits, une pour la Catalogne et l'autre pour le reste de l'État. Un fabricant artisanal peut le faire, mais nous qui sommes au Corte Inglés, à Carrefour ou à Mercadona, nous ne pouvons pas leur dire : écou-tez, ce Viña Sol vous me le séparez, car c'est seulement pour la Catalogne. Ils veulent un seul produit ou alors vous devez l'étiqueter en bilingue. Notre crainte était que dans le reste de l'État, cela ait des conséquences négatives. Nous savons bien qu'il y a une extrême droite espagnole toujours prête à se livrer à ce genre d'actions. Mais cela ne s'est pas produit.[33]

---

[29] Entretien de Bernat Gasull avec l'auteur le 18/11/ 2008 à Barcelone et le 26/11/2009 par téléphone.

[30] Plataforma per la Llengua (2009), *El català en el món socioeconòmic*, *op. cit.*, p. 44.

[31] *Ibid.*, p. 41.

[32] Entretien avec l'auteur le 18/11/2008 à Barcelone.

[33] J. Nebot, Entrevista a Miguel A. Torres, *El Temps*, n° 1220, octobre 2007, p. 6, « P-Pel que fa a l'etiquetatge en català, quina és la seva posició ? – Nosaltres ja tenim gairebé tots els productes etiquetats en català i castellà, i afortunadament no hem

Les trois autres grands fabricants de boissons que sont Ron Bacardi (apéritifs), Font Vella (eau minérale, fait partie du groupe multinational français Danone) et Cobega SA, qui embouteille le Coca-Cola, n'étiquètent pas en catalan. Interrogé fin novembre 2009 par nos soins, le sociologue Bernat Gasull, de la Plateforme pour la Langue, a indiqué que cela n'avait pas changé.[34]

Des produits étiquetés en catalan pourtant boycottés

Mais les risques ne sont pas toujours d'un seul côté. Même sans éti-quette en catalan, les bouteilles d'eau minérale Font Vella ont subi le boycott de produits catalans et basques organisé en 2005 par certains consommateurs du reste de l'Espagne après des propos du président d'Esquerra de l'époque, Josep-Lluís Carod-Rovira.[35] À l'époque, à Murcie notamment, le boycott de l'eau minérale catalane Font Vella avait une forte valeur émotionnelle. Les consommateurs exprimaient ainsi leur refus d'acheter de l'eau à des Catalans qui refusaient de leur céder de l'eau de l'Èbre.

Le contentieux sur le partage des ressources de l'Èbre entre la Cata-logne, Valence et Murcie n'est qu'un des aspects des conflits géopoli-tiques internes à l'Espagne sur l'eau. Le bassin de ce fleuve s'étend sur neuf Communautés Autonomes, mais son delta se situe au sud de la Catalogne, dans la province de Tarragone. Région très sèche, la Com-munauté Autonome de Murcie revendique le transfert d'une partie de l'eau de l'Èbre depuis la Catalogne. Au pouvoir à Murcie et à Valence depuis 1995, le Parti Populaire a fait de la question de l'eau l'un de ses principaux chevaux de bataille.[36] Barcelone, pouvant souffrir de pénu-ries d'eau, refuse ce transfert. Vu du reste de l'Espagne, cela nourrit l'accusation faite aux Catalans d'être égoïstes (*insolidarios*). L'exécutif catalan exprima sa volonté de contrôler le partage des ressources de l'Èbre en décembre 2003 dans le pacte de Tinell entre les trois partis du

---

tingut cap queixa de la resta de l'Estat. Som una empresa gran i no podem fer dues línies de producte, una per Catalunya i una altra per a la resta de l'Estat. Això ho pot fer un elaborador artesà, però nosaltres, que estem a El Corte Inglés, a Carrefour o a Mercadona, no els podem dir : miri, aquest Viña Sol me'l separa, que és només per a Catalunya. Ells volen un sol producte o aleshores l'has d'etiquetar bilingüe. La nos-tra por era que a la resta de l'Estat això portés conseqüències negatives. Ja sabem que hi ha una extrema dreta espanyola sempre preparada per agafar-se a aquestes coses. Però això no s'ha produït ».

[34] Entretien avec l'auteur, par téléphone, le 26/11/2009.

[35] M. Carod-Rovira, leader indépendantiste catalan, s'était exprimé contre la candida-ture de Madrid à l'organisation des Jeux Olympiques de 2012. Voir : *La Vanguardia*, 27/11/2004.

[36] Barbara Loyer (2006), *Géopolitique de l'Espagne*, Paris, Armand Colin, pp. 274-275.

futur gouvernement tripartite catalan,[37] puis dans le nouveau Statut d'autonomie de Catalogne entré en vigueur en 2006.[38] Ce lourd contentieux entre la Catalogne et la Communauté Autonome de Murcie motiva le recours de celle-ci auprès du Tribunal Constitutionnel espagnol contre le Statut d'autonomie catalan de 2006.[39] Il fut l'une des motivations du recours présenté par la Communauté Autonome de Valence contre le texte catalan.[40] De simples bouteilles d'eau minérale de Catalogne peuvent donc cristalliser une intense rivalité géopolitique. En 2003, les eaux et autres boissons non alcoolisées produites en Catalogne représentaient 27,3% des ventes dans ce secteur de l'industrie agroalimentaire espagnole, et 28,8% de ses emplois.[41] En Catalogne, ce secteur représentait quelque 5 500 emplois en 2005.[42]

Le fait que l'absence d'étiquetage en catalan ne protège pas contre les pratiques de boycott contre des produits de Catalogne, était souligné en octobre 2007 par Miguel A. Torres dans l'entretien cité plus haut qu'il avait accordé au magazine valencien *El Temps* :

> Ce que nous avons noté en revanche, a été le boycott contre les produits catalans. Voici un an et quelque, de nombreux restaurants espagnols et quelques-uns de Valence ont retiré nos vins de leur carte. Et au même moment, une partie de la presse catalane critiquait la maison Torres pour l'absence d'étiquetage en catalan.[43]

Des exemples de volontarisme d'entreprises catalanes en faveur de la langue

S'il existe de plus en plus de produits sur lesquels le catalan est introduit, quelques obstacles continuent d'entraver la généralisation de

---

[37] http://www.revistalafactoria.eu/articulo.php?id=259 p. 84, (consulté le 30/11/2009).

[38] http://www.parlament.cat/porteso/estatut/eac_ca_20061116.pdf, Art. 117, pp. 74-75. (consulté le 30/11/2009).

[39] Recurso de inconstitucionalidad n° 8829-2006, en relación al art. 117, apartados 1 c), 2), 3 a), y c), 4 y 5 de la Ley Orgánica 6/2006, de 19 de Julio, de reforma del Estatuto de Autonomía de Cataluña, Madrid, *Boletín Oficial del Estado*, núm. 262, 2/11/2006, art. 19042, p. 38024.

[40] José Carlos Herreras (2008), « Le statut des langues de l'Espagne dans le nouveau "statut d'autonomie" », *La linguistique*, 2008/1, vol. 44, p. 14, Paris, PUF.

[41] Département d'Agriculture de la Generalitat de Catalogne, (consulté le 30/11/2009): http://www20.gencat.cat/docs/DAR/Documents/Arxius/www.gencat.net_darp_c_agr oalim_publiagr_cpub03.htm%20-%206.10.pdf

[42] http://www.idescat.cat/industria/?tc=1&se=12#T1 Institut Catalan de la Statistique, (consulté le 30/11/2009).

[43] « El que sí que vam notar va ser el boicot als productes catalans. Fa un any i escaig, molts restaurants espanyols i alguns de valencians ens van treure els vins de la carta. I mentre això passava, una part de la premsa catalana criticava la casa Torres per no etiquetar en català ». J. Nebot, *El Temps*, *op. cit.*

cette langue. Tout d'abord, une logique générale et croissante d'homogénéisation du marché s'oppose à l'étiquetage en d'autres langues que l'espagnol et le portugais. Les entreprises produisent ainsi depuis Madrid pour toute la péninsule ibérique. Depuis le début de l'extension de la normalisation linguistique au-delà de l'administration, certaines lignes ont bougé. Mais certains patrons ne sont tout simplement pas convaincus, comme les dirigeants de l'Association des Industries de l'Alimentation et Boissons de Catalogne, (Asociación de Industrias de Alimentación y Bebidas de Cataluña, AIABECA) et certains de ses adhérents, opposés depuis le début à l'extension au secteur privé de la législation linguistique.

D'autres entreprises montrent en revanche leur volonté de contribuer à diffuser la langue catalane. C'est le cas des entreprises qui demandent au Secrétariat à la politique linguistique (Secretaria de Política Llinguística), un bilan de la présence du catalan dans leur fonctionnement interne, ou de celles qui, depuis le début de l'immigration extracommunautaire dans les années 1990, donnent des cours de catalan à une partie de leur personnel.

Cette pratique demeure minoritaire. Elle concernait en 2007 14% des PME de services, d'hôtellerie, de commerce et de transports. Cependant, la pratique des cours de catalan dans le cadre professionnel semble se développer puisque l'organisme officiel catalan qui les organise, le Consortium pour la Normalisation Linguistique (Consorci per a la Normalització Llingüística), recensait 77 987 adultes inscrits en 2005-2006, 91 142 en 2006-2007, et 111 335 en 2007-2008.[44] Nous en donnerons deux exemples.

Le premier est celui de la chaîne catalane de supermarchés Bonpreu. Ce groupe étiquette l'ensemble de ses produits en catalan et reste très soucieux de l'usage du catalan par ses employés dans les contacts avec les clients. En 2001, sur six groupes de grande distribution présents en Catalogne, seul Bonpreu affichait 100% de catalan ou de bilinguisme dans l'ensemble de sa communication.[45]

Le site Internet de Bonpreu – www.bonpreu.cat – est disponible en catalan et en espagnol. Il propose entre autres un formulaire de candidature où figure une question sur la connaissance et la pratique du catalan par le candidat. Si le candidat répond « jamais » (*mai*) à la question sur son utilisation du catalan, cela ne signifie pas qu'il n'ait aucun avenir dans le groupe Bonpreu puisque celui-ci donne des cours de catalan à ses employés.

---

[44] Plataforma per la Llengua (2009), « El català en el món socioeconòmic », *op. cit.*, p. 10.

[45] *Ibid.*, p. 50.

Deuxième exemple, Mimcord, PME industrielle familiale implantée comme le siège de Bonpreu dans la comarque nationaliste et anciennement industrialisée d'Osona. Son patron, Joan Rovira, représente les quelque 1 500 PME de la comarque. Il définit le catalan comme « la langue intérieure de l'entreprise » et les cours qu'il organise comme « un élément important ».[46] Ils reflètent autant son attachement à la langue que la nécessité de se comprendre avec des ouvriers issus de l'immigration récente et qui pour certains d'entre eux, d'origine subsaharienne ne parlaient, au début, ni le catalan, ni l'espagnol. Joan Rovira a confirmé que les travailleurs étrangers avec lesquels il est en contact apprennent le catalan et l'espagnol. Il revendique trente ans d'expérience du commerce international, et la société Mimcord exporte dans le reste de l'Europe, mais aussi entre autres, en Colombie, au Pérou, au Vietnam, en Inde, en Indonésie, et en République d'Afrique du Sud.

Plus généralement, on peut observer avec la sociologue catalane Marta Rovira,[47] à la tête d'un groupe de recherche sur l'identité, que, dans les communications internes, le catalan agit probablement plus pour intégrer les employés issus de l'immigration récente alors que l'étiquetage en catalan suppose, lui, un feed-back des consommateurs pour atteindre pleinement son objectif.

Conclusions

Cet article se veut un tour d'horizon, et non un examen exhaustif des pratiques linguistiques des patrons catalans. Selon Amado Alarcón,[48] le thème des choix linguistiques est peu présent dans les préoccupations des futurs entrepreneurs, très soucieux en revanche d'apprendre les langues de leurs futurs marchés, comme l'italien, le français et l'allemand. Rares sont les consommateurs catalans qui n'achètent que les produits étiquetés en catalan, tout comme le sont les entrepreneurs qui n'emploient jamais l'espagnol quitte à perdre des clients potentiels. Toutefois, ces deux comportements existent, et invitent à une réflexion plus générale sur les acteurs non partisans du nationalisme. Les différentes attitudes linguistiques des patrons catalans, reflètent sans doute en partie l'absence actuelle de consensus entre eux sur l'importance actuelle et future du marché espagnol pour l'économie catalane. Mais cette même diversité des usages linguistiques reflète aussi l'écart entre les convictions personnelles des dirigeants, l'image publique de chaque entreprise et ses pratiques. Nous pouvons avancer, à titre d'hypothèse,

---

[46] Entretien avec l'auteur, le 26/09/2008 à Manlleu.
[47] Entretien avec l'auteur, le 19/09/2008.
[48] Entretien avec l'auteur, 24/11/2008.

que l'exigence de la connaissance du catalan pour certains emplois privés, constitue une source majeure de rivalités entre la Catalogne et les citoyens du reste de l'Espagne.

Summary

This article looks at the positions taken by Catalan business leaders on the use of the Catalan language in the context of a globalised economy. In the same way as the Scottish National Party, the Catalan separatist party, Esquerra, has sought the support of the business community. Recent immigration from outside the European Union has had a crucial impact on the debate. The position of Catalan business leaders is largely pragmatic. Although many of them see the language as merely instrumental, there is evidence of companies following different language strategies; this may stem from individual conviction or from changing commercial circumstances. Some business leaders go further than Catalan legislation on the language requires.